주한미군지위협정(SOFA)

공공용역
합동위원회 2

주한미군지위협정(SOFA)

공공용역 합동위원회 2

한국학술정보

| 머리말

미국은 오래전부터 우리나라 외교에 있어서 가장 긴밀하고 실질적인 우호 · 협력관계를 맺어 온 나라다. 6 · 25전쟁 정전 협정이 체결된 후 북한의 재침을 막기 위한 대책으로서 1953년 11월 한미 상호방위조약이 체결되었다. 이는 미군이 한국에 주둔하는 법적 근거였고, 그렇게 주둔하게 된 미군의 시설, 구역, 사업, 용역, 출입국, 통관과 관세, 재판권 등 포괄적인 법적 지위를 규정하는 것이 바로 주한미군지위협정(SOFA)이다. 그러나 이와 관련한 협상은 계속된 난항을 겪으며 한미 상호방위조약이 체결로부터 10년이 훌쩍 넘은 1967년이 돼서야 정식 발효에 이를 수 있었다. 그럼에도 당시 미군 범죄에 대한 한국의 재판권은 심한 제약을 받았으며, 1980년대 후반 민주화 운동과 함께 미군 범죄 문제가 사회적 이슈로 떠오르자 협정을 개정해야 한다는 목소리가 커지게 되었다. 이에 1991년 2월 주한미군지위협정 1차 개정이 진행되었고, 이후에도 여러 사건이 발생하며 2001년 4월 2차 개정이 진행되어 현재에 이르고 있다.

본 총서는 외교부에서 작성하여 최근 공개한 주한미군지위협정(SOFA) 관련 자료를 담고 있다. 1953년 한미 상호방위조약 체결 이후부터 1967년 발효가 이뤄지기까지의 자료와 더불어, 이후 한미 합동위원회을 비롯해 민 · 형사재판권, 시설, 노무, 교통 등 각 분과위원회의 회의록과 운영 자료, 한국인 고용인 문제와 관련한 자료, 기타 관련 분쟁 자료 등을 포함해 총 42권으로 구성되었다. 전체 분량은 약 2만 2천여 쪽에 이른다.

2024년 3월

한국학술정보(주)

| 일러두기

· 본 총서에 실린 자료는 2022년 4월과 2023년 4월에 각각 공개한 외교문서 4,827권, 76만 여 쪽 가운데 일부를 발췌한 것이다.

· 각 권의 제목과 순서는 공개된 원본을 최대한 반영하였으나, 주제에 따라 일부는 적절히 변경하였다.

· 원본 자료는 A4 판형에 맞게 축소하거나 원본 비율을 유지한 채 A4 페이지 안에 삽입하였다. 또한 현재 시점에선 공개되지 않아 '공란'이란 표기만 있는 페이지 역시 그대로 실었다.

· 외교부가 공개한 문서 각 권의 첫 페이지에는 '정리 보존 문서 목록'이란 이름으로 기록물 종류, 일자, 명칭, 간단한 내용 등의 정보가 수록되어 있으며, 이를 기준으로 0001번부터 번호가 매겨져 있다. 이는 삭제하지 않고 총서에 그대로 수록하였다.

· 보고서 내용에 관한 더 자세한 정보가 필요하다면, 외교부가 온라인상에 제공하는 『대한민국 외교사료요약집』 1991년과 1992년 자료를 참조할 수 있다.

| 차례

머리말 4
일러두기 5

SOFA 한.미국 합동위원회 공공용역 분과위원회, 1970-74 7

분류번호	729.418 1970~74	등록번호	528	보존기간	영구
기능명칭	SOFA - 한.미 합동 위원회 공공용역 분과 위원회, 1970~74				
생 산 과	안보담당관실		생산년도	1974	

주; 1. 1970년

2. 1971년

3. 1972년

4. 1973년

5. 1974년.

	M/F No.	

결 번

넘버링 오류

1. 1970년

REPUBLIC OF KOREA - UNITED STATES
UTILITIES SUBCOMMITTEE

29 January 1970

MEMORANDUM FOR: The Joint Committee

SUBJECT: Consultation on Rate/Tariff Changes

1. Subcommittee Members:

Republic of Korea

SUH Suck Joon, Chairman
CHOI Soo Byung, Secretary
LEE Kil Sang, Member
HAN Byung Il, Member
LEE Hea Kwon, Member
CHUNG Jong Taik, Member
SONG Hae Joon, Member
LEE Nak Young, Member
PAIK Sun Will, Member
SHIN, Kyong Shick, Member

United States

COL Gerald L. Haymaker, Chairman
COL Hugh L. Schmitt, Alternate Chairman
Major John C. Lynch, Secretary
CDR Roger D. Simon, Member
LTC Samuel L. Defebo, Member
Major Peter J. Bistany, Member
Mr. Samuel Pollack, Member
Mr. Don Leland, Member
Mr. Francis K. Cook, Member

2. Subject of Recommendation: Agreed Minute 1 to Article VI, ROK-US SOFA, provides that any changes determined by the authorities of the Republic of Korea in priorities, conditions, and rates or tariffs, applicable to the United States Armed Forces shall be the subject of consultation in the Joint Committee prior to their effective date.

3. The Republic of Korea has initiated consultation concerning a change in rates for maintenance and repair service charge on military sidetracks with a proposed effective date of 1 August 1969 (Incl 1).

4. The United States component of the Utilities Subcommittee has received the ROK Memorandum of Consultation and has determined that the requested change in maintenance and repair service charge is no less favorable than those accorded any comparable user. Further, it has been agreed through the consultative process that the effective date of the change in service charge will be 11 September 1969 (Incl 2).

3

SUBJECT: Consultation on Rate/Tariff Changes 29 January 1970

5. It is requested that the Joint Committee accept this memorandum as evidence of consultation contemplated by Article VI of the Status of Forces Agreement.

SUH, Suck Joon
Republic of Korea Chairman
Utilities Subcommittee

GERALD L. HAYMAKER, USA
United States Chairman
Utilities Subcommittee

2 Incl
as

4

REPUBLIC OF KOREA - UNITED STATES
UTILITIES SUBCOMMITTEE

29 January 1970

SUBJECT: Change in Maintenance and Repair Service Charge on U.S. Military Sidetracks

Republic of Korea Chairman, Utilities Subcommittee

1. References:

a. Paragraph 2 and Agreed Minute 1 of Article VI of the Status of Forces Agreement.

b. ROK component of the Utilities Subcommittee Memorandum of Consultation, dated 11 September 1969, subject same as above, pertaining to a change in maintenance and repair service charge on military sidetracks.

2. The ROK memorandum, reference 1b above, has been reviewed and as agreed to during the consultative process the effective date of this rate change will be 11 September 1969. The United States component of the Utilities Subcommittee fully understands the requirement for change in the maintenance and repair service charge on U.S. military sidetracks and will join with the ROK component of the Utilities Subcommittee in presenting a memorandum on the rates to the Joint Committee.

GERALD L. HAYMAKER
Colonel, U.S. Army
U. S. Chairman
Utilities Subcommittee

5.

REPUBLIC OF KOREA-UNITED STATES
UTILITIES SUBCOMMITTEE

September 11, 1969

Subject: Change in Maintenance and Repair Service Charge on U.S. Military Sidetracts Under Article VI of the Status of Forces Agreement.

To: Chairman, U.S. Utilities Subcommittee

1. Reference: Paragraph 2 and Agreed Minute 1 of Article VI of the Status of Forces Agreement.

2. The Government of the United States is informed through this written consultative process that the Republic of Korea proposes to change the following rates/tariffs at locations indicated below:

Rate/Tariff	Location
Maintenance and Repair Service Charge on U.S. Military Sidetracts.	Whole Country

3. The following data is provided.

a. Effective date.
August 1, 1969

b. Rate Schedule of proposed change.
Refer to item "d".

c. Rate Schedule showing rates that are charged all classes of users.
Refer to Attachment I.

d. Calculation of old and new rate base.

6

Unit: Won per year

Classification	Unit	Old Rate	New Rate
Track	per meter	496	524
Highway Crossing	per meter in breadth	2400	2923
Bridge	per meter	1103	1234
Culvert	one place	4941	5563
Drainage	one place	1854	2121

c. Reasons for revision of rates.
Increased prices of repair parts and personal expenditures.

4. The Government of ROK advises the Government of the United States that the priorities, conditions and rates or tariffs being changed are no less favorable than those accorded any other user. The view of the Government of the United States is solicited prior to the effective date of the rate change. You may be assured that your views will be greatly appreciated.

for Suk J. [illegible], Secretary
Chung Jai Duc
Republic of Korea Chairman
Utilities Subcommittee

(Attachment I)

Maintenance and Repair Service Charge on Sidetracts.

Unit: Won per year

Clissification	Unit	Rate
Track	per meter	524
Highway Crossing	per meter in breadth	2923
Bridge	per meter	1234
Culvert	one place	5563
Drainage	one place	2121

Note: Above rate is applicable to all classes of users.

8

REPUBLIC OF KOREA - UNITED STATES
UTILITIES SUBCOMMITTEE

9 January 1970

MEMORANDUM FOR: The Joint Committee

SUBJECT: Consultation on Rate/Tariff Changes

1. Subcommittee Members:

Republic of Korea	United States
SUH Suck Joon, Chairman	COL Gerald L. Haymaker, Chairman
CHOI Soo Byung, Secretary	COL Hugh L. Schmitt, Alternate Chairman
LEE Kil Sang, Member	Major John C. Lynch, Secretary
HAN Byung Il, Member	CDR Roger D. Simon, Member
LEE Hea Kwon, Member	LTC Samuel L. Defebo, Member
CHUNG Jong Taik, Member	Major Peter J. Bistany, Member
SONG Hae Joon, Member	Mr. Samuel Pollack, Member
LEE Nak Young, Member	Mr. Don Leland, Member
PAIK Sun Will, Member	Mr. Francis K. Cook, Member
SHIN, Kyong Shick, Member	

2. Subject of Recommendation: Agreed Minute 1 to Article VI, ROK-US SOFA, provides that any changes determined by the authorities of the Republic of Korea in priorities, conditions, and rates or tariffs, applicable to the United States Armed Forces shall be the subject of consultation in the Joint Committee prior to their effective date.

3. The Republic of Korea has initiated consultation concerning a change in electric rates as follows:

Effective 27 December 1970, cost for electric power purchased from the Korea Electric Company under contract #DAJB03-70-D-6017 will be increased by 10% for contracted demand and power consumed. Further, for those USFK facilities with a demand of 200KW or less, a discount of 30% will be granted from the aforementioned effective date of the electric power increase (Incl 1).

4. The United States component of the Utilities Subcommittee has received the ROK Memorandum of Consultation and has determined that the requested change in rates is no less favorable than those accorded any comparable user (Incl 2).

9

9 January 1970

SUBJECT: Consultation on Rate/Tariff Changes

5. It is requested that the Joint Committee accept this memorandum as evidence of consultation contemplated by Article VI of the Status of Forces Agreement.

Suh Suck Joon
SUH, SUCK JOON
Republic of Korea Chairman
Utilities Subcommittee

Gerald L. Haymaker
COL GERALD L. HAYMAKER, USA
United States Chairman
Utilities Subcommittee

2

10

REPUBLIC OF KOREA-UNITED STATES
UTILITIES SUBCOMMITTEE

December 26, 1969

Subject: Change in Electric Rate Schedule applicable to the US Armed Forces under Article VI of The Status of Forces Agreement

To: US Chairman, Utilities Subcommittee

1. Reference: Paragraph 2 and Agreed Minute 1 of Article VI of the Status of Forces Agreement.

2. The Government of the United States is informed through this written consultative process that the ROK proposes to change the following rates/tariffs at locations indicated below:

Rate/Tariffs	Location
Electric rate schedule applicable to the US Armed Forces	Whole Country

3. The following data is provided:

a. Effective date
27 December, 1969

b. Rate Schedule showing rates that are charged all classes of users. Attached

c. Rate Schedule of proposed change.
10% increase with no exception over the old rate schedule. For detailed information, refer to item "b".

d. Calculation of old and new rate base.
Refer to item "b"

e. Reasons for revision of rate.
To secure fair return and investment fund.

4. The Government of ROK advises the Government of the United States that the priorities, conditions and rates or tariffs being changed are no less favorable than those accorded any other user. The view of the Government of the United States is solicited prior to the effective date of the rate changes. You may be assured that your views will be greatly appreciated.

Suck Joon Suh
Suck Joon, Suh
Director, Office of Price Policy
Republic of Korea Chairman
Utilities Subcommittee

10

12

Incl 1

KOREA ELECTRIC COMPANY
New Electric Rate Schedule
(Effective From 27 Dec. 1969)
TARIFF 1
GENERAL SERVICE A

APPLICABLE:

To residential service without limit and general service of 4kw demand or under.

TYPE OF SUPPLY:

Single or three phase supply at any one of the Company's available standard voltages, 100 v or 200 v.

MONTHLY BILL:

Basic Rate:

Energy Charge::

W 142.50 for the first 3 kwh.
W 13.50 per kwh for the next 27 kwh.
W 10.25 per kwh for the next 180 kwh. *
W 7.90 per kwh for each additional kwh.
* Add 90 kwh at W 10.25 block for each kw in excess of 3kw of demand.

Minimum Charge : W 142.50.

TARIFF 2
GENERAL SERVICE B

APPLICABLE:

To general service of 4 kw of contracted demand and over.

TYPE OF SUPPLY:

Single or three phase supply at any one of the Company's available standard voltages, 20kv, 10kv, 6kv, 5.2kv, 3kv, 200v, 100v or others.

MONTHLY BILL:

Basic Rate:

a. Demand Charge:
W 160.00 per kw for the first 50 kw of contracted demand.
W 127.00 per kw for the next 450 kw of contracted demand.
W 95.00 per kw for each additional kw of contracted demand.

13

b. Energy Charge:

W 8.25 per kwh for the first 90 kwh per kw of contracted demand.
W 5.65 per kwh for the next 90 kwh per kw of contracted demand.
W 4.07 per kwh for the next 180 kwh per kw of contracted demand.
W 2.75 per kwh for each additional kwh.

C. Minimum contracted kw of demand; 4 KW.

TARIFF 3
HIGH TENSION SERVICE

HIGH TENSION SERVICE A

APPLICABLE:

To service of 1 000 kw of contracted demand and over and 20 kv and over

TYPE OF SUPPLY:

Three phase supply at any one of the Company's available standard voltages 20 kv and over.

MONTHLY BILL:

Basic Rate:

a. Demand Charge:

W 132.00 per kw for the first 500 kw of contracted demand.
W 88.00 per kw for each additional kw of contracted demand.

b. Energy Charge:

W 8.25 per kwh for the first 90 kwh per kw of contracted demand.
W 5.37 per kwh for the next 90 kwh per kw of contracted demand.
W 3.74 per kwh for the next 180 kwh per kw of contracted demand.
W 2.36 per kwh for each additional kwh.

c. Minimum contracted kw of demand; 1,000 KW.

HIGH TENSION SERVICE B

APPLICABLE:

To service of 150 kv and over.

4

TYPE OF SUPPLY:

Three phase supply at any one of the Company's available standard voltages, 150 kv and over.

MONTHLY BILL:

Basic Rate:

a. Demand Charge:
W 88.00 per kw of contracted demand.

b. Energy Charge:

W 8.25 per kwh for the first 90 kwh per kw of contracted demand.
W 5.31 per kwh for the next 90 kwh per kw of contracted demand.
W 3.66 per kwh for the next 180 kwh per kw of contracted demand.
W 2.35 per kwh for each additional kwh.

TARIFF 4
IRRIGATION SERVICE

APPLICABLE:

To service required for the operation of pumps which are used to irrigate land for the cultivation and growing of grain for food purpose. Lighting necessary and incidential to the operation of pumps is permitted.

TYPE OF SUPPLY:

Same as "General Service B".

MONTHLY BILL:

Basic Rate:

Demand Charge: W 47.00 per kw for contracted demand.
Energy Charge: W 3.05 per kwh for each kwh.

15

TARIFF 5
STREET LIGHTING SERVICE

APPLICAB LE:

To service for operation of lighting of streets parks and similar places for the benefit and convenience of public.

TYPE OF SUPPLY:

Single phase at either 100 v or 200 v.

MONTHLY BILL:

Basic Rate: W 2.40 per watt for connected load.
Minimum Charge: W 80.00.

TARIFF 6
FLAT RATE LIGHTING SERVICE

APPLICABLE:

To lighting service (including radio substituted on set as one lamp), principally limited to 100 watts of connected load with three lamps or under. One radio set shall be counted as 20 watts.

TYPE OF SUPPLY:

Single phase supply at either 100 v or 200 v.

MONTHLY BILL:

Basic Rate:

W 4.70 per watt for first 60 watts of connected load.
W 3.20 per watt for additional watts of connected load.

Minimum Charge: W 80.00.

SPECIAL PROVISIONS

1. SPECIAL INDUSTRY:

a. To export industry customers with 200 kw of contracted demand or under.
b. To aluminium iron and steel industry customers whose power charges occupy more than 10% of the total production cost.
c. To industry customers whose power charges occuply more than 20% of the total production cost who are designated by the Minister of Commerce and Industry.

DISCOUNT: Monthly bill shall be discounted as follows:

a. 30% duscount: for esport industry customer with 200 kw of contracted demand or under.
b. 20% discount: for the aluminium, iron and steel industry customer whose electric charges occupy 10% and over, of the total production cost.
   25% discount: for the aluminium, iron and steel industry customer whose electric charges occupy 30% and over, of the total production cost.
   30% discount: for the aluminium, iron and steel industry customer whose electric charges occupy 40% and over, of the total production cost.
c. 15% discount: for the industry customer whose electric charges occupy 20% and over, of the total production cost.
   20% discount: for the industry customer whose electric charges occupy 30% and over, of the total production cost.
   25% discount: for the industry customer whose electric charges occupy 40% and over, of the total production cost.
   30% discount: for the industry customer whose electric charge occupy 50% and over, of the total production cost.

2. MUNICIPAL WATER SERVICE:

Rate for Municipal Water Service shall be discounted by 46.7%.

REPUBLIC OF KOREA - UNITED STATES
UTILITIES SUBCOMMITTEE

9 January 1970

SUBJECT: Change in Electric Power Rates under Article VI of the Status of Forces Agreement

TO: Republic of Korea Chairman, Utilities Subcommittee

1. References:

a. Paragraph 2 and Agreed Minute 1 of Article VI of the Status of Forces Agreement.

b. ROK component of the Utilities Subcommittee Memorandum of Consultation, dated 26 December 1969, subject as above, pertaining to a rate/tariff change for electric power supply to the USFK.

2. The ROK memorandum, reference 1b above, has been reviewed and the United States component of the Utilities Subcommittee fully understands the requirement for change in the electric power rates in this instance and will joint with the ROK component of the Utilities Subcommittee in presenting a memorandum on the rates to the Joint Committee.

GERALD L. HAYMAKER
Colonel, United States Army
United States Chairman
Utilities Subcommittee

Incl 2

AGENDA ITEM III ROK Presentation

(1. FOR YOUR INFORMATION: The Korea Electric Company increased its electric power charges by 10 percent, effective 27 December 1969. In accordance with the provisions of Article VI of SOFA and Joint Committee procedures, the Utilities Subcommittee has held consultations regarding the new rate schedule. The US Component of this Subcommittee has agreed that the USFK has been granted as favorable an electric power rate as any other comparable user under the new schedule. The USFK continues to be granted the same power rate as given to Korean export industries, in accordance with the terms of the US-ROK Joint Committee agreement which ended the long dispute over USFK's power rates last April (thirty-seventh Joint Committee meeting, 22 April 1969). This settlement provided that 65 of the 103 USFK electrical connection points, which consume 200 KW or less of contracted demand power per month, are accorded a 30 percent discount on their power, similar to the discount granted to ROK export industries which have similar power usage. The ROK Representative will propose Joint Committee approval of the attached Utilities Subcommittee memorandum.)

2. The United States Representative is happy to concur in the Republic of Korea Representative's proposal that the Joint Committee accept the Utilities Subcommittee memorandum as evidence of completion of the

18

consultation regarding the increased electric power rates, in accordance with the provisions of Article VI of the Status of Forces Agreement and Joint Committee procedures. The United States Representative is also pleased to note that, under the new rate schedule, the United States Forces, Korea, will continue to receive electric power in accordance with priorities, conditions, and rates or tariffs no less favorable than those accorded any other comparable user.

19

특수 산업용 전기요율 할인의 국무회의 상정

1. 상정 내용

제철, 제강, 알미늄제련, PVC용카바이드 제조등 전력비 비중이 과중한 국제경쟁 산업에 대하여 정부가 정책적으로 이들 산업을 육성하기 위하여 전기할인 요율을 각각 20%, 25%, 50%로 확대하려는 것임.

2. 국무회의 상정 보류 경위

동 문제는 69. 7. 10. , 69. 9.4. 2차에 걸쳐 국무회의에 상정되었었으나 다음과 같은 외무부의 의견으로 본안이 보류되어 왔음.
(외무부 의견)

한.미군대지위협정 제6조 2항은 미군의 공공용역 사용에 있어 최혜요율 적용을 규정하고 있으며, 동조 합의 의사록 1항은 요율변경에 있어 미군과의 사전 협의를 규정하고 있으므로 본안이 통과되는 경우 미군도 동일 할인요율적용을 주장 할 가능성이 있으며 협정문귀 해석상으로는 이를 거부할 근거가 박약함. 그렇지 않을 경우 미군 당국으로부터 동일한 할인요율 (50%) 적용을 요구하여 올 경우 이에 적의 응할것을 고려하여야 한다.

* 현재 미군에 적용되는 전기 할인요율은 30% (200kw이하의 수출산업에 적용되는 할인율임)

20

3. 관계부처와의 협의

외무부, 경제기획원, 상공부의 실무자들은 동 할인율적용의 한.미 행정협정상의 문제점을 검토하고 협의하였으며 이에 대하여 미군 당국이 협정문귀의 해석을 이유로 문제를 제기할 가능성은 있으나 이번 할인요율 확대는 미군에 적용될 성질의 것이 아니며 사전에 미군 당국과 협의 할 필요도 없다는 결론을 내리고, 만약 미군이 문제를 제기 할 경우에 대비하여 관계 부처가 협의 필요한 준비를 하기로 합의하고 국무회의에 다시 상정키로 함.

4. 국무회의 재상정

상공부는 69. 9. 19.의 국무회의에 본안을 재상정키로 하였으며 이번에 상정되는 안은 문제가 제기 될 가능성이 있는 요소인 PVC 용 카바이트제조의 50%할인안 (종전 30%할인)을 삭제하였음. 따라서 동안이 국무회의를 통과하고 시행된다 하드라도 미측에서 문제를 제기 할 여지가 없게되었음.

주 1:　한.미군대지위협정 제6조 2항 -

"합중국에 의한 이러한 공익사업과 용역의 이용은 어느 타 이용자에게 부여된것보다 불리하지 아니한 우선권, 조건 및 사용료나 요금에 따라야 한다."

The use of such utilities and services by the United States shall be in accordance with priorities, conditions, and rates or tariffs no less favorable than those accorded any other user.

주 2 :　제6조에 관한 합의 의사록 제1항 -

"합중국 군대에 적용할수 있는 우선권, 조건 및 사용료나 요금에 있어서 대한민국 당국이 결정한 변경은 그 효력발생 일전에 합동위원회의 협의대상이 될것임을 양해한다.

It is understood that any changes determined by the authorities of the Republic of Korea in priorities, conditions, and rates or tariffs, applicable to the United States armed forces shall be the subject of consultation in the Joint Committee prior to their effective date.

상 공 부

동전 1321-144 (73-9375) 1970.2.19

수신 외무부장관

제목 전기요금 개정에 따른 한미행정협정 제6조제2항 문의

1. 물정 331.24-199 (69.8.19) 및 미이-15760 (69.9.2)에 관련입니다

2. 대통령 지시사항인 PVC 공업육성의 일환책으로 특수산업용 전기요금 할인규정중 PVC 용 카바이트에 대한 할인율을 확대적용(전력비 비중에 따라 최고 50% 까지 할인)코저 동 개정안을 국무회의에 상정한바 있었으나 한미행정협정제6조제2항에 관련하여 주한미군측에서 이의를 제기하지 아니할것이라는 확실한 보장이 없어 현재까지 결정을 보지못하고 있읍니다

3. 따라서 본건 개정코저 할시는 "미군측에서 이의 없다는 보장이 없이는 조치키 난하오니 별첨 사항을 참고하시어 이에 대한 귀견을 조속 회보하여 주시기 바랍니다

문서처리인	접수일시	1970.2.19
	접수번호	6008
	분류	

2-1

일

27

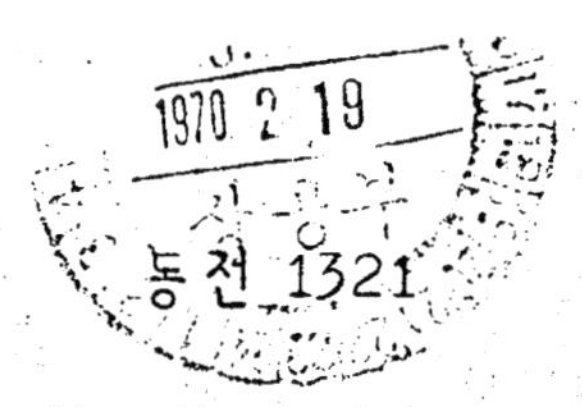

(73-9375) 1970. 2. 19

첨부 : 1. 특수산업용 전기요금 개정에 따른 문제점
2. 물정 331.24-191 (69.8.19) 사본
3. 미이 - 15760 (69.9.2) 사본 . 끝

상 공 부 장 관

2 - 2

24

1. 특수산업용 전기요금 개정에 따른 문제점

가. PVC용 카바이트 할인율을 최고 50%까지 적용토록 개정할지라도 이미 수출산업 요율을 미군에 적용하도록 미측과 합의할 당시 상수도에 대하여는 46.7%의 할인율이 있었음으로 별문제가 없을것이라하나

나. 만약 미군측에서 한미행협 제6.2조의 "최저요금적용"을 내세워 금번 개정할 PVC 용 카바이트 할인율 50%를 미군에도 적용할것을 주장하거나 실지 적용하게되면 대 미군 전기요금액 및 수납에 큰차질을 초래하게 됨

다. 미군요금. 전체에 대한 50% 적용시:
수입감소액은 년 2,033천불이 됨.

25

경 제 기 획 원

물정 331.24-199 (72-9714) 1969.8.19

수신 상공부장관

제목 한미합동위원회 협의요청

1. 동전 1321-1015 (69.8.6)에 대한 응신입니다

2. 물정 331.24-187 (69.7.31) 로 이미 통보한바와 같이 본건은 한미행정 협정 6조 2항 및 합의 의사록 6조 1항에 의하여 미군에 적용되는 것이 아니므로 원칙적으로 한미간 협의가 불필요한 사항입니다.

3. 다만 비공식정으로 미군측 실무자와 접촉한 결과 본건에 대해 미군측에서 문제를 제기할 가능성이 있을것으로 보이나 이 경우 이미 수출산업요율을 미군에 적용하도록 합의할 당시 상수도에 대하여는 46.7% 의 할인을 하고 있던점에 비추어 보아 원래 문제된점이 다시 제기되는 것에 불과한 것입니다. 끝

경 제 기 획 원 장 관

26

외 무 부

미이 — 15760 1969.9.2

수신 상공부장관

제목 한.미합동위원회 협의 문제 회답

1. 동전 1321—1132 (69.8.28)의 회신입니다

2. 귀부의 특수산업 전기요금 할인규정의 개정에 대하여 주한미군 당국은 한.미군대지위협정 제6조2항과 제6조1항에 대한 합의 의사록 1항에 의거하여 문제를 제기할 가능성은 있으나

3. 상기 할인규정의 개정에 앞서 미국측과의 사전 협의는 불필요한것으로 판단됩니다

4. 미국측의 문제 제기에 대비하여 관계부처간에 사전 협의를 통해 한국정부 입장을 미리 준비하는것이 가할것임을 아울러 첨언합니다. 끝

외 무 부 장 관

2ㄲ

증산 수출 건설

기 안 용 지

분류기호 문서번호	미이-	(전화번호)	전결규정 조 항 전결사항
처리기한		기 안 자	결 재 자
시행일자		북미2과 백 성 흴	
보존년한		70. 2. 23.	

보조기관		
	차 관	
	차관보	후결
	국 장	
	북미2과장	
협 조		
경 유 수 신 참 조	상공부 장관	통제관 1970. 2. 24 / 발송 3263 1970. 2. 24 외무부 정서
제 목	전기요금 개정에 따른 한.미군대지위협정 제6조 2항에 대한 문의 회신	

1. 동건 1321-1132(69. 8. 28.), 미이-15760(69.9.2.) 및 동건 1321-144(70. 2. 19)과 관련됩니다.

2. 귀부의 특수산업(PVC 공업) 전기요금할인규정의 개정에 대하여 주한미군 당국은 한.미군대지위협정 제6조 2항과 제 6조 1항에 대한 합의 의사록 1항에 의거하여 문제를 제기할 가능성이 있으므로

3. 미측의 문제 제기에 대비하여 지난번 전기요금 15%인상시(1967. 11.1.부)에 주한미군에 적용될 전기요금을 위요한 한.미간분쟁점, 양국의 입장 및 양국합의점 도달(별첨)등을 참조하시여 미측에서 ~~[illegible]~~ 최혜 대우(본건의 경우는 PVC 공업에 적용되는 전기요금할인율를 주한미군에 적용)을 주장할수 없는 방안을 모색하여야 할것으로 사료됩니다.

공통서식 1-2-1 (갑) 1967. 4. 4. 승인 (18절지) 2급인쇄용지 70g/m² (500,000매 인쇄)

납세의 의무 3780

28

4. 본 처리를 위한 당부의 의견으로는 주한미군의 이의 제기에 대한 대비책으로서 전기요율표의 특별조치 규정(수출산업 및 도시상수도용전기 및 도서지방의 전기요율할인율)과는 별도로, 아래 내용의 임시 조치 규정을 마련하는 방안도 고려할수 있다고 사료됩니다.

가. 불실기업체의 정리를 위한 임시조치의 일환으로써,

나. 당해기업의 경영 및 운영전반에 대한 정부의 직접 감독을 받을 것을 응락하는것을 조건으로

다. 당해기업의 경영 및 운영이 정상궤도에 도달할때까지 임시적으로 정부의 보조금조로 당해기업이 수요하는 한국전력주식회사 전기요금을 임시 할인조치한다.

첨 부: 1967. 11. 1.자로 인상된 전기요금 대 미군적용에 관한 문제요약 1부, 끝

29

외 무 부

미이 -　　　　　　　　　　　　　　　　1970. 2. 24.

수신: 상공부 장관

제목: 전기요금 개정에 따른 한.미군대지위협정 제6조2항에 대한 문의 회신

1. 동건 1321-1132(69. 8. 28.), 미이-15760(69. 9.2.) 및 동건1321-144(70. 2. 19.)과 관련됩니다.

2. 귀부의 특수산업(PVC 공업)전기요금할인규정의 개정에 대하여 주한미군당국은 한.미군대지위협정 제6조2항과 제6조 1항에 대한 합의의사록 1항에 의거하여 문제를 제기할 가능성이 있으므로

3. 미측의 문제 제기에 대비하여 지난번 전기요금 15%인상시(1967. 11. 1부)에 주한미군에 적용될 전기요금을 위요한 한.미간 분쟁점, 양국의 입장 및 양국합의점도달(별첨)등을 참조하시어 미측에서 최혜대우(본건의 경우는 PVC공업에 적용되는 전기요금할인율를 주한미군에 적용)을 주장할수 없는 별도의 방안을 모색하여야 할것으로 사료됩니다.

첨 부: 1967. 11. 1.자로 인상된 전기요금 대 미군적용에 관한 문제 요약 1부. 끝

외 무 부 장 관

30

1967. 11. 1.자로 인상된 전기요금 대 미군 적용에 관한 문제 요약

1. 문제점 및 쌍방 입장

가. 문제점

67.11. 1. 인상 전기요금이 시행되었는바, 신요율표에는 농사용, 상수도 양수용, 도서지역 및 특수산업용에 대한 특혜요율 또는 할인요율이 정하여 지고 있었으며 미측은 특히 특수산업용(수출산업)할인제를 주목하고 협정 6조 2항의 priorities, conditions and rates or tariffs no less favorable than any other user

에 위반한다하여 6조 합의의사록 1항 소정의 협의 절차에서 이의를 제기하여 69. 4. 22. 미군에게도 수출산업에 적용하는 30%(최저율)을 적용할것을 함. 미간에 합 의할때까지 1년이상에 걸쳐 신요율에 의한 사용료를 지불하지 않고 있었음.

나. 당시의 미측 주장

(1) 미측은 전기 4종의 특혜요율중 특히 수출산업에 대한 할인(15%, 20%, 30%)에 대하여 이의를 제기하고 6조 1항 any other user에는 아무런 제한 어구가 없으므로 미군이 최저요율의 적용을 받아야하며, 따라서 전기 할인제를 적용하라고 주장, 미군도 외화로 지불하고 있으며, 이점에서 수출산업과 성질이 같다고 지적하였음.

(2) 미측은 요율수준의 고하를 문제시하고 있는것이 아니고 최혜대우를 받어야한다는 원칙 준수를 요구 함.

31

(3) 한국정부가 정책상 보조금 지급을 결정하는 권한을 행사하는것은 미국이 관여할바 아니나, 보조금이라면 그 취지가 명시되는 방법, 예컨데 국고금 지불, 세금 공제등의 방식을 취하여야 하며, 요율을 할인하는 경우에는 미측도 동일 할인을 받어야 함.

(4) 현 협정하에서는 신요율표를 인정 지불하는 경우, 법적 책임을 불면함.

다. 당시의 한국측 주장

(1) 특수 산업에 대한 할인은 별도 요율이 아니고 내용적으로는 보조금지불의 성격이며, 따라서 6조 1항과는 관계가 없다.

(2) 수출산업에 대한 할인은 외화획득이 주목적이 아니며, 유치산업 보조에 의한 국제경쟁력 강화를 목적으로 하는 것이다.

(3) 4종의 특수요율은 목적별, 용도별이므로 미군에 대하여 차별대우가 아니며 미군도 소정 목적으로 전기를 사용하는 경우에는 동 요율을 적용하는 것이다.

2. 양측 합의점 도달

가. 한.미공공용역분과위원회가 주한미군중 200KW이하를 수요하는 부대에 대하여는 특수 수출산업에 적용하는 당시 최저요율인 30%할인율을 적용하도록 합의하고 1969. 4. 22.자로 제 37차 한.미합동위원회에 각서를 제출 이를 승인함으로서 타결을 봄.

나. 동 합동위원회에서 미국대표는 제 6조 2항에 사용한 "any other user"라는 용어를 " any other generally comparable user "로 미측은 해석한다고 따라서 주한미군은 수출산업에 적용되는 할인율을

31

32

적용받게 되는것이라고 발언하고 이를 동 회의록에 기록했음.

다. 참고로 [illegible] 당시 한.미협의 계류중이든 인천수도요금의 미군 적용 문제에 대하여 미측이 종전에 주장하든 공중목욕탕에 적용하는 입방미터당 21원의 적용을 포기하고 특수수출산업(주한미군이 이 범주에 속한다는 뜻) 에 적용하는 입방미터당 27원을 적용할것에 합의하였음. (69. 8. 28. 제 41차 한.미합동위원회에서)

3. 관계 군대지위협정조항

제 6조 합의의사록

" I. It is understood that any changes determined by the authorities of the Republic of Korea in priorities, conditions, and rates or tariffs, applicable to the United States armed forces shall be the subject of consultation in the Joint Committee prior to their effective date."

제 6조 2항

" 2. The use of such utilities and services by the United States shall be in accordance with priorities, conditions, and rates of tariffs no less favourable than those accorded any other user."

Except from minutes of the thirty-seventh meeting, Joint Committee under SOFA, 22 April 1969.

25 ------ The US authorities have interpreted the phrase "any other user" to mean any other generally comparable user",-------

37

Excerpt from the letter to U.S.Chairman, Utilities Subcommittee sent by ROK Chairman, Utilities Subcommittee, dated August 25, 1969 concerning consultation for the increased rate of water service, Inchon.

----- You will note that the proposed rate is the one applicable to the industrial use, which is most comparable to the U.S. Forces' use in terms of the quantity of water consumtion. --------

계

첨부 5

EXTRACTS OF SOFA'S ON UTILITIES AND SERVICES

Utilities 수도 3/07.

Japan (June 23, 1960)

Article VII

The United States armed forces shall have the use of all public utilities and services belonging to, or controlled or regulated by the Government of Japan, and shall enjoy priorities in such use, under conditions no less favorable than those that may be applicable from time to time to the ministries and agencies of the Government of Japan.

Republic of China - no provisions (Aug. 31, 1965)

Philippines

Article VII Use of Public Services

It is mutually agreed that the United States may employ and use for United States military forces any and all public utilities, other services and facilities,

35

airfields, ports, harbors, roads, highways, railroads, bridges, viaducts, cannals, lakes, rivers and streams in the Philippines under conditions no less favorable than those that may be applicable from time to time to the military forces of the Philippines.

Australia (May 9, 1963)

Article XXIII paragraph (1)

The United States Forces and all persons associated with activities agreed upon by the two Governments may use the public services and facilities owned, controlled or regulated by the Australian Government or its instrumentalities. The terms of use, including charges, shall be no less favorable than those available to other users in like circumstances unless otherwise agreed.

Dominican Republic (March 19, 1957)

Article XXVI

The Government of the United States of America shall have the right to employ and use, in order to carry out the purposes of this Agreement, all public services, including any water rights owned or controlled by the Dominican Republic,

subject to the tariffs established by the Dominican laws and regulations. Utilities and other facilities, bays, roads, highways, bridges and similar channels of transportation belonging, controlled or regulated by the Government of the Dominican Republic shall be used under such terms and conditions as shall be mutually agreed upon by the two Governments.

Nicaragua (Sept. 5, 1958)

No provisions

West Indies (Feb. 10, 1961)

Article VII

Public Services and Facilities

(1) The United States Forces, United States contractors and the members of the United States Forces and contractor personnel may use the public services and facilities belonging to or controlled or regulated by the Federal Government or the Government of the Territory. The terms of use, including charges, shall be no less favorable than those available to other users unless otherwise agreed ...

Ethiopia (May 22, 1953)

The Imperial Ethiopian Government grants to the Government of the United States the right to employ and use public and commercial utilities, services, transportation and communication facilities in Ethiopia in connection with operations under this Agreement. The Government of the United States shall pay for any employment or usage of such facilities at the most favorable rates obtained by other public users who employ and use such facilities.

公益使用者中의 최저사용

Libya (Sept. 9, 1954)

Article V

Public Services and Facilities

Upon the request of the Government of the United States of America and provided that the Government of the United Kingdom of Libya is assured that the public and private interests in Libya will be duly safeguarded, the public services and facilities in Libya shall be made available as far as practicable for the use of the Government of the United States of America and members of the United States forces. The charges therefor shall be the same as those paid by other users, unless otherwise agreed.

39

38

NATO (June 19, 1951)

Article IX

1. Members of a force or of a civilian component and their dependents may purchase locally goods necessary for their own consumption, and such service as they need, under the same conditions as the nationals of the receiving State.

3. Subject to agreements already in force or which may hereafter be made between the authorized representatives of the sending and receiving States, the authorities of the receiving State shall assume sole responsibility for making suitable arrangements to make available a force or a civilian component the buildings and grounds which it requires, as well as facilities and services connected therewith. These agreements and arrangements shall be, as far as possible, in accordance with the regulations governing the accommodation and billeting of similar personnel of the receiving State. In the absense of a specific contract to the contrary, the laws of the receiving State shall determine the rights and obligations arising out of the occupation or use of the buildings, grounds, facilities or services.

39

Germany (Aug. 3, 1959)

Article 47

1. The Federal Republic shall accord to a force or a civilian component treatment in the matter of procurement of goods and services not less favorable than is accorded to the German Armed Forces.

Greece (Sept. 7, 1956)

NATO Agr.

40

경 제 기 획 원

물정 331.24- 1146 1970. 6. 5.

수신 외무부 장관

제목 SOFA 협정에 의한 수도 요금 조정 협의

건설부 장관으로 부터 부산시, 인천시의 상수도 급수 조례 개정으로 인한 상수도 요금을 유엔군에 적용키 위하여 SOFA 협정에 의한 협의를 요청하여 온바 이를 별첨과 같이 미측 공공용역 분과 위원회 위원장에게 제의 하였음을 통보하오니 양지 하시기 바랍니다.

첨부 미측 협의 공문 사본 1부. 끝.

공람	담당	과장	국장

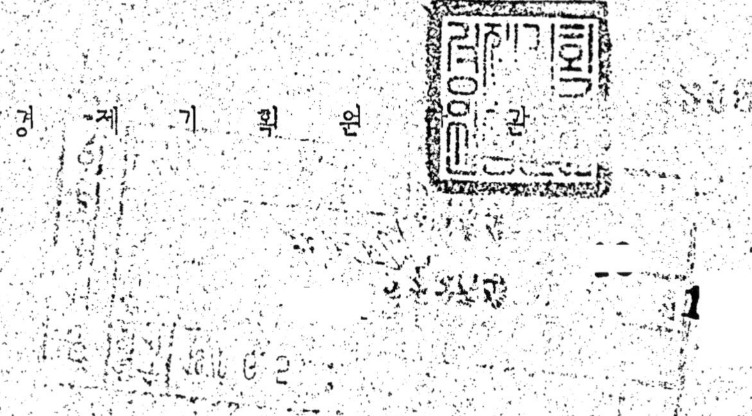

경 제 기 획 원 장관

41

REPUBLIC OF KOREA-UNITED STATES

UTILITIES SUBCOMMITTEE

June 1, 1970

SUBJECT: Change in Water Supply Rate Schedule applicable to the US Armed Forces under Article VI of the Status of Forces Agreement.

TO: US chairman, Utilities Subcommittee

1. Reference: Paragraph 2 and Agreed Minute 1 of Article VI of the Status of Forces Agreement.

2. The Government of the United States is informed through this written consultative process that the Republic of Korea proposes to change the following rates/tariffs at locations indicated below:

Rates/Tariffs	Location
Water Supply rate schedule	The city of Pusan and the city of Inchon including Bupyoung & Kimpo

3. The following data are provided:

a. Effective date.
Although the rate changes are effective from March 2, 1970 in Pusan and March 1, 1970 in Inchon, the new rate will be applied to the U.S Forces' use in accordance with the agreement set forth in the letter dated 15 November, 1969

b. Rate schedule of proposed change.
Refer to item "d".

c. Rate schedule showing rates that are charged all classes of users. (Attachment 1)

d. Calculation of old and new rate.

location	unit	old rate (won)	new rate (won)	Remarks
Pusan city	m^3	21	25	
Inchon city	Basic rate for first $100m^3$	2000	2500	Bupung & Kimpo included
	over charge per m3	27	33	

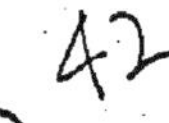

e. Reasons for revision of rate base.

To cover the rising cost.

4. The Government of ROK adivises the Government of the United states that the priorities, conditions and rates or tariffs being changed are no less favorable than those accorded any other user.

The view of the Government of the United States is solisited as soon as possible. You may be assured that your views will be greatly appreciated.

Suck Joon, Suh
Director, Office of Price Policy
Republic of Korea chairman
Utilities Subcommittee

43

(Attachment1,

Water rate of the city of Pusan
****

description	basic (month) Quantity(Ton)	rate(Won)	excess charge (per excess ton)
domestic use : class I	10	130	22
: class II	20	400	25
commercial use : class I	20	600	32
: class II	30	1,200	50
governmental office			25
industrial use	200	5,000	27
public bathing use : classI	500	12,500	27
: classII	500	20,000	50
special public use			25
recreation			100
ship use			34
temporary use			42
common use A(public)			10
B(private)			10
fire fighting exercise		345 por hydrant	345 per each exercise

44

(Attachment 1)

Water rate of the City of Inchon
****

description	MONTHLY BASIC RATE Quantity (Ton)	rate (Won)	EXCESS charge(Per Excess Ton)
Household Use	7	130	23
Business Use	30	900	35
Bath Business Use	300	7,500	30
Public Office Use	30	750	33
Industrial Use	100	2,500	33
Military Use	100	2,500	33
Vessel & Railroad Use	-	-	35
Temporary Use	-	-	35
Special Public Use	30	600	25
Common Use			
A (Private)	25	450	20
B (Public)	1	18	
Fire fighting exercise	200 Per hydrant		200 Per each exercise

REPUBLIC OF KOREA - UNITED STATES
UTILITIES SUBCOMMITTEE

11 September 1970

MEMORANDUM FOR: The Joint Committee

SUBJECT: Consultation on Rate/Tariff Change

1. Subcommittee Members:

Republic of Korea	United States
SUH Suck Joon, Chairman	COL Gerald L. Haymaker, Chairman
CHOI Soo Byung, Secretary	COL Hugh L. Schmitt, Alternate Chairman
LEE Kil Sang, Member	MAJ Virgil V. Carlsen, Secretary
NOH Jin Shick, Member	LCDR Bruce B. Bower, Member
HAN Jung Soo, Member	LTC Samuel L. Defebo, Member
CHUNG Jong Taik, Member	MAJ James A. Tolcher, Member
SONG Hae Joon, Member	Mr. Samuel Pollack, Member
LEE Nak Young, Member	Mr. Don Leland, Member
LEE Seung Kon, Member	Mr. Francis K. Cook, Member
SHIN Kyong Shick, Member	

2. Subject of Recommendation: Agreed Minute 1 to Article VI, ROK/US SOFA, provides that any changes determined by the authorities of the Republic of Korea in priorities, conditions and rates or tariffs applicable to the United States Forces, Korea, shall be the subject of consultation in the Joint Committee prior to their effective date.

3. The Republic of Korea has initiated consultation concerning a change in rates or tariffs for the cost of water for the cities of Inchon and Pusan in addition to Bupyoung and Kimpo, effective 1 June 1970, under contract #DAJB03-69-C-0275 (see Inclosure 1).

4. The United States component of the Utilities Subcommittee has received the ROK request for consultation and has determined that the requested change in rates or tariffs is no less favorable than those accorded any other comparable user (see Inclosure 2).

46

SUBJECT: Consultation on Rate/Tariff Change

5. It is recommended that the two inclosures referenced in paragraphs 3 and 4 be accepted by the Joint Committee as evidence of consultation contemplated by Article VI of the Status of Forces Agreement.

SUH SUCK JOON
Republic of Korea Chairman
Utilities Subcommittee

COL GERALD L. HAYMAKER, USA
United States Chairman
Utilities Subcommittee

2

45-1.E

47

REPUBLIC OF KOREA-UNITED STATES

UTILITIES SUBCOMMITTEE

June 1, 1970

SUBJECT: Change in Water Supply Rate Schedule applicable to the US Armed Forces under Article VI of the Status of Forces Agreement.

TO: US chairman, Utilities Subcommittee

1. Reference: Paragraph 2 and Agreed Minute 1 of Article VI of the Status of Forces Agreement.

2. The Government of the United States is informed through this written consultative process that the Republic of Korea proposes to change the following rates/tariffs at locations indicated below:

Rates/Tariffs	Location
Water Supply rate schedule	The city of Pusan and the city of Inchon including Bupyoung & Kimpo

3. The following data are provided:

a. Effective date.
Although the rate changes are effective from March 2, 1970 in Pusan and March 1, 1970 in Inchon, the new rate will be applied to the U.S Forces' use in accordance with the agreement set forth in the letter dated 15 November, 1969

b. Rate schedule of proposed change.
Refer to item "d".

c. Rate schedule showing rates that are charged all classes of users. (Attachment 1)

d. Calculation of old and new rate.

location	unit	old rate (won)	new rate (won)	Remarks
Pusan city	m^3	21	25	
Inchon city	Basic rate for first $100m^3$	2000	2500	Bupung & Kimpo included
	over charge per m3	27	33	

48

e. Reasons for revision of rate base.
To cover the rising cost.

4. The Government of ROK adivises the Government of the United states that the priorities, conditions and rates or tariffs being changed are no less favorable than those accorded any other user.
The view of the Government of the United States is solisited as soon as possible. You may be assured that your views will be greatly appreciated.

Suck J. Suh
Suck John, Suh
Director, Office of Price Policy
Republic of Korea chairman
Utilities Subcommittee

46-1. E

49

(Attachment1)

Water rate of the city of Pusan
****

description	basic (month)		excess charge (per excess ton)
	Quantity(Ton)	rate(Won)	
domestic use : class I	10	130	22
: class II	20	400	25
commercial use : class I	20	600	32
: class II	30	1,200	50
governmental office			25
industrial use	200	5,000	27
public bathing use : classI	500	12,500	27
: classII	500	20,000	50
special public use			25
recreation			100
ship use			34
temporary use			42
common use A(public)			10
B(private)			10
fire fighting exercise	345 per hydrant		345 per each exercise

60

(Attachment 1)

Water rate of the City of Inchon
****

description	MONTHLY BASIC RATE		EXCESS charge(Per Excess Ton)
	Quantity (Ton)	rate (Won)	
Household Use	7	130	23
Business Use	30	900	35
Bath Business Use	300	7,500	30
Public Office Use	30	750	33
Industrial Use	100	2,500	33
Military Use	100	2,500	33
Vessel & Railroad Use	-	-	35
Temporary Use	-	-	35
Special Public Use	30	600	25
Common Use			
A (Private)	25	450	20
B (Public)	1	18	
Fire fighting exercise	200 Per hydrant		200 Per each exercise

51

REPUBLIC OF KOREA - UNITED STATES
UTILITIES SUBCOMMITTEE

9 September 1970

SUBJECT: Change in Water Supply Rate Schedule Applicable to the US Armed Forces under Article VI of the Status of Forces Agreement

ROK Chairman, Utilities Subcommittee

1. Reference:

a. Paragraph 2 and Agreed Minute 1 of Article VI of the Status of Forces Agreement.

b. ROK component of the Utilities Subcommittee Memorandum, dated 15 November 1969, pertaining to effective date of any rate/tariff change.

c. ROK component of the Utilities Subcommittee Memorandum of Consultation, dated 1 June 1970, subject as above, pertaining to a rate/tariff change for water service to the USFK.

2. The ROK memorandum, reference 1c above, has been reviewed and the United States component of the Utilities Subcommittee fully understands the requirement for change in the water rates in this instance and will join with the ROK component of the Utilities Subcommittee in presenting a memorandum on the rates to the Joint Committee.

GERALD L. HAYMAKER
Colonel, U.S. Army
United States Chairman
Utilities Subcommittee

62

기 안 용 지

분류기호 문서번호	미이 742 -	(전화번호 :)	전결규정 조 항 전결사항
처리기한		기 안 자	결 재 자
시행일자		북미2과 이승곤	
보존년한		70. 9. 25.	국 장
보조기관	과 장		
협 조			
경 유 수 신 참 조	경제기획원장관	통제	정서
제 목	한.미 행정협정에 의한 합동위원회의 인상 수도 요율 적용에 관한 합의.		

1. 물정 331.24 - 146 (70. 6. 5.) 공한과 관련입니다.

2. 9. 24. 에 개최된 한.미 행정협정에 의한 합동위원회는 부산직할시 및 인천시의 1970. 3. 2.자 및 1970. 3.1.자로 인상된 수도 요율을 한.미 행정협정 제6조 에 관한 합의의사록 에 의하여 주한미군 에게도 1970. 6. 1.부터 적용키로 합의하였음을 알려드립니다.

첨부 : 전기 건에 관한 양측 합의문서 (사본) 1 부. 끝

공용서식 1-2-1 (갑)
1967. 4. 4. 승인

(18절지) 2급인쇄용지 70g/m²
(조달청 ,50,000매 인쇄)

외 무 부

미이 742 - 1970. 9. 25.

수 신 : 경제기획원 장관

제 목 : 한.미 행정협정에 의한 합동위원회의 인상 수도 요율 적용에 관한 합의.

1. 물정 331.24 - 146 (70. 6. 5.) 공한과 관련입니다.

2. 9. 24.에 개최된 한.미 행정협정에 의한 합동위원회는 부산직할시 및 인천시의 1970. 3. 2.자 및 1970. 3. 1.자로 인상된 수도 요율을 한.미 행정협정 제 6조에 관한 합의의사록에 의하여 주한미군에게도 1970. 6. 1. 부터 적용키로 합의하였음을 알려드립니다.

첨부 : 전기 건에 관한 양측 합의문서(사본) 1 부. 끝

외 무 부 장 관

54

경 제 기 획 원

물정 331.24-282 (72-9714) 1970. 12. 15.

수신 외무부장관

23

제목 SOFA협정에 의한 수도요금 조정 협의

건설부장관으로 부터 대구시의 상수도 급수 조례 개정으로 인한 상수도 요금을 유엔군에 적용키 위하여 SOFA 협정에 의한 협의를 요청하여 온바 이를 별첨과 같이 미측 공공용역분과 위원회 위원장에게 제의 하였음을 통보하오니 양지하시기 바랍니다.

첨부 미측 협의 공문 사본 1부. 끝.

경 제 기 획 원

55

16 DEC '70 15:29
52501

REPUBLIC OF KOREA-UNITED STATES
UTILITIES SUBCOMMITTEE

December 9, 1970

SUBJECT: Change in Water Supply Rate Schedule applicable to the US Armed Forces under Article VI of the Status of Forces Agreement.

TO: US chairman, Utilities Subcommittee

1. Reference: Paragraph 2 and Agreed Minute 1 of Article VI of the Status of Forces Agreement.

2. The Government of the United States is informed through this written consultative process that the Republic of Korea proposes to change the following rates/tariffs at locations indicated below:

Rates/Tariffs	Location
Water supply rate schedule	The city of Taegu

3. The following data are provided:

a. Effective date
Although the rate changes are effective from January 1, 1970 in the city of Taegu, the new rate will be applied to the U.S Forces' use in accordance with the agreement set forth in the letter dated November 15, 1969.

b. Rate schedule of proposed change.
Refer to item " d ".

c. Rate schedule showing rates that are charged all classes of users. (Attached)

56

d. Calculation of old and new rate

location	unit	old rate(won)	New rate(won)
the city of Taegu	m^3	22	27

e. Reason for revision of rate base.

To cover the rising cost.

4. The Government of ROK advises the Governmentof the United States that the priorities, conditions and rates or tariffs being changed are no less favorable than those accorded any other user. The view of the Government of the United States is solicited as soon as possible. You may be assured that your views will be greatly appreciated.

Suh

Suck Joon, Suh
Director, Office of Price Policy
Republic of Korea chairman
Utilities Subcommittee

57

Attachment

Water Supply Rate of all classes of users

class	Basic Charge		Over charge(per Excess M^3)	
	quantity(M^3)	rate(won)	over quantity(M^3)	rate(won)
Domestic Use	10	150	11-50 Above 50	23 24
Industrial Use	100	1,800	101-1000 Above 1000	23 25
Commercial Use	10	240	10-50 Above 50	33 37
Public Bath Use	100	1,500	101-1000 Above 1000	25 29
Temporary or Recreational Use	-	-	-	50
Military Use	-	-	-	27
Common Use				
A (Private)	10	130	Above 10	20
B (Public)	100	1,000	Above 100	17

58

2. 1971년

59

72-9704
북미2과 사무관

외 무 부

년 월 일

問題点 : —37 J.C. '69.

1. 왜 military use 를 Industrial use 로 바꾸었느냐?

To mean any other generally comparable user.

2. 이번 大邱市의 수도료 인상이 industrial use 에 대로 적용되느냐? 또한 USFK 도 적용되느냐?

북미 2 과 장

무자리 왜?

58

410

외 무 부

년 월 일

3. 大邱市에 12个了 稅法에 있어, USFK 혜택을 통하여는 大邱市 조례를 고쳐야 한다.

의견 :

① Any other user 는 "All" 이 아님.

1229

② Industrial use 는 고어의 성격을 갖느냐 개념은 항상 발전하고 현실적이야 되니까 재검토 要. —— different in nature 이니까 使用料이 同一하다는 사실이 同一한 것이라 봅니다.

41

③ 韓美 12条에 적용하는 요금이 참고할 Any other Generally Comparable User 임.

북미 2 과 장

59

60

72 9704
북 2과 사무관
3/11

외 무 부

년 월 일

問題點 : —37 J.C. '69.

1. 왜 military use 를 Industrial use로 변경 했느냐 ?
To mean any other generally comparable user.

2. 이번 大統領의 수도 料 인상이 industrial use 에대로 적용되나 ? 오직 USFK 만 적용되나 ?

북 미 2 과 장
후자라면 왜 ? 58 410
1228

외 무 부

년 월 일

3. 大統領에 12개 種類 인데, USFK 혜택을 부하려는 大統領 조례를 고쳐야 한다.
의뢰중

① Any other user 는 "All" 이 아님. 1229

② Industrial use 는 2개의 선례를 맺으나 개념은 항상 발전하고 현실적이야 하니까, 재검토 要. — different in nature 이니까 使用量이 同一한 것은 性質이 同一한것 아님니다.

41

북 미 2 과 장 59
③ 韓國 12種에 적용하는 요율이 원칙인 Any other Generally Comparable User임.

60

외 무 부

Minutes on U 년 월 일

1. P770.

Garbage disposal services will be exempted from

2. P770 . p 783.

料金을 소급하는 경우는

인상요금 적용 ——

협의 승인 새요금 적용.

(will retroactively pay the new rates from the effective date set by ROK.)

북 미 2 과 장

61

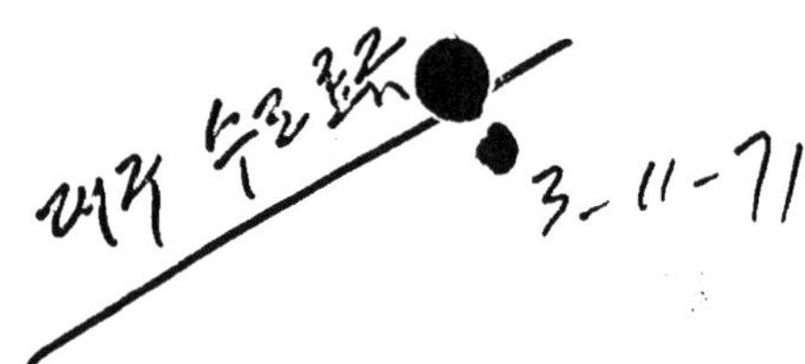

韓國側 主張:

1. 特定産業 (Industrial Rate referred by US)에 대한 저율적용(할인)은 별도 요금이 아니고, 내용적으로는 보조금 지불의 성격임. 그로 SOFA 협정 6조 1항과는 관계가 없음.

2. 수출산업 (Industrial Rate referred by US)에 한 할인은 외화획득이 목적이 아니고, 육성산업 보조형식으로 간주한 저율적용임.

3. 1 및 2項의 특수요금은 목적별, 용도별이므로 USFK에 대한 차별대우가 아님. 뿐만 아니라 "Any other user" (6조 2항)의 정의는(concept) 대한민국 정부가 시행하고 있는 공공용역 운영상 정상적인, 일반적인 (General Term) 利用者를 칭하며, 예외적인 特定産業 取扱 받는 case를 지칭함은 아님.

61

62

외 무 부

ROK側 : 년 월 일

1. 大仲介의 物価等의 앙등에 대비한것 (local gait 임금협정에서 농촌노동자와 비교)

2. 한국 모범고용에 비교해서 同一水準임 — 當然 最下限선을 (강제로 책정한것임)

3. 1 및 2 項에 의하여 less favorable 한 條件이 아님.

4.

북 미 2 과 장

63

REPUBLIC OF KOREA-UNITED STATES
UTILITIES SUBCOMMITTEE

30 January, 1971

SUBJECT: Change in Water Supply Rate Schedule applicable to the US Armed Forces under Article VI of the Status of Forces Agreement.

TO: US chairman, Utilities Subcommittee

1. Reference:

a. Paragraph 2 and Agreed Minute 1 of Article VI of the Status of Forces Agreement.

b. Korean component of the Utilities Subcommittee Memorandum of Consultation, dated 9 December 1970.

2. Concerning the water rate in the city of Taegu, we referred to the city of Taegu and received the following opinions:

a. Comparably low rate of industrial use is the reflection of the policy of the City to maintain the low industrial cost. This policy cannot be applied to other uses.

b. The proposed military rate is already made effective to Korean military uses from 1 January 1970. The U.S. military use is most comparable, in nature, to the Korean military use.

c. The U.S. rate is more favorable in Taegu, as compared to that of Inchon.

d. The military rate is already set at reasonably low level, referring to other uses such as business, bathing and recreation.

3. Taking the above points into consideration, I would like to request you that you would proceed the consultation as soon as possible. Your cooperation will be highly appreciated.

Suck Joon, Suh
Director, Office of Price Policy
Republic of Korea chairman
Utilities Subcommittee

65

REPUBLIC OF KOREA-UNITED STATES

UTILITIES SUBCOMMITTEE

December 9, 1970

SUBJECT: Change in Water Supply Rate Schedule applicable to the US Armed Forces under Article VI of the Status of Forces Agreement.

TO: US chairman, Utilities Subcommittee

1. Reference: Paragraph 2 and Agreed Minute 1 of Article VI of the Status of Forces Agreement.

2. The Government of the United States is informed through this written consultative process that the Republic of Korea proposes to change the following rates/tariffs at locations indicated below:

Rates/Tariffs	Location
Water supply rate schedule	The city of Taegu

3. The following data are provided:

a. Effective date
Although the rate changes are effective from January 1, 1970 in the city of Taegu, the new rate will be applied to the U.S Forces' use in accordance with the agreement set forth in the letter dated November 15, 1969.

b. Rate schedule of proposed change.
Refer to item " d ".

c. Rate schedule showing rates that are charged all classes of users. (Attached)

66

d. Calculation of old and new rate

location	unit	old rate(won)	New rate(won)
The city of Taegu	m^3	22	27

e. Reason for revision of rate base.

To cover the rising cost.

4. The Government of ROK advises the Governmentof the United States that the priorities, conditions and rates or tariffs being changed are no less favorable than those accorded any other user. The view of the Government of the United States is solicited as soon as possible. You may be assured that your views will be greatly appreciated.

Suck Joon, Suh
Director, Office of Price Policy
Republic of Korea chairman
Utilities Subcommittee

Attachment

Water Supply Rate of all classes of users

class	Basic Charge		Over charge(per Excess M^3)	
	quantity(M^3)	rate(won)	over quantity(M^3)	rate(won)
Domestic Use	10	150	11-50	23
			Above 50	24
Industrial Use	100	1,800	101-1000	23
			Above 1000	25
Commercial Use	10	240	10-50	33
			Above 50	37
Public Bath Use	100	1,500	101-1000	25
			Above 1000	29
Temporary or Recreational Use	-	-	-	50
Military Use	-	-	-	27
Common Use				
A (Private)	10	130	Above 10	20
B (Public)	100	1,000	Above 100	17

공 란

공 란

공 란

공 란

공 란

공　　　란

(Art. 6, 2 para — no less fav.
Agreed Mi' Art 6. 1 paragh — phrase their effective date.

Ⅱ pending 외: 부

년 월 일

① Referring to Article 6, 2nd phrase which provide that the use of such utilities & services by the US shall be in accordance with priorities, conditions, & rates of tariffs no less favorable than those accorded any other user."

In the 37th JC meeting the US authorities have interpreted the phrase "any other users" to mean any other generally comparable user.

북미 2 과 장

Any user of ... all including exceptional.

69

* The industrial use
1. Subsidy, a kind of ... aid.
2. An exceptional, particular, not general & usual case.

외 무 부

년 월 일

② It is my understanding that the precedent done by both parties that the Industrial use was most comparable to USFK use in terms of the quantity of water consumption was not reasonable. Because the same quantity of water consumption is one thing, the quality & the nature of use of water is quite another thing.

70

북 미 2 과 장

(Art. 6, 2 para — no less fav.
Agreed Min Art 6. 1 paragh — priority
their effective date

III pending 외: 水道料

외 무 부

년 월 일

① Referring to Article 6, 2nd phrase which provide that the use of such ~~public~~ utilities & services by the US shall be in accordance with priorities, conditions, & rates of tariffs no less favorable than those accorded any other user."

In the 37th JC meeting the US authorities have interpreted the phrase "any other user" to mean any other generally comparable user.

북미 2과 장

Any ... including exceptional.

69

* The industrial use { 1. Subsidy, a kind of ... 2. An exceptional, particularly, not general & usual case.

외 무 부

년 월 일

② It is my understanding that the precedent done by both parties that the industrial use was most comparable to ~~the~~ USFK use in terms of the quantity of water consumption was not reasonable. Because the same quantity of water consumption is one thing, the quality & the nature of use of water is quite ...

70

북미 2과 장

175

모범주長 - 交通部

외 무 부

년 월 일

③ It is my understanding & conviction that the proposed rate should be the one applicable to the Korean military use, which I think is most comparable to the USFK use in terms of nature of use & quality of water consumed.

북미2과장

hipothetical　　각종산업 category

외 무 부

년 월 일

i) 日本의 조항은 정부기관에 (To the ministries & Agencies of Gov't) 적용하는 것보다 不利하지 않은 條件으로. (Ethiopia는 일본은 public user와 같은 조건보다 不利하지 않은)

ii) 필리핀 조항은 필리핀 군대 (Germany 同一) 에 적용할수 있는 조건보다 不利하지 않은 條件으로.

iii) Australia는 類似한 條件에 있는 여타 使用者보다 不利하지 않은 條件으로

북미2과장

76

외 무 부

년 월 일

③ It is my understanding & conviction that the proposed rate should be the one applicable to the Korean military use, which I think is most comparable to the USFK use in terms of nature of use & quality of water consumed.

북 미 2 과 장

외 무 부

년 월 일

i) ○○의 조항은 정부기관에 (To the ministries & Agencies of Gov't) 적용하는 것보다 불리하지 않은 條件으로. (Ethiopia는 public user 보다 불리하지 않게)

ii) 필리핀 조항은 필리핀 군대 (Germany에) 적용할 수 있는 조건보다 불리하지 않은 條件으로.

iii) Australia는 類似 條件에 있는 여타 使用者보다 불리하지 않은 條件으로

북 미 2 과 장

76

Summer Fun

USO, Clubs Set Tours of Korea

TAEGU, Korea (Special) — If you want to see some of Korea this summer but don't have much money and don't want to go through the trouble of trying to plan different tours, your problems are solved.

The USOs in Seoul and Taegu and Armed Forces' Service Clubs throughout Korea provide inexpensive and easy means for you to see the attractions of Korea. All you need is a little initiative.

The following is a list of travel activities the two USOs and various service clubs in the KORSCOM area have scheduled for the summer months:

SEOUL

The Moyer Service Club at Yongsan has tours every Saturday and Sunday to sites of interest in Seoul and outlying areas. In the summer the tours start at 10 a.m. and run all day. Fifteen cents pays for the transportation with the only additional expenses being any entrance fees encountered. A knowledgeable tour guide goes along on the 35-passenger bus. The tours are flexible. If the group decides to stay longer at one stop, it can do so.

In addition, during the summer months, the club is planning swimming, hiking and picnicking trips on Sunday to resort areas near Seoul. These trips will start at 9 a.m. and last all day.

The Seoul USO has daily tours to sites of interest in and around the capital. The tours start at 2 p.m. and end at five. Twenty-five cents covers the cost of transportation. As at Moyer, a tour guide accompanies the bus.

On weekends the USO conducts two tours, one at 10 a.m. and another at 2 p.m. The 10 a.m. tour is often a day-long trip to outlying sites of interest. All four weekend tours are free.

If you like to hike, talk to Mr. Kim, a counselor at the USO. On May 2 he led a spring hike to the top of Mt. Do Bong. He plans more for the summer. Total price, including hiking clothes, rubber soled shoes and lunch, is $1.20.

In conjunction with its travel service, the USO has planned major weekend trips for the summer months.

On a still unspecified date in June the USO will sponsor an all-day trip to Kang Wah Island for $2.50.

On July 4th weekend (July 4-7) the USO will run a trip to Cheju Island, the beautiful resort island off the southern tip of Korea. Total cost is $84.

You can sign up for any of these trips at the Seoul USO and should do so early because space will be limited.

TAEGU

The Taegu USO recently received a new 30-seat bus and plans to run tours Monday-Thursday to sites of interest in Korea's third largest city. The bus will leave each afternoon from the USO at 1:30. All tours will be free.

The USO also plans to use the bus for day-long trips to outlying spots on selected weekends during the summer. Many of these trips will be to the excellent beaches in Pusan where you'll be able to swim and soak up the sun. Like the daily tours, all trips will be free except for expenses.

The trips are scheduled for the following dates: June 5, 6, 17 and 18; July 3, 4, 5, 17, 18, and 31; Aug. 1, 14 and 15; and Sept. 4 and 5. USO Director John King urges anyone interested to sign up early because space will be limited.

The Riviera Service Club at Camp Henry schedules one free tour every weekend. On two weekends the tour lasts all-day and goes to a site of historical interest or a resort in the Pusan-Taegu area. The other weekends the tour lasts half a day and goes to different factories in Taegu. An experienced Korean guide accompanies every tour.

In addition, once a month the club runs a "dutch treat" restaurant tour for those interested in sampling culinary delights of the Orient.

PUSAN

The Idle Hours Service Club at Hialeah Compound runs all-day tours to sites of interest in Pusan each Sunday during the summer beginning at 10 a.m. The tours are free and a Korean guide is provided.

Also, on weekends, a bus leaves every 30 minutes from Hialeah Compound for Haeundae Beach.

WAEGWAN

The Caroline Service Club runs two tours a month, usually on Sunday. Some are all-day tours, beginning at 8 a.m., to outlying sites of interest. Others are half-day tours, beginning at 12:30 p.m., to markets and factories in Taegu. All are free and accompanied by a Korean guide.

Also, approximately once every three months the club sponsors a weekend trip to Pusan. The bus leaves early Saturday morning and returns Sunday night. On Saturday travelers tour sites of interest in Pusan. Sunday is spent at one of Pusan's many beaches. Food and overnight lodging are provided at Hialeah Compound.

The club has arranged special hikes and overnight campouts in the surrounding area during the warm weather months. The first one is scheduled for June 10.

BUPYONG

The At Ease Service Club at Ascom has free afternoon tours every Sunday, usually to sites of interest in neighboring Seoul, but sometimes to the port city of Inchon, and to Suwon and Panmunjom. All the tours begin at 1 p.m.

PYONGTAEK

The Jordan Service Club at Camp Humphreys schedules a tour every Saturday and Sunday to sites of interest in Seoul, Inchon, and Suwon. The tours begin at 10:30 a.m. are always free and accompanied by a Korean guide.

Action '71-7-26.

문제점

군산 비행장 미 공군측이 전북 옥구 저수지의 농업용수 사용에 대한 요율 인상에 대해 군산 비행장 미 공군측은 SOFA 협정 제 6조에 의한 SOFA 협의를 거칠것을 계속 요구하고 있음.

정부 입장

1. 한.미 군대지위협정 제 6조 1항은 미군의 공공용역 사용에 있어서 대한민국 정부 또는 그 지방 행정기관이 소유 (owned), 관리 (controlled), 또는 규제 (regulated)하는 공익사업과 용역만을 규정하고 있으며, 개인 또는 사설단체가 주관하는 용역에는 일체의 규정이 없음.

2. 전북 농지 개량 조합은 대한민국 수도법 제 2조 및 제 17조에 의한 수도사업을 영위함이 아니고, 단지 자체의 용수 해결을 위해 저수지를 (수원) 소유하고 있는 것임.
따라서 미 공군측은 농지 개량 조합과의 사계약에 의해 농지 개량 조합 소유의 수원을 이용하고 이에 대한 보상을 지불하고 있는 형식이며, 동시에 농지 개량 조합은 정부의 요율 시행령 적용은 일체 받지않고 있음.

3. 1968. 8. 2. 한국측 공공용역 분과위원장 이희일 (Hee Il Lee) 씨가 미군측 분과위원장 호톡스 대령에게 보낸 서신으로 분과 위원회의 level 에서 상기 문제가 SOFA 협의의 대상이 아님을 확인한바 있음.

4. 본건은 상기 1. 2. 3.의 이유로 SOFA 협의의 대상이 아니라고 결론 지을수 있음.

118

경 제 기 획 원 80

물정 331.24-160 (72-9704) 1971. 7. 22

수신 외무부장관

제목 군산비행장 용수 사용료

전북농지개량조합에서는 1961.1. 1 일부터 옥구 저수지의 농업용수 일부를 군산비행장미공군측에 공급하여 미공군은 이를 자체양수장을 축조하여 당해 저류수를 인수하여 음료수를 사용하고 있는바 현재 원수 1,000개론 당 16.27 원을 적용하여 공급하고 있으나 동요율을 개정코자 1969. 12. 6 및 1971. 1. 20 양차에 걸쳐 계약갱신을 요청하였으나 주한 미육군 구매처에서는 SOFA 협정 제 6조에 의한 SOFA 협의를 거칠것을 요구한다하여 당원에서는 별첨과 같이 SOFA 협의 대상이 아님을 미측에 통보하였으니 동문제 해결을 위한 귀부의 협조가 있으시길 바랍니다.

유첨 한국측 해명서

전북농지개량조합 공한사본. 끝.

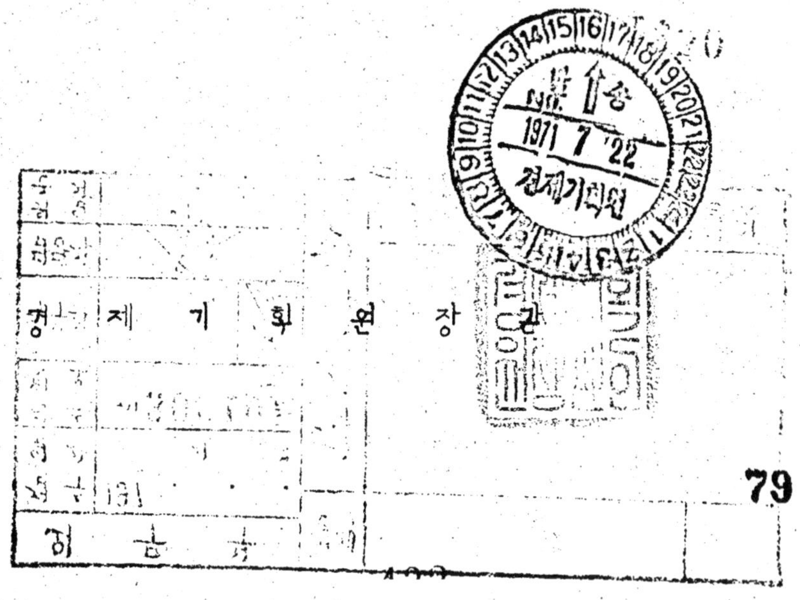

경제기획원장관

79

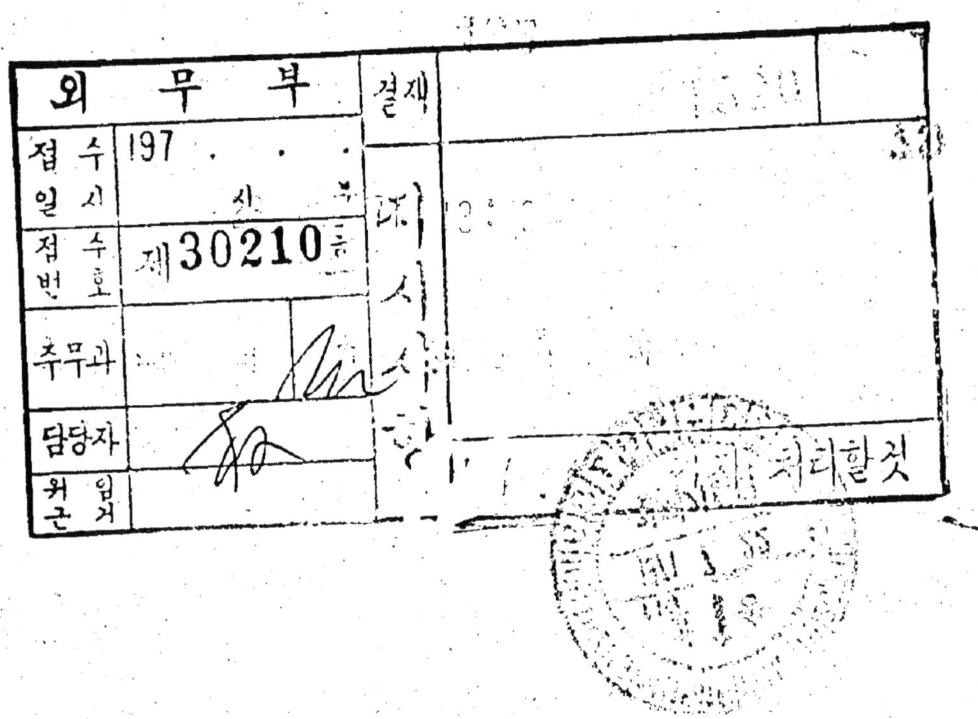

외 무 부		결재	
접수 일시	197 . . .		
접수 번호	제30210호		
추무과			
담당자			
위임 근거			처리할 것

민원서류

처리기한 71. 7. 28

전 북 농 지 개 량 조 합

전북농조 재 1162-1607(301) 1971, 7, 9,

수신 경제기획원 장관

참조 물가정책실

제목 군산 비행장 용수 사용료 인상

1. 당조합 설립목적은 조합 구역안의 농업경영의 합리화와 농업 생산력의 발전을 위하여 농지개량시설을 유지 관리하고 구역 정리사업및 농지개량사업등을 수행함으로서 조합원의 농업생산력의 증대에 이바지 하고 있으며

2. 전항 목적 수행에 있어 첫째 조건인 농업용수 현황을 살펴보면 당조합 저수량이 몽리면적에 비하여 용수부족을 면치 못하고 있는 실정에 있음에도 불구하고 당조합 인접에 위치한 군산 비행장 미공군 부대에서는 당조합 최말단 구역 2,000정보의 급수 해결을 위하여 설치한 옥구저수지는 약 200키가 떨어진 당조합 원천지에서 비관개기에 양수하여 년간 막대한 경비를 투입하여 양수 저류된 용수를

3. 군산비행장 미공군 측에서 자체내의 음료수 해결을 위하여 당조합 옥구 저수지 제방 밑에 자체 양수장을 축조하여 당해 저류수를 인수하여 음료수로 사용함에 대하여

4. 1961.1.1 1,000개론당 4원으로 미육군 구매처장과 당조합간에 계약을 체결하고 그후 동 계약서 DATB03-70-C -6048 제5조 "요율의 변경"에 따라 전계약처인 주한 미육군 구매처 와 당조합간에 상호 협의하여 1966년도 까지 계속 인상하였으나

5. 1967년도 1,000개론당 13.21 원으로 인상당시 미측에서 1966,7,9 자 조인된 한미 행정협정 조약 제6조에 의거 한미 합동 위원회 의 심의 대상이라 하여 당시 한미 합동 위원회에 건총한

81

433

80

— 1 —

전북농조 재 1971, 7, 9,

결과 별지 사본과 같이 심의 대상이 아니라고 판시되어 당조합에서 요청한 안대로 추가 계약하였으며 1968년도 역시 1,000개톤당 13.91 원을 16.27 원으로 한미 합동 위원회의 심의 없이 추가 인상하였으나

6. 1969년에 1,000개톤당 현행 16.27 원을 19.95 원으로 1970년도에 1,000개톤당 19.95 원을 24.50 원으로 각각 인상 요구를 하였으나

7. 피계약처인 주한 미육군 구매처에서는 미8군 사령부의 인준을 득하여야 한다고 차일 피일 책임을 미8군 사령부에 전가하여

8. 미8군 사령부 용역처와 절충하여 전5항에 대한 경유를 설명한바 미8군 사령관 앞으로 인상 요청을 하라하옵기 별지 사본과 같이 인상요청한바 한미 합동위원회 미측에서 한미합동위원회의 심의 사항이라 고집하니 한국측 대표와 절충하여 조속한 시일내에 부의가 되도록 조치하라 하여

9. 부득이 심의 대상이 아님을 열거하여 상신 하오니 첨부된 관계 참고 서류를 검토하여 조속한 시일내에 추가 인상계약이 되도록 선처하여 주시기 바랍니다.

가. 당조합은 법인체 이며

나. 영조물 사용에 대하여는 조합장이 임의로 용익대상자와의 협의하에 계약 체결하여 당조합 정관에 명시된 바와 같이 조합비외 수입으로 수입하므로서 계약 행위임.

10. 용수사용처 — 군산 비행장 미공군 3rd 전투 비행단

첨부 1. 1968년도 용수사용료 인상에 따른 관계서류 1부

2. 군산비행장 용수 사용료 부가징수내역 1부

3. 단가 인상 경유 1부

4. 관계 법조문 발췌 1부

5. 정관 발췌 1부. 끝.

전 북 농 지 개 량 조 합

71. 7. 13

82

81

REPUBLIC OF KOREA-UNITED STATES
UTILITIES SUBCOMMITTEE

21 July, 1971

SUBJECT : Change in Water Supply Rate applicable to the U.S. Air Force in Kunsan Air Base

TO : U.S. Chairman, Utilities Subcommittee

1. References:

a. Paragraph 1, 2 and Agreed Minutes I of Article VI of SOFA.

b. Chonpuk Water Utilization Association's letters to Commanding Officer U.S. Army Korea Procurement Agency, dated 6 December 1969 and 20 January 1971.

2. This is concerned with the water rate increase of Chonpuk Water Utilization Association in Kunsan Air Base.

3. Referring to the letter, dated 2 August 1968, of Mr. Hee Il Lee, Korean Chairman, to Col. Horrocks, U.S. chairman, I would like to call your attention to the fact that the rate increase is not subject to the SOFA consultation. The past changes of the rates were not consulted. I would like to ask you to study the past records on this problem, and your cooperation in this matter will be highly appreciated.

Suck Joon, Suh
Director, Office of Price Policy
Republic of Korea Chairman
Utilities Subcommittee

82

ECONOMIC PLANNING BOARD
REPUBLIC OF KOREA
Seoul, Korea

2 August, 1968

Col. Horrocks, Chairman
U.S. Utility Subcommittee

Dear Col. Horrocks:

Reference is made to Captain B. L. Higgins' letter, dated 2 July, 1968, to Mr. Chae Yung Suk of Chon Pik Water Utilization Association concerning the applicability of the consultation under Article VI of SOFA to the water rate increase of the Association. In the mentioned letter, Captain Higgins indicated the opinion of Staff Judge Advocate of the Eighth U. S. Army to the effect that the Association is a water supply enterprise within the meaning of Article 17 of the ROK Water Supply Law, requiring therefore the SOFA consultation.

However, I would like to mention that Staff Judge Advocate missed the provision of Article 2 of the Water Supply Law which defines the water supply enterprises of Article 17 of the Law. You are hereby informed that the water rates of the Association is not subject to the regulation of the ROK Government, because Article 17 of the Law is applicable only to the enterprises which supply refined water as defined under Article 2 of the Law. In the case of the water supply of the Association to the U.S. Air Base in Kunsan, pre-refined raw water is supplied by the Association, refinement being performed by the Air Base itself. All this puts the Association outside the scope of the Water Supply Law.

Your understanding in and early solution to the problem will be very highly appreciated.

Sincerely,

Signed.
Hoe Il Lee
Chairman
ROK Utility Sub-Committee

83

경 제 기 획 원

물정 331. 24-270 (72-9704) 1971. 9. 28

수신 외무부장관

제목 대전지구 유엔군 급수 계약 변경을 위한 SOFA 협의 제의

대전시 수도 조례 개정으로 대전지구 유엔군 급수 계약을 변경키 위한 SOFA 협의를 미측 공공용역분과 위원장에게 별첨과 같이 제의 하였음을 통보 하오니 양지 하시기 바랍니다.

유첨 협의 제의 공문사본 1부. 끝.

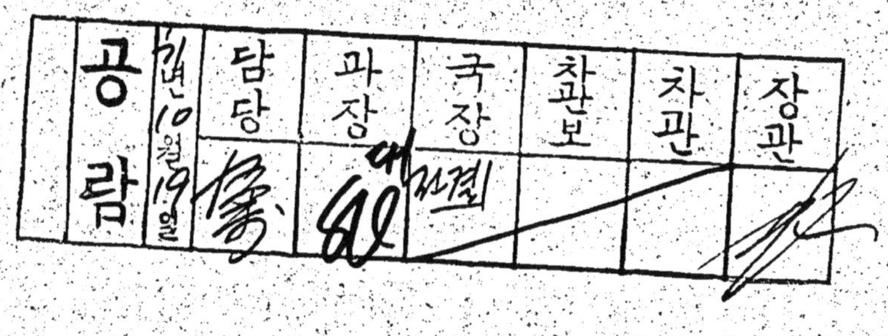

공람	년 10월 19일	담당	과장	국장	차관보	차관	장관

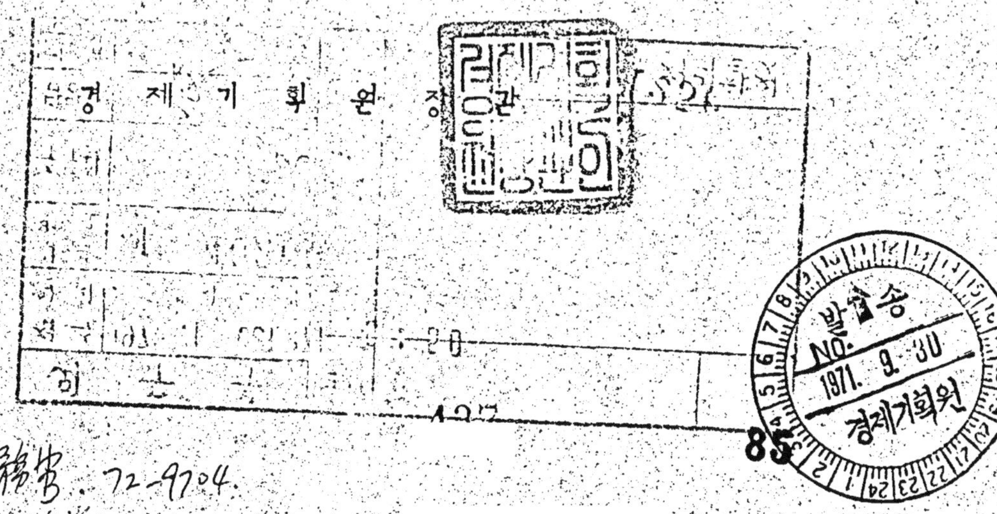

경 제 기 획 원 장

발송 NO. 1971. 9. 30 경제기획원

85

* 企劃院 物資局 72-9704.
84.1.01 美側과 會議

외 무 부		결재		
접수 일시	197 .1 OCT '71 9 : 50 시 분			
접수 번호	제 40260 호			
주무과				
담당자			197 . . . 까지 처리할것	
기안 근거				

85-1.E

REPUBLIC OF KOREA-UNITED STATES
UTILITIES SUBCOMMITTEE

27 September, 1971

SUBJECT : Change in Water Supply Rate Schedule applicable to the US Armed Forces under Article VI of the Status of Forces Agreement.

TO : US Chairman, Utilities Subcommittee

1. Reference : Paragraph 2 and Agreed Minute 1 of Article VI of the Status of Force Agreement.

2. The Government of the United States is informed through this written consultative procese that the Republic of Korea proposes to change the following rate/tariff at locations below:

Rate/Tariff	Location
Water Supply	The city of Taejon

3. The following date are provide:

a. Effective date.
Although the rate change are effective from 1 May, 1970 in Taejon, the new rate will be applied to the US Forces' use in accordance with the agreement set forth in the letter dated 15 November, 1969.

b. Rate schedule of proposed change.
Refer to item " d ".

c. Rate schedule showing rates that are charged all classes of users. (attached)

85

d. Calculation of old and new rate

description	old rate (won)	new rate (won)
Basic rate for the first $30m^3$	300	700
Excess charge per m^3	15	40

e. Reason for revision of rate base.

To cover the rising prime cost.

4. The Government of ROK advises the Government of the United States that priorities, conditions, and rates or tariffs being changed are no less favorable than those accorded any other user. The view of the Government of the United States is solicited as soon as possible. You may be assured that your views will be greatly appreciated.

Suck Joon Suh

Suck Joon Suh
Chairman
ROK Utilities Subcommittee

(attached)

Water Rate Schedule of the city of Taejon

Description	Unit	Monthly basic rate		Charge above Minimum (per 1 m^3)
		Q'ty(m^3)	Rate(won)	
Special use	1 house 1 place	30	700	40
Commercial	"	20	450	40
Recreation	1 place	-	-	40
Bath house	1 house 1 place	200	4,000	25
Construction	1 place	-	-	35
Industrial use	1 house 1 place	20,000	200,000	15
Domestic	1 house	10	150	20
Public	1 house	5	60	20

10-11-'71

한국 정부측 주장 :

1. 수출산업 (Industrial Rate referred by US) 에 대한 저율적용 (할인)은 별도 요율이 아니고, 내용적으로는 보조금 지불의 성격임. 고로 SOFA 협정 6조 1항과는 관계가 없음.

2. 수출산업 (Industrial Rate referred by US) 에 대한 할인은 외화 획득이 주목적이 아니고, 유치산업 보조 형식으로 간주한 저율 적용임.

3. 1. 과 2.항의 특수 요율은 목적별, 용도별이므로 USFK 에 대한 차별대우가 아님. 뿐만 아니라 "Any other user" (6조 2항)의 정의 (Concept)는 대한민국 정부가 시행하고 있는 공공용역 운영상 정상적인, 일반적인 (General Term) 이용자를 칭하며, 예외적인 수출을 취급받는 case 를 지칭함은 아님.

88

3. 1972년

89

한 국 전 력 주 식 회 사
(22-5101-277)

한전영(영)910-610　　　　　　　　　　　　1972. 2. 1

수 신　외무부 장관

제 목　전력요금 인상에 따른 업무협조

1. 1972. 2월분 요금조정시 부터 전력요금이 15% 인상케 됨에 따라 인상전력 요금을 주한미군 수용가에 적용하기 이전에 한,미 행정협정에 의한 한국정부와 미국정부간의 협의에 대한 사항입니다

2. 한,미 행협, 한,미 공공용역분과 위원회 및 합동 위원회에서 주한 미군수용가에 대한 "인상전력요금 적용" 문제가 협의 되어야 하옵기 요청하오니 본 문제를 관련 미측 위원회와 협의 주한미군 수용가에게도 인상된 전력요금이 조속히 적용 될수 있도록 협조하여 주시기 바랍니다.

첨부: 인상 전력 요금표 1부. 끝.

사　장　김　상

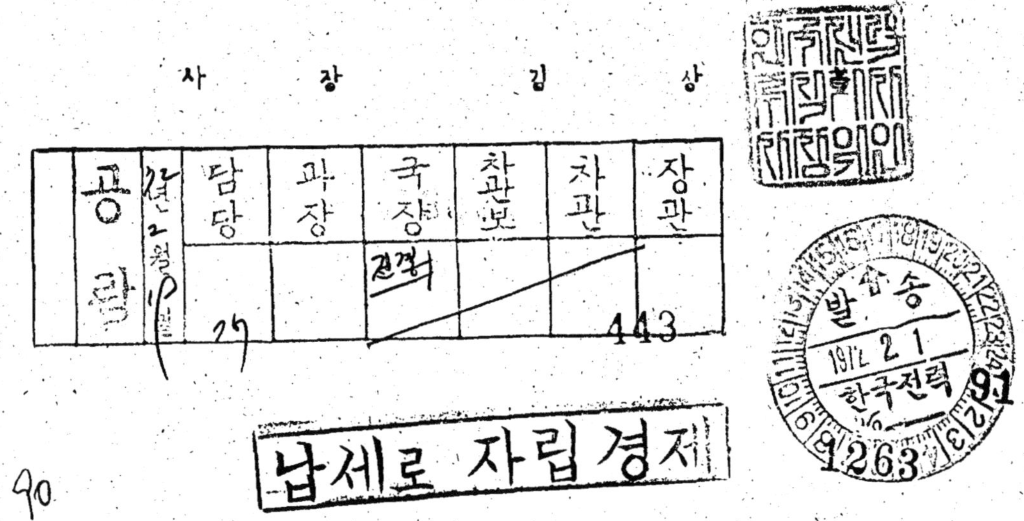

공람	72년 2월 1일	담당	과장	국장	차관보	차관	장관
		27		전결			

443

90

[illegible]

3. [illegible]

구분	수요요금		전력량요금		비고
	[illegible]	[illegible]	[illegible]	[illegible]	[illegible]

4. 농사용 전력

	수요요금	전력량요금	비고
	[illegible] 원	1kWh당 3원 [illegible] 전	

5. 가로등

	[illegible]	1kWh당 2원 [illegible] 전	최저요금 92원

6. [illegible]

	1. 부하설비용량이 [illegible] 60W 이하	1kWh당 5원 41전	최저요금 92원
	2. 60W 초과 [illegible]	〃 3원 48전	

7. 특수산업요금

카바이드, 합금철 [illegible] P.V.C 제조업 [illegible] 200kW 이상 [illegible]

㈎ 카바이드, 합금철 [illegible] P.V.C 제조업 [illegible] 200kW 이상의 수용가에 대하여는 30%

㈏ [illegible] (전력비가 총제조원가의 [illegible])

전력비가 총제조원가에 차지하는 비율	할인율
① 10% 이상 30% 미만은 ② 30% 이상 40% 미만은 ③ 40% 이상은	20 25 30 %

㈐ [illegible]

전력비가 총제조원가에 차지하는 비율	할인율
① 20% 이상 30% 미만은 ② 30% 이상 40% 미만은 ③ 40% 이상 50% 미만은 ④ 50% 이상은	15 20 25 30 %

8. 상수도용 전력요금

상수도(용 전력)요금은 감면할 수 없읍니다. 단 [illegible] 적용합니다.

9. 도서요금

전기공급 계통상 고립된 도서지방에 대하여는 상공부장관의 인가로 별도요금을 설정할 수 있읍니다.

三. 요금의 적용

1972년 2월분(요금조정) 부터 본 요금을 적용합니다.

※ 개정된 요금에 대하여 문의 사항은 가까운 [illegible] 사업소에 물어주시면 상세히 안내하여 드리겠읍니다.

91

1. 일반전기 요금표

1. 일반전등 (4kW 이하의 기타 수용)

구분	전력량 요금	요금	비고
	[illegible]	[illegible]	[illegible]

[illegible]

2. 일반전력을 (4kW 이상의 모든 수용)

구분	수용 요금		전력량 요금		비고
	계약 전력	요금	전력량	요금	
가.	[illegible]	[illegible]	[illegible]	[illegible]	1265
나.	[illegible]		[illegible]	[illegible]	[illegible]

3. 특수용 전력

구분		수용 요금		전력량 요금		비고
		계약 전력	요금	전력량	요금	
가.	A	[illegible]	[illegible]	[illegible]	[illegible]	[illegible]
	B	[illegible]	[illegible]	[illegible]	[illegible]	[illegible]
나.		[illegible]		[illegible]	[illegible]	[illegible]

4. 농사용 전력

	수용 요금	전력량 요금	비고
	[illegible]	[illegible]	

5. 가로등

	[illegible]	[illegible]	[illegible]

6. 임시 전등

	[illegible]	[illegible]	[illegible]

7. [illegible]

[illegible]

[illegible]	[illegible]
① [illegible] ② [illegible] ③ [illegible]	[illegible]

[illegible]

경 제 기 획 원

물정 331.24- 35 (70-3022) 1972. 2. 8

수신 외무부장관

제목 전기및 철도 화물 요금 개정에 따른 SOFA 협의

금반 전기및 철도 화물요금의 개정에 따라 UN 군과의 계약을 경신코저 한미행정 협정에 의한 협의를 미측 공공용역 분과 위원장에게 별첨과 같이 제의 하였음을 통보 합니다.

첨부 한국측 제의 공문 사본 1부. 끝.

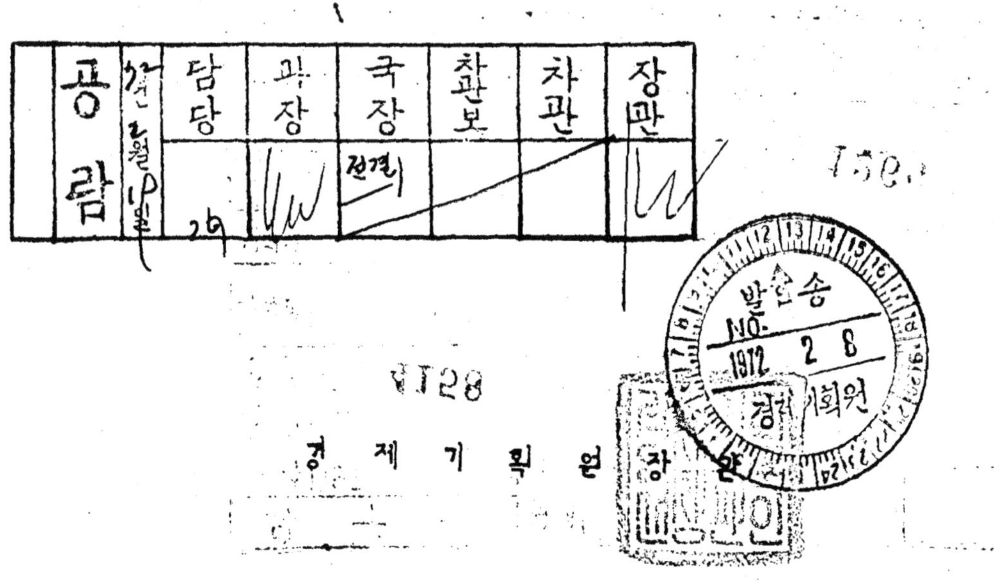

공람	72년 2월 10일	담당	과장	국장	차관보	차관	장관
		29		전결			

발송 NO. 1972 2 8 경제기획원

경 제 기 획 원 장 관

92

REPUBLIC OF KOREA-UNITED STATES
UTILITIES SUBCOMMITTEE

5 February, 1972

Subject : Change in Electric Power Rates applicable to the US Armed Forces under Article VI of the Status of Forces Agreement.

To : US Chairman, Utilities Subcommittee

1. Reference : Paragraph 2 and Agreed Minute 1 of Article VI of the Status of Forces Agreement.

2. The Government of the United States is informed through this written consultative process that ROK proposes to change the following rate/tariff at locations indicated below;

Rate/Tariff	Location
Electric rate schedule applicable to the US Armed Forces	Whole Country

3. The fallowing data is provided;

a. Effective date

Although the rate changes are effective from 1 February, 1972, the new rates will be applied to the US Forces' use in accordance with the agreement set forth in the letter dated 15 November, 1969.

b. Rate Schedule showing rates that are charged all classes of users. Attached.

c. Rate schedule of proposed change.

15% increase with no exception over the old rate schedule. For detailed information, refer to item "b."

d. Calculation of old and new rate base.

Refer to item "b."

e. Reasons for revision of rate.

To secure fair return and investment fund.

97

4. The Government of ROK advises the Government of the United States that priorities, conditions and rates or tariffs being changed are no less favorable than those accorded any other user.
You may be assured that your early views will be greatly appreciated.

Suck Joon Suh
Director, Office of Price Policy
Republic of Korea Chairman
Utilities Subcommittee

94

(Attached)

PROPOSED NEW ELECTRIC RATE SCHEDULE

TARIFF 1
GENERAL SERVICE A

APPLICABLE:

To residential service without limit and general service of 4kw demand or under.

TYPE OF SUPPLY:

Single or three phase supply at any one of the Company's available standard voltages, 100 v or 200 v.

MONTHLY BILL:

Basic Rate:

Energy Charge:

W163.88 for the first 5 kwh.
W 15.55 per kwh for the next 27 kwh.
W 11.79 per kwh for the next 180 kwh.*
W 9.09 per kwh for each additional kwh.
* Add 90 kwh at W11.79 block for each kw in excess of 5kw of demand.

Minimum Charge: W163.88.

TARIFF 2
GENERAL SERVICE B

APPLICABLE:

To general service of 4 kw of contracted demand and over.

TYPE OF SUPPLY:

Single or three pahse supply at any one of the Company's available standard voltages, 20kv, 10kv, 6kv, 5.2kv, 3kv, 200v, 100v or others.

MONTHLY BILL:

Basic Rate:

a. Demand Charge:

W184.00 per kw for the first 50 kw of contracted demand.
W146.00 per kw for the next 450 kw of contracted demand.
W109.00 per kw for each additional kw of contracted demand.

96

b. Energy Charge:

W9.49 per kwh for the first 90 kwh per kw of contracted demand.
W6.50 per kwh for the next 90 kwh per kw of contracted demand.
W4.68 per kwh for the next 180 kwh per kw of contracted demand.
W3.16 per kwh for each additional kwh.

c. Minimum contracted kw demand: 4 kw.

TARIFF 3
HIGH TENSION SERVICE

HIGH TENSION SERVICE A

APPLICABLE:

To service of 1,000 kw of contracted demand and over, and 20 kv and over.

TYPE OF SUPPLY:

Three phase supply at any one of the Company's available standard voltages, 20 kv and over.

MONTHLY BILL:

Basic Rate:

a. Demand Charge:

W152.00 per kw for the first 500 kw of contracted demand.
W101.00 per kw for each additional kw of contracted demand.

b. Energy Charge:

W9.49 per kwh for the first 90 kwh per kw of contracted demand.
W6.18 per kwh for the next 90 kwh per kw of contracted demand.
W4.30 per kwh for the next 180 kwh per kw of contracted demand.
W2.71 per kwh for each additional kwh.

c. Minimum contracted kw demand: 1,000 kw.

HIGH TENSION SERVICE B

APPLICABLE:

To service of 150kv and over.

TYPE OF SUPPLY:

Three phase supply at any one of the Company's available standard voltages, 150 kv and over.

98

97

MONTHLY BILL:

Basic Rate:

a. Demand Charge:

W101.00 per kw of contracted demand.

b. Energy Charge:

W9.49 per kwh for the first 90 kwh per kw of contracted demand.
W6.11 per kwh for the next 90 kwh per kw of contracted demand.
W4.21 per kwh for the next 180 kwh per kw of contracted demand.
W2.70 per kwh for each additional kwh.

TARIFF 4
IRRIGATION SERVICE

APPLICABLE;

To service required for the operation of pumps which are used to irrigate land for the cultivation and growing of grain for food purpose. Lighting necessary and incidental to the operation of pumps is permitted.

TYPE OF SUPPLY:

Same as "General Service B".

MONTHLY BILL:

Basic Rate:

Demand Charge: W54.00 per kw for contracted demand.
Energy Charge: W5.51 per kwh for each kwh.

TARIFF 5
STREET LIGHTING SERVICE

APPLICABLE:

To service for operation of lighting of streets, parks and similar places for the benefit and convenience of public.

TYPE OF SUPPLY:

Single phase at either 100 v or 200v.

MONTHLY BILL:

Basic Rate: W2.76 per watt for connected load.
Minimum Charge: W92.00.

TARIFF 6

FLAT RATE LIGHTING SERVICE

APPLICABLE:

To lighting service (including radio substituted one set as one lamp), principally limited to 100 watts of connected load with three lamps or under. One radio set shall be counted as 20 watts.

TYPE OF SUPPLY:

Single phase supply at either 100v or 200 v.

MONTHLY BILL:

Basic Rate:

W5.41 per watt for the first 60 watts of connected load.
W3.68 per watt for additional watts of connected load.

Minimum Charge: W92.00.

99

SPECIAL PROVISIONS

1. SPECIAL INDUSTRY:

a. To export industry customers with 200 kw of contracted demand or under.
b. To p. v. c. manufacturing industry customers who use carbide and acetylene in p.v.c. manufacturing process. (only applied to the industry which is financed by the foreign loan and guaranteed by the Government for repayment).
c. To aluminium, iron and steel industry customers whose power charges occupy more than 10% of the total production cost. (only limited to pig iron and ingot iron).
d. To industry customers whose power charges occupy more than 20% of the total production cost, who are designated by the Minister of commerce and Industry.

DISCOUNT RATE: Monthly bill shall be discounted as follows:

a. 30% discount: For export industry customer with 200 kw of contracted demand or under.
b. 30% discount: For p. v. c. manufacturing industry customers who use carbide and acetylene in p.v.c. manufacturing process.
c. 20% discount: For the aluminium, iron and steel industry customers whose electric charges occupy 10% and over, of the total production cost.
25% discount: For the aluminium, iron and steel industry customers whose electric charges occupy 30% and over, of the total production cost.
30% discount: For the aluminium, iron and steel industry customers whose electric charges occupy 40% and over, of the total production cost.
d. 15% discount: For the industry customer whose electric charges occupy 20% and over, of the total production cost.
20% discount: For the industry customer whose electric charges occupy 30% and over, of the total production cost.
25% discount: For the industry customer whose electric charges occupy 40% and over, of the total production cost.
30% discount: For the industry customer whose electric charges occupy 50% and over, of the total production cost.

2. MUNICPAL WATER SERVICE:

Electric rate for Municipal Water Service may be discounted, but the discount rate shall be determined by Minister of Commerce and Industry.

100

REPUBLIC OF KOREA-UNITED STATES
UTILITIES SUBCOMMITTEE

5 February, 1972

Subject: Change in Freight Rates of Railroad applicable to the US Armed Forces under Article VI of the Status of Forces Agreement.

To : US Chairman, Utilities Subcommittee.

1. Reference: Paragraph 2 and Agreed Minute 1 of Article VI of the Status of Forces Agreement.

2. The Government of the United States in informed through this written consultative process that ROK proposes to change the following rate/tariff at locations indicated below;

Rate/Tariff	Location
Freight rate schedule of Railroad applicable to the US Armed Forces	Whole Country

3. The following data is provided;

a. Effective date

Although the rate changes are effective from 1 February, 1972, the new rates will be applied to the US Forces' use in accordance with theagreement set forth in the letter dated 15 November, 1969.

b. Rate Schedule showing rates that are charged all classes of users.(Attachment I)

c. Rate Schedule of proposed change.
Refer to item " d."

d. Calculation of old and new rate.
(Attachment II)

101

c. Reasons for revision of rate.

To secure transportation cost and investment fund.

4. The Government of ROK advises the Government of the United States that priorities, conditions and rates or tariffs being changed are no less favorable than those accorded any other user.
You may be assured that your early views will be greatly appreciated.

Suck Joon Suh
Director, Office of Price Policy
Republic of Korea Chairman
Utilities Subcommittee

102

Attachment I

THE NEW FREIGHT RATE SCHEDULE

Description	Unit	Rate (won)
1. Basic Rates		
a. Less Than Carload Freight		
1st class	per 100kg/per 50km	52
2nd class	"	30
3rd class	"	29
4th class	"	28
5th class	"	27
b. Carload Freight		
1st class	per ton/per 50km	133
2nd class	"	113
3rd class	"	97
4th class	"	83
5th class	"	73
c. Privately Owned Freight Car	Per car	25% Discount for General Carload Freight Fare
2. Minimum Charge		
a. Less Than Carload Freight	per Case	48
b. Carload Freight (Include privately Owned Freight Car)	per car	4,120
c. Reserved Train	per train	285,600
3. Collection and Delivery Charge	1. within 2km	
	a. within 50kg	52
	b. per 50kg over 50kg	21
	2. within 4km	
	a. within 50kg	64
	b. per 50kgover 50kg	25

103

4. Storage Charge		
a. Less than Carload Freight	per100kg/perunit of 24hrs	15
b. Carload Freight	per ton/perunit of 6 hrs	161
5. Impounding Charge	½of Storage Charge	
6. Demurrage	1. per ton/1st 6hrs	40
	2. per ton/perunit of 6rs over 6 hrs	80
7. Transfer Charge	per ton	153
8. Conversion		
a. Cancellation of Ordered		
1. Less Than Carload	per case	28
2. Carload Freight	per car	
i) Before Supply of Freight Car		116
ii) After Supply of Freight Car		1,200
3. Reserved Train	per Train	7,750
b. other		
1. Before Dispatch of Consignment Note	per Case	37
2. After Dispatch of Goods and Consignment note		
i) Before Advice of Arrival		
0. Less Than Carload	per case	57
0. Carload Freight	per car	58
ii)		

104

ii) After Advice of Arrival		
O. Less than Carload	per case	48
O. Carload Freight	Per car	2,400
9. Convoyer Charge	per km	1 20
10. Delivery note	per case/per time	37
11. Using Freight Car Scale	per car	1,397
12. Copy of Consignment note	per copy	36
13. Bill of Lading	per copy	60
14. Additional Charge		
a. Convoyer without Leave	per km	2 40
b. Dangerous Goods		
i) powder	per kg 181	181
ii) other	per kg	60
15. Equipment Rental	per Car/per day	
a. To 30 Freight car		1,700
b. To 40 Freight Car		1,040
c. over 41 Freight car		1,300
16. Switching for Special Team Track (KNR owned)	per car/per km	208
17. Privately Owned Track		
a. Switching Charge.	per Engine/perkm	623
b. Using Freight Car (per car)	a. within 5hrs	410
	b. within 11 hrs	1,763
	c. per unit of 6hrs over 11hrs	2,716
18. Freight car for internal Yard use only	per car	
a. To 29 Freight car		600
b. over 30 Freight car		1,200

108

29. Privately owned Freight car		
a. Scheduled General Inspection and Repair (Every 24 months) Excluding Owner's Imposition parts	per car	70,168 * by Fy 72 KNR's Budget

106

Attachment II

CALCULATION OF OLD AND NEW RATE BASE

(US Army)

Applicable Tech spec	Description	Unit	old rate(won)	New rate(won)
3. 1. 2	Carload Freight			
a.	Basic rate using Carrier's car	per car/ per km	58 15	70
b.	Basic rate using US Owned car	"	37 80	25% Discount for Basic Freight Fare
c.	Minimum Charge for Carload of Rented and US Owned car	per car	2,080	4,120
3. 1. 3	Special Train Service Minimum Charge	per train	125,730	150,000
3. 1. 4	Demurrage	per car per unit of 6 hrs	1,006	1,200
3. 1. 5	Diversion or Reconsignment	per car	2,016	2,400
3. 1. 6	Cancellation of car ordered	"	1,004	1,200
3. 1. 7	Switching Charge	"	523	623
3. 1. 8	Stop off in Transit	"	939	1,120
3. 1. 9	Equipment Rental	per car/ per day	798	950
3. 1. 11	Deadhead Movement of Rented or US Owned Car	per car/ per km	14 30	18

109

- 2 -

3. 1. 12	Surcharge for oversized Freight	per car/ per km	14 50	51
3. 3. 2	US Government Owned Car			
a.	Scheduled General Inspection and Repair Excluding painting (every 24 months)	per car	32,000	38,100
(PACEX)	Carload Freight			
	a. Basic Rate	per car/per km	67 80	81
	b. Minimum Charge	per car	2,120	4,120
	Demurrage	per car per unit of 6hrs	1,006	1,200
	Deversion or Reconsignment	per car	2,016	2,400
	Cancellation of car ordered	"	1,004	1,200
	Switching charge	"	523	623
	Stop off in transit	"	939	1,120
	Surcharge for oversized Freight	per car/per km	42 60	51

108

경 제 기 획 원

물정 331·24-44 (70-3022) 1972. 2. 17

수신 외무부장관

제목 서울시 급수조례 개정에 따른 유엔군 급수 계약 경신

서울시 급수조례 개정에 따른 유엔군과의 급수 계약을 변경코저 한미행정에 의한 협의를 별첨과 같이 미측 공공요역 분과위원장에게 제의 하였음을 통보하오니 양지 하시기 바랍니다.

첨부 대 미측 공공용역 분과 위원장 공문 사본 1부. 끝.

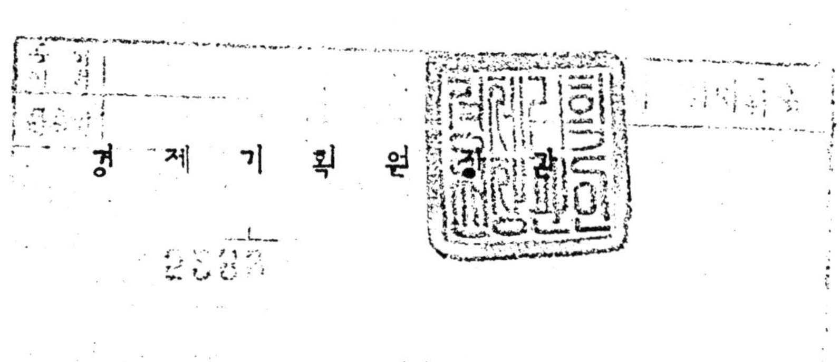

공람	72년 2월 18일	담당	과장	국장	참관보	차관	장관
				전결			

109

REPUBLIC OF KOREA-UNITED STATES
UTILITIES SUBCOMMITTEE

16 February, 1972

Subject : Change in Water Supply Rates applicable to the US Armed Forces under Article VI of the Status of Forces Agreement.

To : US Chairman, Utilities Subcommittee.

1. Reference: Paragraph 2 and Agreed Minute I of Article VI of the Status of Forces Agreement.

2. The Government of the United States is informed through this written consultative process that ROK proposes to change the following rate/tariff at locations indicated below;

Rate/Tariff	Location
Water supply rate schedule applicable to the US Armed Forces	The city of Seoul

3. The following data is provided

a. Effective date

Although the rate changes are effective from 1 January, 1972, the new rates will be applied to the US Forces' use in accordance with the agreement set forth in the letter dated 15 November, 1969.

b. Rate schedule showing rates that are charged all classes of users. (Attached)

c. Rate schedule of proposed change refer to item"d."

d. Calculation of old and new rate base

old rate(won)	new rate(won)
10 per m^3	20 per m^3

e. Reasons for revision of rate

To cover the rising cost and investment fund.

110

4. The Government of ROK advises the Government of the United States that priorities, conditions and rates of tariffs being changed are no less favorable than accorded any other user.
You may be assured that your early views will be greatly appreciated.

Suck Joon Suh
Director, Office of Price Policy
Republic of Korea Chairman
Utilities Subcommittee

111

(Attached)

Water supply rates schedule

Rates / Use		Basic rates		excessive rates	
		quantity(m^3)	rate (won)	quantity(m^3)	rate per m^3(won)
Home use		10	150	11 - 20 21 - 30 31 - 40 over 41	15 20 30 40
Business use	class 1	30	1,350	31 - 200 201 - 1,000 over 100	70 90 120
	class 2	30	900	per m^3	35
industrial use		200	6,000	"	35
Piblic bath	class A	600	48,000	601 - 1,000 1,001 - 3,000 over 3,000	100 160 200
	class B	600	12,000	per m^3	25
Public use		100	1,000	"	10
Special use (Government, Army etc)		20 won per 1 m^3			
Fire extinguishing use		100 won per month			

112

DISPOSITION FORM

For use of this form, see AR 340-15; the proponent agency is The Adjutant General's Office.

REFERENCE OR OFFICE SYMBOL	SUBJECT
USFK DJ	Notification of Changed Installation Communications Charges

TO USAKPA
ATTN: Contracting Officer
Services Section

FROM ACofS, J4

DATE 16 Mar 72 CMT 1
Mr. Cook/ib/3417

1. This Division has requested the ACofS, J5, to review the letter of notification of changed installation communications charges at Inclosure 1.

2. The ACofS, J5 was requested to determine whether the form of notification was appropriate and in accordance with established Joint Committee consultation procedures on utility matters contained as Inclosure 11 to the minutes of the twenty-second meeting of the Joint Committee on 14 March 1968.

3. This Division has been informed by the ACofS, J5, that it does not meet the requirements of the aforementioned consultation procedures. An examination of Inclosure 1 to Inclosure 11 of the referenced minutes will indicate the format for a memorandum of consultation on utility matters, which is to be signed by the Republic of Korea Chairman of the Utilities Subcommittee of the Joint Committee, who is an officer of the Economic Planning Board of the Government of the Republic of Korea. Such a memorandum initiating the consultation process cannot validly be issued or signed by any other agency or person in the Government of the Republic of Korea.

4. Accordingly, it is recommended that Inclosure 1 be returned to sender, with an explanation of the above reasoning in this matter, with a request that the Ministry of Communications transmit its notice to the Republic of Korea Chairman of the Utilities Subcommittee for further processing in accordance with established Joint Committee procedures in utilities matters.

I Incl
as

RICHARD T. CANN
Colonel, USA
ACofS, J4
US Chairman, Utilities Subcommittee

113

DA FORM 1 FEB 62 2496 REPLACES DD FORM 96, EXISTING SUPPLIES OF WHICH WILL BE ISSUED AND USED UNTIL 1 FEB 63 UNLESS SOONER EXHAUSTED. ☆ GPO : 1970 O - 399-410

MINISTRY OF COMMUNICATIONS

REPUBLIC OF KOREA

SEOUL, KOREA

TELECOMMUNICATIONS BUREAU.
Our Ref: MOC/TB

Telex Number: 2298 GENTEL
Cable Address: GENTEL SEOUL

Contracting Officer
U.S.Korea Procurement Agency
APO Sanfrancisco 96301

2 March, 1972

Dear Sir,

This reference is to the notification of the changed installation charges which effected on 1st February, 1972.

According to No. 16 RATES FOR SERVICE, General Provisions of the Telecommunications Services Contract (Contract No. DAJB03-69-D-0154), I give you a notice of the changed installation charges herewith enclosed.

Sincerely yours,

K S Chung

Kyou Suk CHUNG
Director-General
Telecommunications Bureau

Enclosed: Description of the changed installation Charges

Coordinated with LTC TURNER, J4
on 8 March 1972 -
T.C.W

115

114

Description of Changed Installation Charges

1.16 Installation Charges

1.161 Ordinary telephone, per station

Class		Amount
1st Class		9,000 Won
2nd "		12,000 "
[illegible] "		12,000 "
4th "		15,000 "
5th "	Automatic	37,500 "
	Manual	21,000 "
[illegible] "	Automatic	60,000 "
	Manual	31,500 "
7th "		75,000 "
8th "		90,000 "
9th "		105,000 "
10th "		120,000 "
11th "		135,000 "
12th "		150,000 "
13th "		165,000 "

115

바로보자 거짓평화 막아내자 적화야욕

경 제 기 획 원

물정 331·24-138　　　　　　　　　　　　　　　1972. 5. 22

수신 외무부장관

제목 전화 가설비 개정에 따른 SOFA 협의

표기의 건에 대한 SOFA 협의를 미측 공공용역분과 위원회 위원장에게 별첨과 같이 제출하였아오니 양지 하시기 바랍니다.

첨부 대 미측 공공용역 분과 위원장 제의 공문사본 1부. 끝.

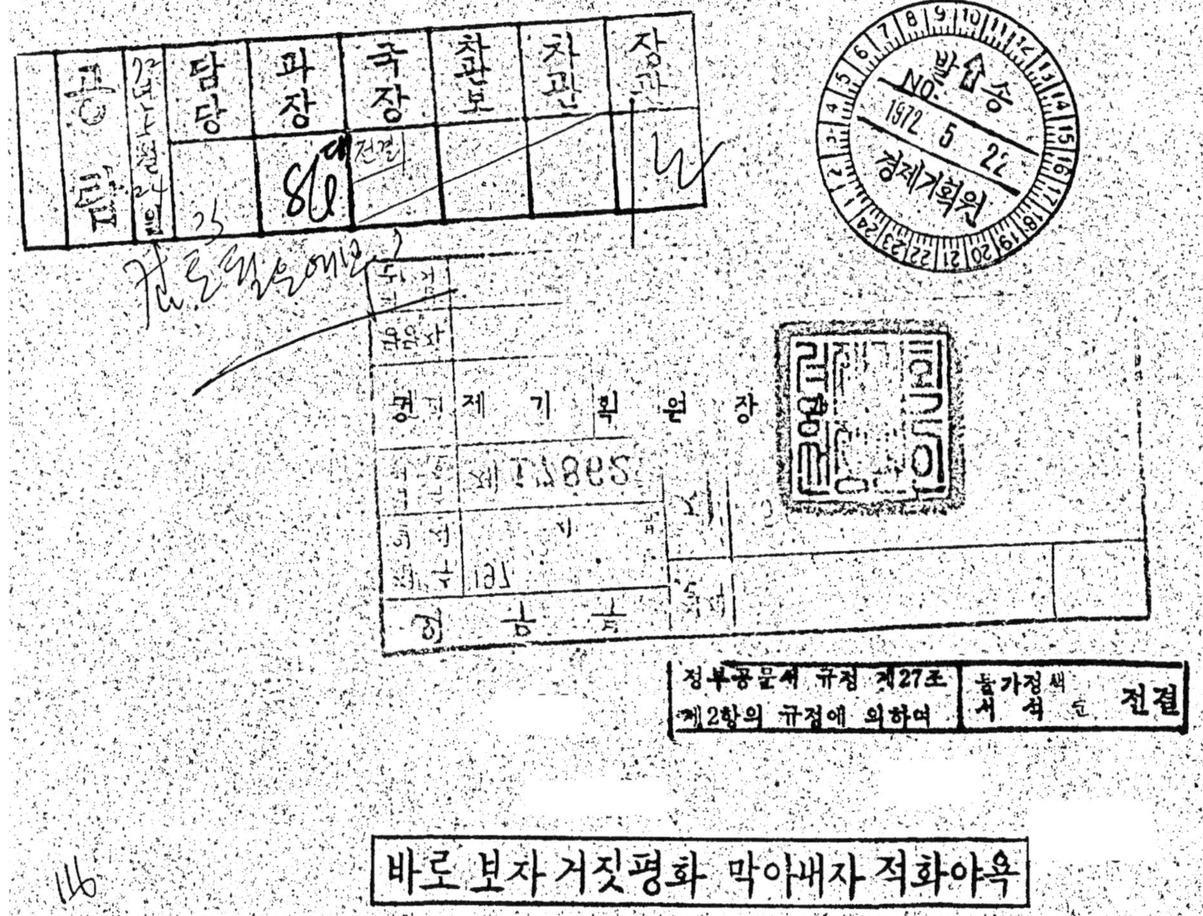

공람	72년 5월 24일	담당	과장	국장	차관보	차관	장관
				전결			

발송 No. 1972. 5. 22. 경제기획원

경제기획원장

정부공문서 규정 제27조 제2항의 규정에 의하여 | 농가정책 서 석 순 전결

바로보자 거짓평화 막아내자 적화야욕

116

REPUBLIC OF KOREA-UNITED STATES
UTILITIES SUBCOMMITTEE

May 18, 1972

SUBJECT : Chang in Telephone Installation Charges applicable to the US Armed Forces under Article VI of the Status of Forces Agreement

TO : US Chairman, Utilities Subcommittee

1. Reference ; Paragraph 2 and Agreed Minute I of Article VI of the Status of Forces Agreement.

2. The Government of the United States is informed through this written consultative process that ROK proposes to change the following rate/tariff at location indicated below;

Rate/Tariff	Location
Telephone installation charges	The whole country

3. The following data are provided;

a. Effective date

Although the rate changes are effective from 1 February, 1972, the new charges will be applied to the US Forces' use from 2 March, 1972, the date when the Ministry of Communications informed you of the changes.

b. Rate schedule showing rates that are charged all classes of users. (Attachment I)

c. Rate schedule of proposed change refers to item " b ".

d. Calculation of old and new rate base. (Attachment II)

e. Reason for revision of rate

To cover the rising cost and provide investment Fund.

4. The Government of ROK advises the Government of the United States that priorities, conditions and rates or tariffs being changed are no less favorable than those accorded any other user. The view of the Government of the United States is solicited as soon as possible. You may be assured that your views will be greatly appreciated.

Suck J. Suh
Suck Joon Suh
ROK Chairman
Utilities Subcommittee

118

(Attachment I)

Description of Changed Installation Charges of Ordinary Telephone

Class		Unit	Charge (Won)
1st class		per station	9,000
2nd "		"	12,000
3rd "		"	12,000
4th "		"	15,000
5th "	Automatic	"	37,500
	Manual	"	21,000
6th "	Automatic	"	60,000
	Manual	"	31,500
7th "		"	75,000
8th "		"	90,000
9th "		"	105,000
10th "		"	120,000
11th "		"	135,000
12th "		"	150,000
13th "		"	165,000

119

(Attachment II)

Calculation of Old and New Charges

(Won)

Class	Unit	Old charges	New charges
1st class	per station	6,000	9,000
2nd "	"	8,000	12,000
3rd "	"	8,000	12,000
4th "	"	10,000	15,000
5th " Automatic	"	25,000	37,500
Manual	"	14,000	21,000
6th " Automatic	"	40,000	60,000
" Manual	"	21,000	31,5000
7th "	"	50,000	75,000
8th "	"	60,000	90,000
9th "	"	70,000	105,000
10th "	"	80,000	120,000
11th "	"	90,000	135,000
12th "	"	100,000	150,000
13th "	"	110,000	165,000

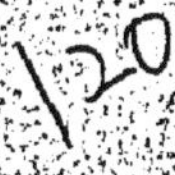

REPUBLIC OF KOREA-UNITED STATES
UTILITIES SUBCOMMITTEE

11 May 1972

MEMORANDUM TO: The Joint Committee

SUBJECT: Consultation on Rate/Tariff Changes

1. Subcommittee Members:

ROK	US
Mr. SUH Suck Joon, Chairman	COL Richard T. Cann, Chairman
Mr. PARK Woon Suh, Secretary	COL Norman W. Hammes, Alt Chairman
Mr. KIM Woon Cho, Member	LTC Charles J. Turner, Secretary
Mr. CHO Chang Suk, Member	CDR John P. Smith, Member
Mr. CHUNG Chae Jin, Member	Mr. William E. Woodford, Member
Mr. KIM Jong Ho, Member	MAJ Robert E. Frazier, Member
Mr. SONG Hae Joon, Member	Mr. Samuel Pollock, Member
Mr. PAIK Joong Sup, Member	Mr. Don Leland, Member
Mr. SHIN Kyong Shick, Member	MAJ Jewell D. Raymond, Member
Mr. KIM Sung Shil, Member	Mr. Francis K. Cook, Member

2. Subject of Recommendation: Agreed Minute 1 to Article VI, ROK-US SOFA, provides that any changes determined by the authorities of the Republic of Korea in priorities, conditions, and rates or tariffs, applicable to the United States armed forces shall be the subject of consultation in the Joint Committee prior to their effective date.

3. The Republic of Korea has initiated consultation concerning a change in rates or tariffs for the cost of water purchased from the City of Seoul, effective 16 February 1972, under contract DAJBO3-69-C-0275 (Inclosure 1).

4. The United States component of the Utilities Subcommittee has received the ROK request for consultation and has determined that the requested change in rates or tariffs is no less favorable than those accorded any other comparable user (see Inclosure 2).

121

5. It is recommended that the two inclosures referenced in paragraphs 3 and 4 be accepted by the Joint Committee as evidence of consultation contemplated by Article VI of the Status of Forces Agreement.

2 Incl

SUH SUCK JOON
Republic of Korea Chairman
Utilities Subcommittee

for RICHARD T. CANN, COL, USA
United States Chairman
Utilities Subcommittee

122

122-1.E

REPUBLIC OF KOREA-UNITED STATES
UTILITIES SUBCOMMITTEE

16 February, 1972

Subject : Change in Water Supply Rates applicable to the US Armed Forces under Article VI of the Status of Forces Agreement.

To : US Chairman, Utilities Subcommittee.

1. Reference: Paragraph 2 and Agreed Minute I of Article VI of the Status of Forces Agreement.

2. The Government of the United States is informed through this written consultative process that ROK proposes to change the following rate/tariff at locations indicated below;

Rate/Tariff	Location
Water supply rate schedule applicable to the US Armed Forces	The city of Seoul

3. The following data is provided

a. Effective date

Although the rate changes are effective from 1 January, 1972, the new rates will be applied to the US Forces' use in accordance with the agreement set forth in the letter dated 15 November, 1969.

b. Rate schedule showing rates that are charged all classes of users. (Attached)

c. Rate schedule of proposed change refer to item"d."

d. Calculation of old and new rate base

old rate(won)	new rate(won)
10 per m^3	20 per m^3

e. Reasons for revision of rate

To cover the rising cost and investment fund.

123

4. The Government of ROK advises the Govrnment of the United States that priorities, conditions and rates of tariffs being changed are no less favorable than accorded any other user.
You may be assured that your early views will be greatly appreciated.

Suck J. Suh
Suck Joon Suh
Director, Office of Price Policy
Republic of Korea Chairman
Utilities Subcommittee

124

1234.E

(Attached)

Water supply rates schedule

Rates / Use		Basic rates: quantity(m^3)	Basic rates: rate (won)	excessive rates: quantity(m^3)	excessive rates: rate per m^3(won)
Home use		10	150	11 - 20	15
				21 - 30	20
				31 - 40	30
				over 41	40
Business use	class 1	30	1,350	31 - 200	70
				201 - 1,000	90
				over 100	120
	class 2	30	900	per m^3	35
industrial use		200	6,000	"	35
Public bath	class A	600	48,000	601 - 1,000	100
				1,001 - 3,000	160
				over 3,000	200
	class B	600	12,000	per m^3	25
Public use		100	1,000	"	10
Special use (Government, Army etc)		20 won per 1 m^3			
Fire extinguishing use		100 won per month			

125

REPUBLIC OF KOREA - UNITED STATES
UTILITIES SUBCOMMITTEE

8 May 1972

SUBJECT: Change in Water Supply Rates Applicable to the US Armed Forces, City of Seoul, under Article VI of the Status of Forces Agreement

Republic of Korea Chairman, Utilities Subcommittee

1. References:

a. Paragraph 2 and Agreed Minute 1 of Article VI of the Status of Forces Agreement.

b. ROK component of the Utilities Subcommittee Memorandum of Consultation, dated 16 February 1972, subject as above, pertaining to a rate change for water supply, City of Seoul.

2. The ROK memorandum, reference 1b above, has been reviewed and the United States component of the Utilities Subcommittee fully understands the requirement for change in the water supply rates in this instance and will join with the ROK component of the Utilities Subcommittee in presenting a memorandum on the rates to the Joint Committee.

Norman W. Hommes, COL
for
RICHARD T. CANN
Colonel, US Army
United States Chairman
Utilities Subcommittee

126

REPUBLIC OF KOREA-UNITED STATES
UTILITIES SUBCOMMITTEE

11 May 1972

MEMORANDUM TO: The Joint Committee

SUBJECT: Consultation on Rate/Tariff Changes

1. Subcommittee Members:

ROK	US
Mr. SUH Suck Joon, Chairman	COL Richard T. Cann, Chairman
Mr. PARK Woon Suh, Secretary	COL N. W. Hammes, Alt Chairman
Mr. KIM Woon Cho, Member	LTC Charles J. Turner, Secretary
Mr. CHO Chang Suk, Member	CDR John P. Smith, Member
Mr. CHUNG Chae Jin, Member	Mr. William E. Woodford, Member
Mr. KIM Jong Ho, Member	MAJ Robert E. Frazier, Member
Mr. SONG Hae Joon, Member	Mr. Samuel Pollock, Member
Mr. PAIK Joong Sup, Member	Mr. Don Leland, Member
Mr. SHIN Kyong Shick, Member	MAJ Jewell D. Raymond, Member
Mr. KIM Sung Shil, Member	Mr. Francis K. Cook, Member

2. Subject of Recommendation: Agreed Minute 1 to Article VI, ROK-US SOFA, provides that any changes determined by the authorities of the Republic of Korea in priorities, conditions, and rates or tariffs, applicable to the United States armed forces shall be the subject of consultation in the Joint Committee prior to their effective date.

3. The Republic of Korea has initiated consultation concerning a change in rates or tariffs for the cost of electric power furnished to USFK throughout the Republic of Korea, effective 5 February 1972, under contract DAJB03-70-D-6017 (Inclosure 1).

4. The United States component of the Utilities Subcommittee has received the ROK request for consultation and has determined that the requested change in rates or tariffs is no less favorable than those accorded any other comparable user (see Inclosure 2).

121

5. It is recommended that the two inclosures referenced in paragraphs 3 and 4 be accepted by the Joint Committee as evidence of consultation contemplated by Article VI of the Status of Forces Agreement.

2 Incl

SUH SUCK JOON Republic of Korea Chairman Utilities Subcommittee	for RICHARD T. CANN, COL, USA United States Chairman Utilities Subcommittee

128

REPUBLIC OF KOREA-UNITED STATES
UTILITIES SUBCOMMITTEE

5 February, 1972

Subject : Change in Electric Power Rates applicable to the US Armed Forces under Article VI of the Status of Forces Agreement.

To : US Chairman, Utilities Subcommittee

1. Reference : Paragraph 2 and Agreed Minute 1 of Article VI of the Status of Forces Agreement.

2. The Government of the United States is informed through this written consultative process that ROK proposes to change the following rate/tariff at locations indicated below;

Rate/Tariff	Location
Electric rate schedule applicable to the US Armed Forces	Whole Country

3. The following data is provided;

a. Effective date

Although the rate changes are effective from 1 February, 1972, the new rates will be applied to the US Forces' use in accordance with the agreement set forth in the letter dated 15 November, 1969.

b. Rate Schedule showing rates that are charged all classes of users. Attached.

c. Rate schedule of proposed change.

15% increase with no exception over the old rate schedule. For detailed information, refer to item "b."

d. Calculation of old and new rate base.

Refer to item "b."

e. Reasons for revision of rate.

To secure fair return and investment fund.

129

4. The Government of ROK advises the Government of the United States that priorities, conditions and rates or tariffs being changed are no less favorable than those accorded any other user.
You may be assured that your early views will be greatly appreciated.

Suck Joon Suh
Director, Office of Price Policy
Republic of Korea Chairman
Utilities Subcommittee

130

(Attached)

PROPOSED NEW ELECTRIC RATE SCHEDULE

131

TARIFF 1
GENERAL SERVICE A

APPLICABLE:

To residential service without limit and general service of 4kw demand or under.

TYPE OF SUPPLY:

Single or three phase supply at any one of the Company's available standard voltages, 100 v or 200 v.

MONTHLY BILL:

Basic Rate:

Energy Charge:

W163.88 for the first 3 kwh.
W 15.53 per kwh for the next 27 kwh.
W 11.79 per kwh for the next 180 kwh. *
W 9.09 per kwh for each additional kwh.
* Add 90 kwh at W11.79 block for each kw in excess of 3kw of demand.

Minimum Charge: W163.88.

TARIFF 2
GENERAL SERVICE B

APPLICABLE:

To general service of 4 kw of contracted demand and over.

TYPE OF SUPPLY:

Single or three pahse supply at any one of the Company's available standard voltages, 20kv, 10kv, 6kv, 5.2kv, 3kv, 200v, 100v or others.

MONTHLY BILL:

Basic Rate:

a. Demand Charge:

W184.00 per kw for the first 50 kw of contracted demand.
W146.00 per kw for the next 450 kw of contracted demand.
W109.00 per kw for each additional kw of contracted demand.

132

b. Energy Charge:

W9.49 per kwh for the first 90 kwh per kw of contracted demand.
W6.50 per kwh for the next 90 kwh per kw of contracted demand.
W4.68 per kwh for the next 180 kwh per kw of contracted demand.
W3.16 per kwh for each additional kwh.

c. Minimum contracted kw demand: 4 kw.

TARIFF 3
HIGH TENSION SERVICE

HIGH TENSION SERVICE A

APPLICABLE:

To service of 1,000 kw of contracted demand and over, and 20 kv and over.

TYPE OF SUPPLY:

Three phase supply at any one of the Company's available standard voltages, 20 kv and over.

MONTHLY BILL:

Basic Rate:

a. Demand Charge:

W152.00 per kw for the first 500 kw of contracted demand.
W101.00 per kw for each additional kw of contracted demand.

b. Energy Charge:

W9.49 per kwh for the first 90 kwh per kw of contracted demand.
W6.18 per kwh for the next 90 kwh per kw of contracted demand.
W4.30 per kwh for the next 180 kwh per kw of contracted demand.
W2.71 per kwh for each additional kwh.

c. Minimum contracted kw demand: 1,000 kw.

HIGH TENSION SERVICE B

APPLICABLE:

To service of 150kv and over.

TYPE OF SUPPLY:

Three phase supply at any one of the Company's available standard voltages, 150 kv and over.

137

MONTHLY BILL:

Basic Rate:

a. Demand Charge:

W101.00 per kw of contracted demand.

b. Energy Charge:

W9.49 per kwh for the first 90 kwh per kw of contracted demand.
W6.11 per kwh for the nest 90 kwh per kw of contracted demand.
W4.21 per kwh for the next 180 kwh per kw of contracted demand.
W2.70 per kwh for each additional kwh.

TARIFF 4
IRRIGATION SERVICE

APPLICABLE:

To service required for the operation of pumps which are used to irrigate land for the cultivation and growing of grain for food purpose. Lighting necessary and incidential to the operation of pumps is permitted.

TYPE OF SUPPLY:

Same as "General Service B".

MONTHLY BILL:

Basic Rate:

Demand Charge: W54.00 per kw for contracted demand.
Energy Charge: W3.51 per kwh for each kwh.

TARIFF 5
STREET LIGHTING SERVICE

APPLICABLE:

To service for operation of lighting of streets, parks and similar places for the benefit and convenience of public.

TYPE OF SUPPLY:

Single phase at either 100 v or 200v.

MONTHLY BILL:

Basic Rate: W2.76 per watt for connected load.
Minimum Charge: W92.00.

134

TARIFF 6

FLAT RATE LIGHTING SERVICE

APPLICABLE:

To lighting service (including radio substituted one set as one lamp), principally limited to 100 watts of connected load with three lamps or under. One radio set shall be counted as 20 watts.

TYPE OF SUPPLY:

Single phase supply at either 100v or 200 v.

MONTHLY BILL:

Basic Rate:

W5.41 per watt for the first 60 watts of connected load.
W3.68 per watt for additional watts of connected load.

Minimum Charge: W92.00.

135

SPECIAL PROVISIONS

1. **SPECIAL INDUSTRY:**

   a. To export industry customers with 200 kw of contracted demand or under.
   b. To p. v. c. manufacturing industry customers who use carbide and acetylene in p.v.c. manufacturing process. (only applied to the industry which is financed by the foreign loan and guaranteed by the Government for repayment).
   c. To aluminium, iron and steel industry customers whose power charges occupy more than 10% of the total production cost. (only limited to pig iron and ingot iron).
   d. To industry customers whose power charges occupy more than 20% of the total production cost, who are designated by the Minister of commerce and Industry.

   DISCOUNT RATE: Monthly bill shall be discounted as follows:

   a. 30% discount: For export industry customer with 200 kw of contracted demand or under.
   b. 30% discount: For p. v. c. manufacturing industry customers who use carbide and acetylene in p.v.c. manufacturing process.
   c. 20% discount: For the aluminium, iron and steel industry customers whose electric charges occupy 10% and over, of the total production cost.
      25% discount: For the aluminium, iron and steel industry customers whose electric charges occupy 30% and over, of the total production cost.
      30% discount: For the aluminium, iron and steel industry customers whose electric charges occupy 40% and over, of the total production cost.
   d. 15% discount: For the industry customer whose electric charges occupy 20% and over, of the total production cost.
      20% discount: For the industry customer whose electric charges occupy 30% and over, of the total production cost.
      25% discount: For the industry customer whose electric charges occupy 40% and over, of the total production cost.
      30% discount: For the industry customer whose electric charges occupy 50% and over, of the total production cost.

2. **MUNICPAL WATER SERVICE:**

   Electric rate for Municipal Water Service may be discounted, but the discount rate shall be determined by Minister of Commerce and Industry.

136

REPUBLIC OF KOREA - UNITED STATES
UTILITIES SUBCOMMITTEE

8 May 1972

SUBJECT: Change in Electric Power Rates Applicable to the US Armed Forces under Article VI of the Status of Forces Agreement

Republic of Korea Chairman, Utilities Subcommittee

1. References:

a. Paragraph 2 and Agreed Minute 1 of Article VI of the Status of Forces Agreement.

b. ROK component of the Utilities Subcommittee Memorandum of Consultation, dated 5 February 1972, subject as above, pertaining to a rate change for electric power applicable to the US Armed Forces.

2. The ROK memorandum, reference 1b above, has been reviewed and the United States component of the Utilities Subcommittee fully understands the requirement for change in the electric power rates in this instance and will joint with the ROK component of the Utilities Subcommittee in presenting a memorandum on the rates to the Joint Committee.

Norman W. Hammes, COL
for
RICHARD T. CANN
Colonel, US Army
United States Chairman
Utilities Subcommittee

139

REPUBLIC OF KOREA-UNITED STATES
UTILITIES SUBCOMMITTEE

6 June 1972

MEMORANDUM TO: The Joint Committee

SUBJECT: Consultation on Rate/Tariff Changes

1. Subcommittee Members:

ROK	US
Mr. SUH Suck Joon, Chairman	COL Richard T. Cann, Chairman
Mr. PARK Woon Suh, Secretary	COL N. W. Hammes, Alt Chairman
Mr. KIM Woon Cho, Member	LTC Charles J. Turner, Secretary
Mr. CHO Chang Suk, Member	CDR John P. Smith, Member
Mr. CHUNG Chae Jin, Member	Mr. William E. Woodford, Member
Mr. KIM Jong Ho, Member	MAJ Robert E. Frazier, Member
Mr. SONG Hae Joon, Member	Mr. Samuel Pollock, Member
Mr. PAIK Joong Sup, Member	Mr. Don Leland, Member
Mr. SHIN Kyong Shick, Member	MAJ Jewell D. Raymond, Member
Mr. KIM Sung Shil, Member	Mr. Francis K. Cook, Member

2. Subject of Recommendation: Agreed Minute 1 to Article VI, ROK-US SOFA, provides that any changes determined by the authorities of the Republic of Korea in priorities, conditions, and rates or tariffs, applicable to the United States armed forces shall be the subject of consultation in the Joint Committee prior to their effective date.

3. The Republic of Korea has initiated consultation concerning a change in rates for telephone installation charges applicable to the United States Armed Forces throughout the Republic of Korea, effective 2 March 1972, under contract DAJBO3-69-D-0154 (Inclosure 1).

4. The United States component of the Utilities Subcommittee has received the ROK request for consultation and has determined that the requested change in rates or tariffs is no less favorable than those accorded any other comparable user (see Inclosure 2).

138

5. It is recommended that the two inclosures referenced in paragraphs 3 and 4 be accepted by the Joint Committee as evidence of consultation contemplated by Article VI of the Status of Forces Agreement.

2 Incl

RICHARD T. CANN, COL, USA
United States Chairman
Utilities Subcommittee

SUH SUCK JOON
Republic of Korea Chairman
Utilities Subcommittee

APPROVED BY THE JOINT COMMITTEE

KIM DONG-WHIE
Republic of Korea
Representative

ROBERT N. SMITH
Lieutenant General
United States Air Force
United States Representative

139

REPUBLIC OF KOREA-UNITED STATES
UTILITIES SUBCOMMITTEE

May 18, 1972

SUBJECT : Chang in Telephone Installation Charges applicable to the US Armed Forces under Article VI of the Status of Forces Agreement

TO : US Chairman, Utilities Subcommittee

1. Reference ; Paragraph 2 and Agreed Minute I of Article VI of the Status of Forces Agreement.

2. The Government of the United States is informed through this written consultative process that ROK proposes to change the following rate/tariff at location indicated below;

Rate/Tariff	Location
Telephone installation charges	The whole country

3. The following data are provided;

a. Effective date

Although the rate changes are effective from 1 February, 1972, the new charges will be applied to the US Forces' use from 2 March, 1972,the date when the Ministry of Communications informed you of the changes.

b. Rate schedule showing rates that are charged all classes of users. (Attachment I)

c. Rate schedule of proposed change refers to item " b ".

d. Calculation of old and new rate base. (Attachment II)

Inclosure 1

140

e. Reason for revision of rate

To cover the rising cost and provide investment Fund.

4. The Government of ROK advises the Government of the United States that priorities, conditions and rates or tariffs being changed are no less favorable than those accorded any other user. The view of the Government of the United States is solicited as soon as possible. You may be assured that your views will be greatly appreciated.

Suck J. Suh

Suck Joon Suh
ROK Chairman
Utilities Subcommittee

141

(Attachment I)

Description of Changed Installation Charges of Ordinary Telephone

Class		Unit	Charge (Won)
Ist class		per station	9,000
2nd "		"	12,000
3rd "		"	12,000
4th "		"	15,000
5th "	Automatic	"	37,500
	Manual	"	21,000
6th "	Automatic	"	60,000
	Manual	"	31,500
7th "		"	75,000
8th "		"	90,000
9th "		"	105,000
10th "		"	120,000
11th "		"	135,000
12th "		"	150,000
13th "		"	165,000

142

(Attachment II)

Calculation of Old and New Charges

(Won)

Class	Unit	Old charges	New charges
1st class	per station	6,000	9,000
2nd "	"	8,000	12,000
3rd "	"	8,000	12,000
4th "	"	10,000	15,000
5th " Automatic	"	25,000	37,500
Manual	"	14,000	21,000
6th " Automatic	"	40,000	60,000
7th " Manual	"	21,000	31,5000
7th "	"	50,000	75,000
8th "	"	60,000	90,000
9th "	"	70,000	105,000
10th "	"	80,000	120,000
11th "	"	90,000	135,000
12th "	"	100,000	150,000
13th "	"	110,000	165,000

REPUBLIC OF KOREA - UNITED STATES
UTILITIES SUBCOMMITTEE

26 May 1972

SUBJECT: Change in Telephone Installation Charges Applicable to the US Armed Forces Under Article VI of the Status of Forces Agreement

TO: Republic of Korea Chairman, Utilities Subcommittee

1. References:

a. Paragraph 2 and Agreed Minute 1 of Artice VI of the Status of Forces Agreement.

b. ROK component of the Utilities Subcommittee Memorandum of Consultation, dated 18 May 1972, subject as above, pertaining to a rate change for telephone installation charges.

2. The ROK memorandum, reference 1b above, has been reviewed and the United States component of the Utilities Subcommittee fully understands the requirement for change in the telephone installation charges in this instance and will join with the ROK component of the Utilities Subcommittee in presenting a memorandum on the rates to the Joint Committee.

Incl 2

RICHARD T. CANN
Colonel, US Army
United States Chairman
Utilities Subcommittee

144

REPUBLIC OF KOREA-UNITED STATES
UTILITIES SUBCOMMITTEE

6 July 1972

MEMORANDUM TO: The Joint Committee

SUBJECT: Consultation on Rate/Tariff Changes

1. Subcommittee Members:

ROK	US
Mr. SUH Suck Joon, Chairman	COL Richard T. Cann, Chairman
Mr. PARK Woon Suh, Secretary	COL N. W. Hammes, Alt Chairman
Mr. KIM Woon Cho, Member	LTC Charles J. Turner, Secretary
Mr. CHO Chang Suk, Member	CDR John P. Smith, Member
Mr. CHUNG Chae Jin, Member	Mr. William E. Woodford, Member
Mr. KIM Jong Ho, Member	MAJ Robert E. Frazier, Member
Mr. SONG Hae Joon, Member	Mr. Samuel Pollock, Member
Mr. PAIK Joong Sup, Member	Mr. Don Leland, Member
Mr. SHIN Kyong Shick, Member	MAJ Jewell D. Raymond, Member
Mr. KIM Sung Shil, Member	Mr. Francis K. Cook, Member

2. Subject of Recommendation: Agreed Minute 1 to Article VI, ROK-US SOFA, provides that any changes determined by the authorities of the Republic of Korea in priorities, conditions, and rates or tariffs, applicable to the United States armed forces shall be the subject of consultation in the Joint Committee prior to their effective date.

3. The Republic of Korea has initiated consultation concerning a change in rates or tariffs for the cost of railroad freight services supplied to USFK throughout the Republic of Korea, effective 5 February 1972, under contract DAJB03-70-D-3109 (Inclosure 1).

4. The United States component of the Utilities Subcommittee has received the ROK request for consultation and has determined that the requested change in rates or tariffs is no less favorable than those accorded any other comparable user (see Inclosure 2).

145

5. It is recommended that the two inclosures referenced in paragraphs 3 and 4 be accepted by the Joint Committee as evidence of consultation contemplated by Article VI of the Status of Forces Agreement.

2 Incl

SUH SUCK JOON
Republic of Korea Chairman
Utilities Subcommittee

RICHARD T. CANN, COL, USA
United States Chairman
Utilities Subcommittee

146

146-1.E

REPUBLIC OF KOREA-UNITED STATES
UTILITIES SUBCOMMITTEE

5 February, 1972

Subject: Change in Freight Rates of Railroad applicable to the US Armed Forces under Article VI of the Status of Forces Agreement.

To : US Chairman, Utilities Subcommittee.

1. Reference: Paragraph 2 and Agreed Minute 1 of Article VI of the Status of Forces Agreement.

2. The Government of the United States in informed through this written consultative process that ROK proposes to change the following rate/tariff at locations indicated below;

Rate/Tariff	Location
Freight rate schedule of Railroad applicable to the US Armed Forces	Whole Country

3. The following data is provided;

a. Effective date

Although the rate changes are effective from 1 February, 1972, the new rates will be applied to the US Forces' use in accordance with theagreement set forth in the letter dated 15 November, 1969.

b. Rate Schedule showing rates that are charged all classes of users.(Attachment I)

c. Rate Schedule of proposed change.

Rafer to item " d."

d. Calculation of old and new rate.

(Attachment II)

Inclosure 1

149

e. Reasons for revision of rate.

To secure transportation cost and investment fund.

4. The Government of ROK advises the Government of the United States that priorities, conditions and rates or tariffs being changed are no less favorable than those accorded any other user.

You may be assured that your early views will be greatly appreciated.

Suck J. Suh

Suck Joon Suh
Director, Office of Price Policy
Republic of Korea Chairman
Utilities Subcommittee

148

Attachment I

THE NEW FREIGHT RATE SCHEDULE

Description	Unit	Rate (won)
1. Basic Rates		
a. Less Than Carload Freight		
1st class	per 100kg/per 50km	32
2nd class	"	30
3rd class	"	29
4th class	"	28
5th class	"	27
b. Carload Freight		
1st class	per ton/per 50km	133
2nd class	"	113
3rd class	"	97
4th class	"	83
5th class	"	73
c. Privately Owned Freight Car	Per car	25% Discount for General Carload Freight Fare
2. Minimun Charge		
a. Less Than Carload Freight	per Case	48
b. Carload Freight (Include privately Owned Freight Car)	per car	4,120
c. Reserved Train	per train	285,600
3. Collection and Delivery Charge	1. within 2km	
	a. within 50kg	52
	b. per 50kg over 50kg	21
	2. within 4km	
	a. within 50kg	64
	b. per 50kg over 50kg	25

149

4. Storage Charge		
a. Less tham Carload Freight	per100kg/perunit of 24hrs	13
b. Carload Freight	per ton/perunit of 6 hrs	161
5. Impounding Charge	½of Storage Charge	
6. Demurrage	1. per ton/1st 6hrs	40
	2. per ton/perunit of 6rs over 6 hrs	80
7. Transfer Charge	per ton	133
8. Conversion		
a. Cancellation of Ordered		
1.Less Tham Carload	per case	28
2.Carload Freight	per car	
i)Before Supply of Freight Car		116
ii)After Supply of Freight Car		1,200
3.Reserved Train	per Train	7,750
b. other		
1. Before Dispatch of Consignment Note	per Case=	37
2. After Dispatch of goods and Consignment note		
i) Before Advice of Arrival		
O. Less Tham Carload	per case	37
O. Carload Freight	per car	58

150

ii) After Advice of Arrival		
O. Less tham Carload	per case	48
O. Carload Freight	Per car	2,400
9. Convoyer Charge	per km	1 20
10. Delivery note	per case/per time	37
11. Vsing Freight Car Scale	per car	1,397
12. Copy of Consignment note	per copy	36
13. Bill of Lading	per copy	60
14. Additional Charge		
a. Convoyer without Leave	per km	2 40
b. Damgerous Goods		
i) powder	per kg 181	181
ii) other	per kg	60
15. Equipment Rental	per Car/per day	
a. To 30 Freight car		780
b. To 40 Freight Car		1,040
c. over 41 Freight car		1,300
16. Switching for Special Team Track (KNR owned)	per car/per km	208
17. Pricately Owned Track		
a. Switching Charge	per Engine/perkm	623
b. Vsing Freight Car (per car)	a. within 5hrs	410
	b. within 11 hrs	1,768
	c. per unit of 6hrs over 11hrs	2,716
18. Freight car for internal Yard use only	per car	
a. To 29 Freight car		600
b. over 30 Freight car		1,200

(15)

19. Privately owned Freight car a. Scheduled General Inspection and Repair (Every 24 months) Exchuding Owner's Imposition parts	per car	* by Fy 72 KNR's Budget	70,168

152

Attachment II

CALCULATION OF OLD AND NEW RATE BASE

(US Army)

Applicable tech spec	Description	Unit	old rate(won)	New rate(won)
3. 1. 2	Carload Freight			
a.	Basic rate using Carrier's car	per car/ per km	58 15	70
b.	Basic rate using US Owned car		37 80	25% Discount for Basic Freight Fare
c.	Minimum Charge for Carload of Rented and US Owned car	per car	2,080	4,120
3. 1. 3	Special Train Service Minimum Charge	per train	125,730	150,000
3. 1. 4	Demurrage	per car per unit of 6 hrs	1,006	1,200
3. 1. 5	Diversion or Reconsignment	per car	2,016	2,400
3. 1. 6	Cancellation of car ordered	"	1,004	1,200
3. 1. 7	Switching Charge	"	523	623
3. 1. 8	Stop off in Transit	"	939	1,120
3. 1. 9	Equipment Rental	per car/ per day	798	950
3. 1. 11	Deadhead Movement of Rented or US Owned Car	per car/ per km	14 30	18

157

3. 1. 12	Surcharge for oversized Freight	per car/ per km	14 30	51
3. 3. 2	US Government Owned Car			
a.	Scheduled General Inspection and Repair Excluding painting (every 24 months)	per car	32,000	38,100
(PACEX)	Carload Freight			
	a. Basic Rate	per car/per km	67 80	81
	b. Minimum Charge	per car	2,120	4,120
	Demurrage	per car per unit of 6hrs	1,006	1,200
	Deversion or Reconsignment	per car	2,016	2,400
	Cancellation of car ordered	"	1,004	1,200
	Switching charge	"	523	623
	Stop off in transit	"	939	1,120
	Surcharge for oversized Freight	per car/per km	42 60	51

154

REPUBLIC OF KOREA - UNITED STATES
UTILITIES SUBCOMMITTEE

19 June 1972

SUBJECT: Change in Freight Rates of Railroad Applicable to the US Armed Forces under Article VI of the Status of Forces Agreement

Republic of Korea Chairman, Utilities Subcommittee

1. References:

a. Paragraph 2 and Agreed Minute 1 of Article VI of the Status of Forces Agreement.

b. ROK component of the Utilities Subcommittee Memorandum of Consultation, dated 5 February 1972, subject as above, pertaining to a change in freight rates of railroads.

2. The ROK memorandum, reference 1b above, has been reviewed and the United States component of the Utilities Subcommittee fully understands the requirement for a change in the freight rates of railroad in this instance, and will join with the ROK component of the Utilities Subcommittee in presenting a memorandum on the rates to the Joint Committee.

Richard T. Cann
RICHARD T. CANN
Colonel, US Army
United States Chairman
Utilities Subcommittee

Inclosure 2

155

경 제 기 획 원

물정 331・24-

(70-3022)

1972・ 8・ 3

수신 외무부장관

제목 인천시 및 춘천시 급수 조례 개정에 따른 유엔군 급수 계약 경신

인천 및 춘천시 급수조례 개정에 따른 유엔군과의 급수 계약을 변경코저 한미 행정 협정에 의한 협의를 별첨과 같이 미측 공공용역 분과 위원장에게 제의 하였음을 통보 하오니 양지 하시기 바랍니다. 끝.

유첨 대 미측 공공용역 분과 위원장 공한사본 1부. 끝.

공람	72년 8월 5	담당	과장	국장	차관보	차관	장관
				전결			

156

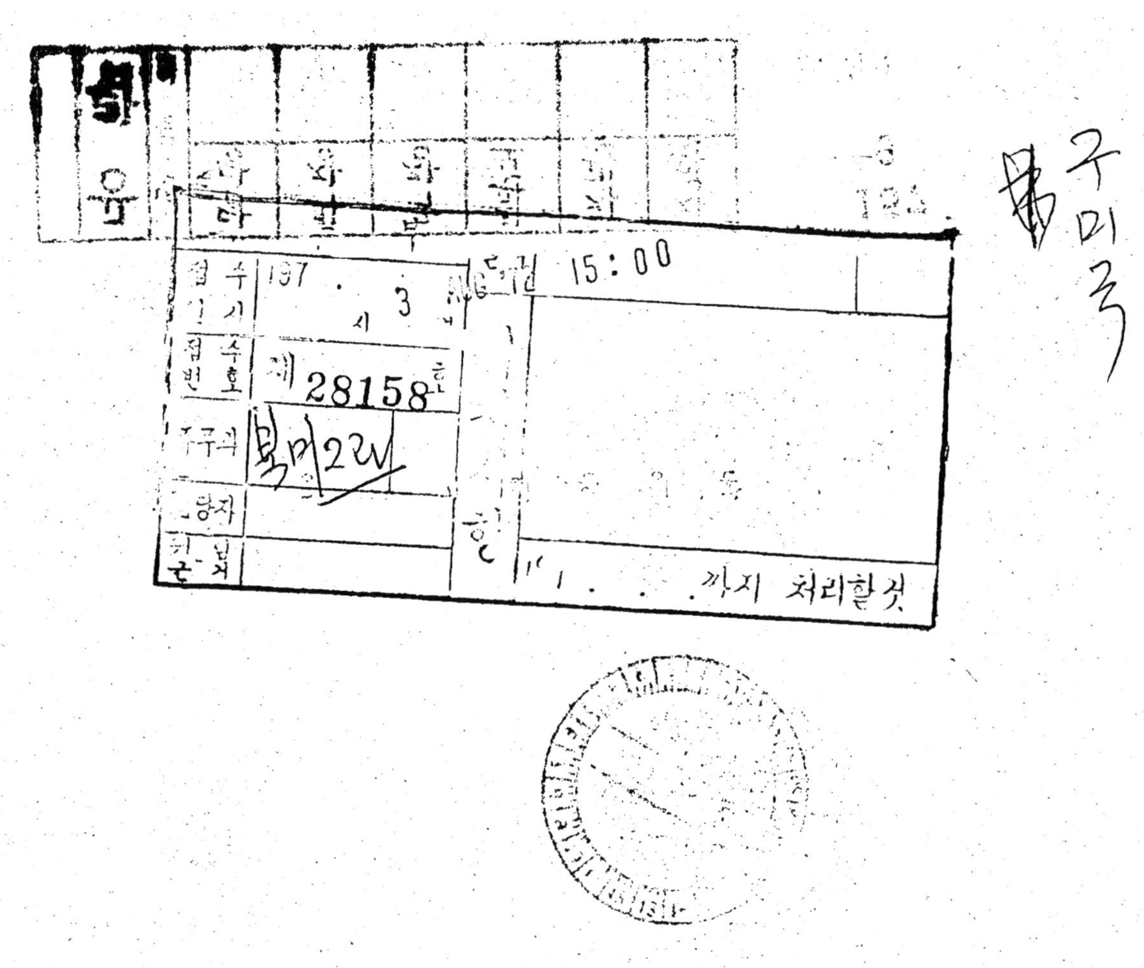

접수일시	197 . 3 . 15:00
접수번호	제 28158 호
주무과	북미2과
담당자	
처리기간	. . 까지 처리할것

158

REPUBLIC OF KOREA-UNITED STATES
UTILITIES SUBCOMMITTEE

1 August, 1972

Subject : Change in Water Supply Rates applicable to the US Armed Forces under Article VI of Status of Forces Agreement.

To : US Chairman, Utilities Subcommittee.

1. Reference : Paragraph 2 and Agreed Minute I of Article VI of the Status of Forces Agreement.

2. The Government of the United States is informed through this written consultative process that ROK proposes to change the following rate/tariff at locations indicated below;

Rate/Tariff	Location
Water supply rate schedule applicable to the US Armed Forces	The city of Inchon and the city of Chunchon

3. The following data are provided;

a. Effective date

Although the rate changes are effective from 1 June, 1972, the new rates will be applied to the US Forces' use from 1 August, 1972 in accordance with the agreement set forth in the letter dated 15 November, 1969.

b. Rate schedule showing rates that are charged all classes of users. (Attached)

c. Rate schedule of proposed change, refer to item "d".

d. Calculation of old and new rate base.

157

Name of City	Description	Old rate(won)	New rate(won)
Inchon	Basic rate for first 100 m^3	2,500	3,300
	Excess charge per m^3	33	35
Chunchon	Basic rate for first 30 m^3	300	600
	Excess charge per m^3	10	30

e. Reasons for revision of rate;

To cover the rising prime cost, especially due to 15% increase and 46.7% discount abolishment of electric power rate from Feb 1972.

4. The Government of ROK advises the Government of the United States that priorities, conditions, and rates or tariffs being changed are no less favorable than those accorded any other user.

You may be assured that your early views will be greatly appreciated.

Sincerely yours,

Suck Joon Suh
Director, Office of Price Policy
Chairman, Republic of Korea
Utilities Subcommittee

158

(Attached)

Water supply rate schedule

a. The city of Inchon

Rates / use	Basic Rates		Excessive Rate	
	Q'ty(m^3)	rate(won)	Q'ty(m^3)	rate (won)
Home use	7	160	8 - 50 per m^3 above 51 "	26 28
Business use	30	1,200	31-100 " 101-500 " above 501 "	41 43 45
Public Bath	300	9,900	301-1,000 " 1001-2,000 " above 2001 "	37 40 43
Government use	30	900	"	37
Industrial use	100	3,300	"	35
Military use	100	3,300	"	35
Railroad, ship use	-	-	"	40
Temporary use	-	-	"	50
Special Public use	30	810	"	30

159

b. The city of Chunchon

Rates / use	Basic Rates		Excessive Rates	
	Q'ty(m^3)	rate (won)	Q'ty(m^3)	rate(won)
Home use	10	190	11-30 per m^3	17
			31-50 "	20
			51-100 "	25
			above 101 "	34
Business use	30	690	31-50 "	36
			51-100 "	55
			above 101 "	73
Industrial use	60	1,350	"	35
Public Bath A	20	550	21-50 "	36
			51-100 "	55
			101-200 "	73
			201-300 "	110
			above 301 "	147
Public Bath B	20	460	21-50 "	27
			51-100 "	36
			101-200 "	45
			above 201 "	54
Military use	30	600	"	30
Temporary & Recreational use	10	460	11-20 "	46
			21-30 "	55
			31-50 "	64
			51-70 "	73
			71-100 "	82
			101-150 "	92
			151-200 "	128
			above 201 "	184

160

Railroad & ship use	200	4,500	per m^3	36
Gov't and Public Organization use	20	450	"	36
Private common use	20	4,400	"	27
Public common use	50	1,080	"	27

161

신 . 구 요 율 계 산

		구요율 (원)	신요율 (원)
인 천	기본 요율 (100 m^3)	2,500	3,300
	초과 요율 (m3)	33	35
춘 천	기본 요율 (30 m^3)	300	600
	초과 요율 (m^3)	10	30

162

외 무 부

년 월 일

제6조 1항에 "합중국 군대는 대한민국 정부 또는 그 지방행정 기관이 소유, 관리 또는 규제하는 모든 공익사업과 용역을 이용한다" 로 규정되어 있어, 개인이나 사 단체가 운영하는 공익사업과 써비스는 SOFA 가 적용될수 없고, 당해 개인이나 사 단체와 합중국 군대간의 일반 사법관계로 처리되어야 하며, 제6조 제2항은 합중국 군대가 대한민국 정부 또는 그 지방행정 기관이 소유, 관리 또는 규제하는 공익사업과 용역을 이용하는 경우에 한하여 적용이 된다고 봄.

북 미 2 과

163

기 안 용 지

분류기호 문서번호	미이 723 -	(전화번호)	전결규정 조 항 국장 전결사항
처리기간			
시행일자	72. 9. 8.		국장 9/8.
보존년한			
보조기관	과장		협
기안책임자	김성실	북미 2과	
경유 수신 참조	고통부장관 (조이부과장)	발신 No.29086 1972. 9. 8 외무부	검열 1972. 9. 9 통제관
제목	영업용 고속버스 요금 할인에 대한 의견 문의		

1. 별첨 서한과 같이 주한 미군당국은 72. 6. 1. 발표한 영업용 고속 버스 운송요금 할인제에 있어, 공무원이 공무 출장일때 이에 해당되는 것으로 알고있으며, 미군 및 미 군속의 공무 출장일 때는 미군당국의 비용으로 영업용 고속 버스를 이용하게 되므로,

2. 한.미 군대지위협정 제 6조 제 2항 규정이 공무 출장일 때는 적용된다고 보고 타 이용자에 불리하지 않은 우선권, 조건 및 요율이어야 함에 따라, 영업용 고속 버스 이용의 경우, 그들도 요금 할인의 혜택을 받도록 하여 달라고 요청하고 있읍니다.

3. 이에 대한 귀부의 의견을 회시하여 주시기 바랍니다.

첨부 : 미측 서한 1 부. 끝.

정서 관인 발송

164

공통서식1-2(갑) 1967. 4. 4. 승인

190mm ×268mm (1급인쇄용지70g/m²) 조달청 (500,000매 인쇄)

JOINT COMMITTEE
UNDER
THE REPUBLIC OF KOREA AND THE UNITED STATES
STATUS OF FORCES AGREEMENT

6 SEP 1972

Dear Mr. Kim:

It has been brought to my attention that certain categories of personnel have been granted discounts for commercial express bus service by the Republic of Korea Ministry of Transportation, effective 1 June 1972. Reportedly among these categories is that of government officials when their travel is in connection with the performance of official duties.

As you may be aware, this command utilizes commercial express bus carriers in the transportation of United States Forces, Korea military and civilian personnel in an official duty travel status. Such travel is performed upon a US Government Transportation Request, which is an official order on a commercial transportation firm to furnish passenger transportation and related service at the expense of the US Government and which also serves as a supporting document for payment to the carrier of applicable transportation costs for service rendered.

It would appear that the provisions of paragraph 2 of Article VI of the ROK-US SOFA are applicable to the official duty travel by personnel of this command referenced in the above paragraph. Accordingly, the use of the transportation services in question should be in accordance with priorities, conditions, and rates or tariffs no less favorable than those accorded any other user.

Your review of this matter would be most appreciated. I am looking forward to receipt of your notification concerning the results of this review.

Sincerely,

ROBERT N. SMITH
Lieutenant General, USAF
United States Representative

Mr. KIM, Dong-Whie
Republic of Korea Representative

165

KWON 피12

교 통 부

육진 1540- 3128　　　　　　　　　　　　　　1972. 9. 16.

수신　외무부장관

제목　영업용 고속버스 요금 할인에 대한 의견회신

1. 미이 723-29086(72. 9. 9)에 대한 회신입니다.

2. 공무원으로서 회의및 공무여행을 할 경우 고속버스 운임의 20%범위내에서 할인할수 있도록 조치하고 있으므로

3. 한미군대 지위협정 규정에 따라 미군및 미군속이 공무여행을 할 경우 우리나라 공무원과 같이 고속버스 운임의 할인을 받을수 있읍니다. 끝.

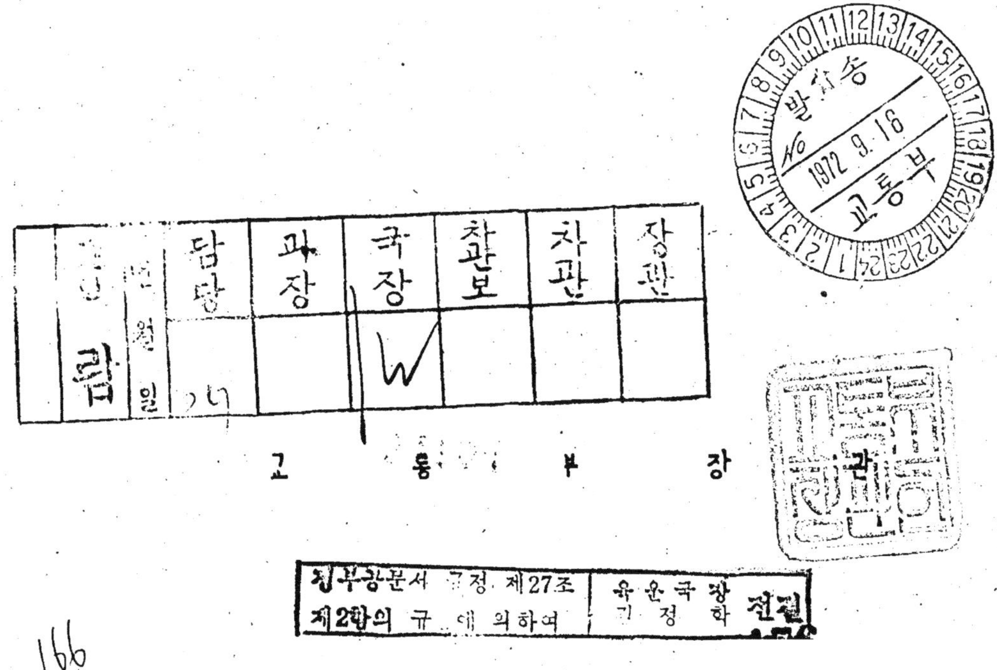

	담당	과장	국장	참관보	차관	장관
월 일						

교 통 부 장 관

정부공문서 규정 제27조 제2항의 규정에 의하여 유운국장 전결

166

외		
접수 일시	197 . . . 18 SEP '72 15 : 26	
접수 번호	제 34154	
주무과		
담당자		
위임 근거		처리할 것

176-1.E

교 통 부

육진 1540—1714 1972. 5. 20

수신 전국고속버스운송사업조합 이사장 이민하

제목 자동차(고속버스)운임할인 제도 승인

전고버조 제282호(72. 5. 9)로 신청한 운임할인제 인가 신청에 대하여는 다음과 같이 승인함

1. 시행일자 : 1972. 6. 1.

2. 할인대상

가. 왕복이용객(매표후 5일간유효)및 통근권

나. 학생(방학기간 및 통학생)

다. 공무원(고직자, 경찰, 고도관포함)으로 통근자와 회의및공무여행의경우

라. 군경유가족(원호처인정)

마. 단체(10인이상)

3. 할인율

가. 20%를 상한선으로 할인함.

나. 경쟁구간을 해당업체간에 합의에 의하여 할인율 결정

다. 단독 노선은 할인율 적용에 재량을 부여함.

4. 할인제도 실시를 사유로 대민써비스및 안전운행에 차질이 있다고 판단되는 경우 본 제도 승인을 취소함. 끝.

교 통 부 장 관

1619

전국 고속버스 운송사업조합

전고버조 제282호

수신 교통부장관

제목 운임 할인제 인가신청

72. 2. 1 고속버스 운임인상 이후 승객의 격감 추세에 당면하여 국가기관 및 사회공익에 기여하는 계층에 대한 봉사적 실리제공과 이른 아침승객없이 왕래하는 차량 및 재화의 효율성 제고 내지 불황타개의 일환책으로서 다음과 같은 특정대상에게 운임 할인제를 적용하기 위하여 운수사업법 제8조 (운임과요금의인가)에 의거 인가신청 하오니 특의 선처 있으시기를 바랍니다.

"다 음"

1. 적용기간 : 72. 5월 15일부터
72. 12월 31일까지

2. 적용대상 : 가. 학생및 교직원
나. 경찰및 일반공무원
다. 군경 유가족(직계존비속)
라. 단체 (10인이상)
마. 왕복 이용객(매표후 5일간 유효)
바. 이른아침 이용객 (9시이전)

3. 할인율및 구간 : 가. 경인간을 제외한 전구간, 일괄20% 상한선으로 할인하되 독자노선업체의 할인율은 당해회사 임의재량으로 한다.

나. 2개업체 이상 복합노선은 당해 회사간 합의하에 동일율을 할인한다.

168

4. 할인사유 : 가. 철도를 비롯한 여타 교통수단의 할인사례에 준거

나. 국가 및 사회공공복리에 기여하는 계층과 원호대상자에게 교통비 부담을 절감

다. 단체 및 왕복이용자, 이른아침 이용자에게 특혜 써비스 제공으로 승객을 유치

5. 할인방법 : 가. 학생및 교직원 경찰및 일반공무원과 군경유가족에게 조합발행 할인권(20%에 국한)을 당해기관 소요만큼 공급, 발부대장에 등재하고 일련번호제로 한다.

나. 매표창구에서 신분증을 제시하는 할인권 소지자에게 소정율 만큼 할인한다.

다. 단체 및 왕복이용객, 아침이용객은 소정할인액을 공제한 운임으로 매표하고 일반 승차권과 구분하여 기표한다.

별첨 : 운임인상후 승객감소 현황 1부. 끝.

전국고속버스여객자동차운송사업조합

이사장 이 민 하

169

경 제 기 획 원

물정 331.24-239 (70-5022) 1972. 9. 15

수신 외무부장관

제목 대구및 부산시 급수조례 개정에 따른 유엔군 급수 계약 갱신

대구및 부산시 급수조례 개정에 따른 유엔군과의 급수 계약을 변경코저 한미행정 협정에 의한 협의를 별첨과 같이 미측 공공용역 분과 위원장에게 제의 하였음을 통보 하오니 양지 하시기 바랍니다.

유첨 대 미측 공공용역 분과 위원장 공한사본 1부. 끝.

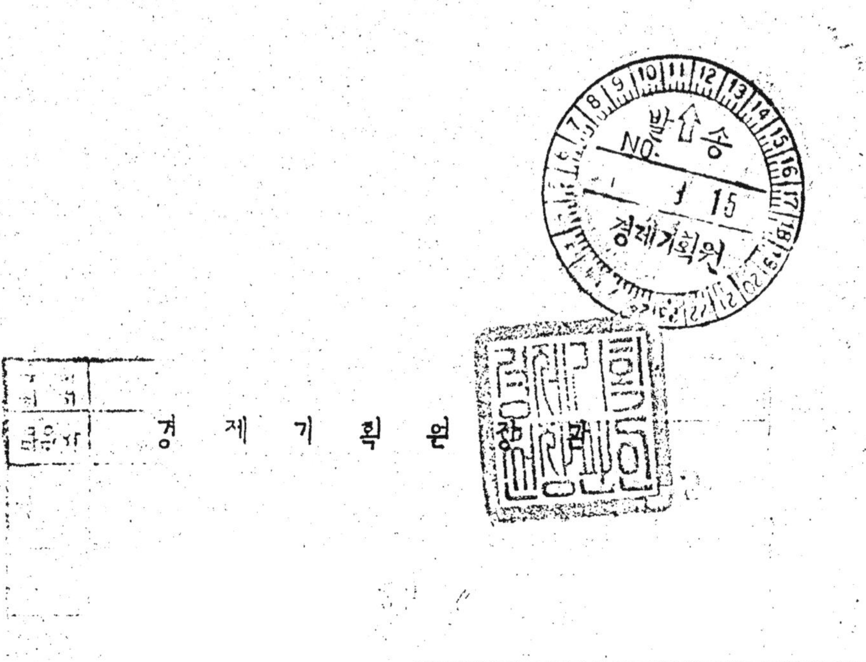

경 제 기 획 원 장 관

정부공문서 규정 제27조 제2항의 규정에 의하여 물가정책과 서석준 전결

170

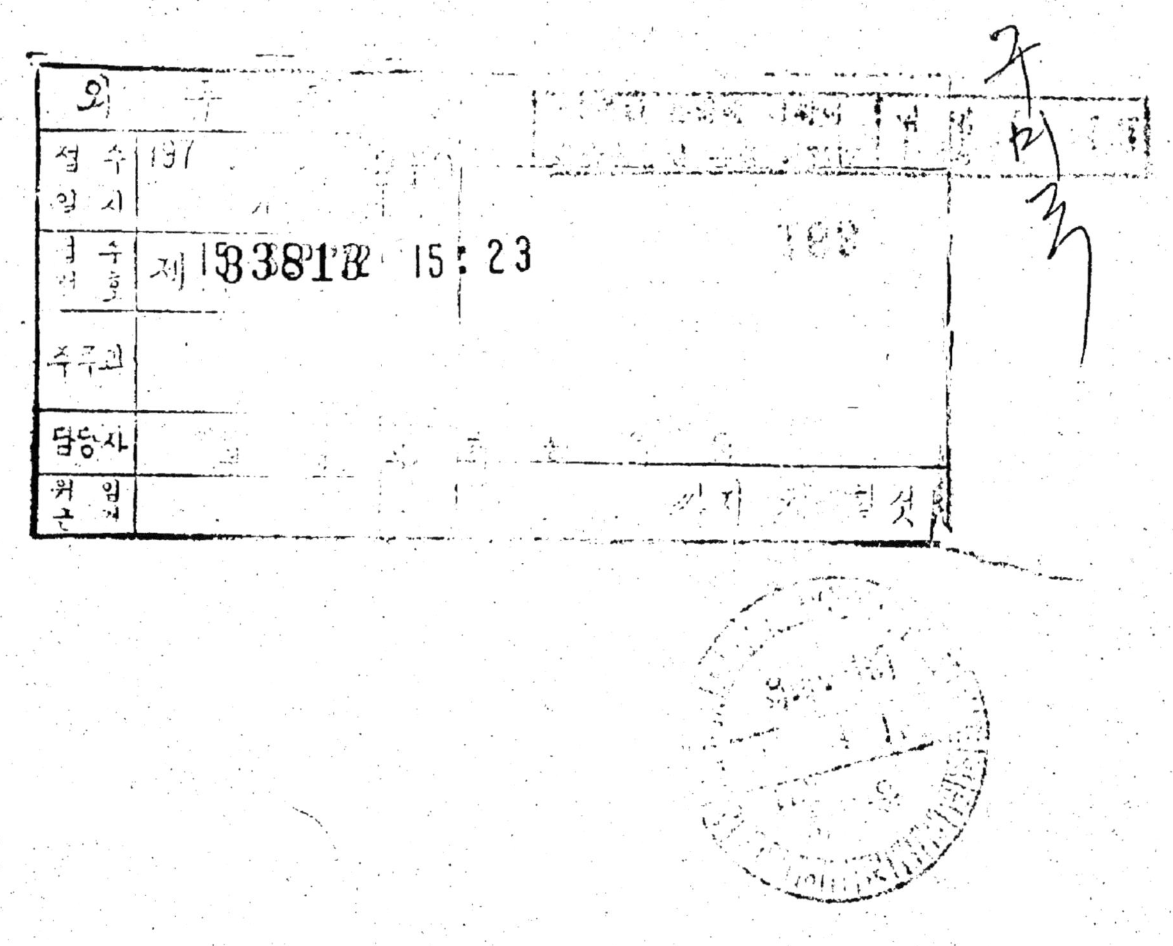

REPUBLIC OF KOREA-UNITED STATES
UTILITIES SUBCOMMITTEE

11 September, 1972

Subject : Change in Water Supply Rates applicable to the US Armed Forces under Article VI of Status of Forces Agreement.

To : US Chairman, Utilities Subcommittee.

1. Reference : Paragraph 2 and Agreed Minute I of Article VI of the Status of Forces Agreement.

2. The Government of the United States is informed through this written consultative process that ROK proposes to change the following rate/tariff at locations indicated below;

Rate/Tariff	Location
Water supply rate schedule applicable to the US Armed Forces	The city of Daegu and the city of Busan

3. The following data are provided;

a. Effective date

Although the rate changes of Daegu and Busan are effective from 1 May, 1972, and 5 June, 1972, the new rates will be applied to the US Forces' use 11 September, 1972 in accordance with the agreement set forth in the letter dated 15 November, 1969.

b. Rate schedule showing rates that are charged all classes of users. (Attached)

c. Rate schedule of proposed change refer to item "d".

d. Calculation of old and new rate base.

171

	Old rate	New rate
	per m^3	per m^3
Daegu	25 won	35 won
Busan	25 "	30 "

e. Reasons for revision of rate;

To cover the rising prime cost, especially due to 15% increase and 46.7% discount abolishment of electric power rate from 1 Feb, 1972.

4. The Government of ROK advises the Government of the United States that priorities, conditions, and rates of tariffs being changed are no less favorable than those accorded any other user.

You may be assured that your early views will be greatly appreciated.

Sincerely yours,

Suck Joon Suh
Director, Office of Price Policy
Chairman, Republic of Korea
Utilities Subcommittee

112

TABLE OF WATER CHARGE ON MONTHLY BASES

a. The city of Daegu

User	Basic Charge		Excessive Charge	
	Q'ty (m^3)	Rate (Won)	Q'ty (m^3)	Rate(Won/m^3)
Domestic	10	200	11 - 30	30
			31 - 50	40
			51 - 100	50
			Over 100	60
Industrial	100	1,800	101-1000	23
			Over 1000	25
Business: Class 1	10	320	11 - 50	45
			51 - 100	80
			Over 100	100
Class 2	10	320	11 - 50	45
			Over 50	50
Bath : Class 1	100	3,000	101-300	35
			301-500	65
			501-1000	100
			1001-1500	150
			Over 1500	230
Class 2	100	2,000	101-1000	30
			Over 1000	
Temporary or recreational	-	-	- 8	70
ROK Army and U.N. Forces	-	-	-	35

b. The city of Busan

User	Basic Charge		Excess Rate	
	Q'ty (m^3)	Rate (Won)	Q'ty(m^3)	Rate (Won/m^3)
Domestic Class 1	10	156		26
Domestic Class 2	20	480	21 - 50 Over 51	36 60
Business Class 1	20	720		42
Business Class 2	30	1,440	31 - 100 Over 101	75 150
Bath Class 1	500	12,500		35
Bath Class 2	500	38,000	501-1,000 Over 1000	200 300
Industrial	200	5,000		32
Gov't Office				30
Special Public				30
Recreation Garden Sparkling				450

179

JOINT COMMITTEE
UNDER
THE REPUBLIC OF KOREA AND THE UNITED STATES
STATUS OF FORCES AGREEMENT

October 27, 1972

Dear General Smith:

In reference to your letter of September 6, 1972, relating to discounts for the commercial express bus services, I would like to inform you that the certain Korean commercial express bus companies are ready to grant discounts privileges to the U.S. military personnel and civilian government employees (under governmental payroll) when their travel is performed on official duties, just like to the Korean government officials on official duties.

Sincerely yours,

Kim Dong Whie
Republic of Korea
Representative
ROK-US Joint Committee

Lt. Gen. Robert N. Smith, USAF
United States Representative
ROK-US Joint Committee

양 고	년 월 일	담 당	과 장	국 장	차관보	차 관	장 관
				전결		177	

175

경 제 기 획 원

물정 331·24-280 (70-3022) 1972. 10. 27

수신 외무부장관

제목 군산시 급수조례 개정에 따른 유엔군 급수 계약 갱신

군산시 급수조례 개정에 따른 유엔군과의 급수 계약을 변경코저 한미행정 협정에 의한 협의를 별첨과 같이 미측 공공용역분과 위원장에게 제의 하였음을 통보 하오니 양지 하시기 바랍니다.

유첨 대 미측 공공용역 분과 위원장 공한사본 1부. 끝.

발송 NO. 1972. 10. 27 경제기획원

공람	72 10월 30일	담당	과장	국장	차관보	차관	장관

경 제 기 획 원

정부공문서규정 제27조 제2항의 규정에 의하여 물가정책관 서석준 전결

REPUBLIC OF KOREA-UNITED STATES
UTILITIES SUBCOMMITTEE

26 October, 1972

Subject : Change in Water Supply Rates applicable to the US Armed Forces under Article VI of Status of Forces Agreement.

To : US Chairman, Utilities Subcommittee.

1. Reference : Paragraph 2 and Agreed Minute I of Article VI of the Status of Forces Agreement.

2. The Government of the United States is informed through this written consultative process that ROK proposes to change the following rate/tariff at location indicated below;

Rate/Tariff	Location
Water supply rate schedule applicable to the US Armed Forces	The city of Gunsan

3. The following data are provided;

a. Effective date

Although the rate changes of Gunsan are effective from 1 July, 1972, the new rates will be applied to the US Forces' use from 26 October, 1972 in accordance with the agreement set forth in the letter dated 15 November, 1969.

b. Rate schedule showing rates that are charged all classes of users. (Attached)

c. Rate schedule of proposed change refer to item "d".

d. Calculation of old and new rate base.

Old rate : Per m^3, 15 won
New rate : Per m^3, 27 won

e. Reasons for revision of rate;

To cover the rising prime cost, especially due to 15% increase and 46.7% discount aboilishment of electric power rate from 1 Feb, 1972.

4. The Government of ROK advises the Government of the United States that priorities, conditions, and rates of tariffs being changed are no less favorable than those accorded any other user.

You may be assured that your early views will be greatly appreciated.

Sincerely yours,

Suck Joon Suh
Director, Office of Price Policy
Chairman, Republic of Korea
Utilities Subcommittee

178

TABLE OF WATER CHARGE ON MONTHLY BASES

(The city of Gunsan)

User	Basic Charge		Excessive Charge	
	Q'ty(m³)	Rate(won)	Q'ty(m³)	Rate(won/m³)
Houshold	10	170	11. - 30	22
			31. - 50	28
			51. - 100	34
			over 101	44
Speciality	30	680		25
Business(A)	20	700	21. - 50	38
			51. - 100	57
			over 101	75
Business(B)	20	450		33
Bath House (A)	150	7,000	151 - 300	40
			301 - 500	48
			501 - 1,000	63
			1,001 - 1,500	77
			over 1,501	96
Public Bath House (B)	150	3,800		31
Private installation for Common use	20	340		20
Public installation for Common use	20	340		20
Ship	50	900		33
United Nation's Military				27

기 안 용 지

분류기호 문서번호	미이 723 -	(전화번호)	전결규정 조 항 국장 전결사항
처리기간			
시행일자	1972. 10. 30.		
보존년한			국 장
보조기관 과 장			협조
기안책임자	김성실	북미 2 과	
경 유		발신	통제
수 신	고통부장관		
참 조	육운국장		
제 목	영업용 고속 버스 요금할인 시행		

연 : 육진 1540 - 3128 (72. 9. 16)

1. 주한미군 및 군속의 영업용 고속 버스 요금할인에 관하여 미측에 별첨서한과 같이 통보하였아오니, 시행에 차질이 없도록 조치하여 주시기 바라며,

2. 주한미군 이라함은 한국에 주둔하는 미국의 현역 군인을 말하며, 주한미군 군속이라함은 미 국적을 가진 민간인으로서 미국정부에 고용된 공무원으로, 주한미군 사령부 및 그 예하부대에 근무하고 있는 자를 말하는 것이오니, 참고 바랍니다.

첨부 : 동 서한. 끝.

정서 / 관인 / 발송

공통서식1-2(갑)
1967. 4. 4. 승인

190mm ×268mm (1급인쇄용지70g/m²)
조달청 (500,000매 인쇄)

4. 1973년

181

Mr. Kim

경 제 기 획 원

물정331.24-100 (70.3101) 1973.3.16.

수신 수신처 참조

제목 한미공공용역분과위원회 개최

한미위원간 직접인사와 유엔군 사용요율 갱신문제 타결을 위하여 한미간에 합동공공용역위원회를 아래와 같이 개최코자 하오니 필히 참석하여 주시기 바랍니다.

(1) 일시 : 73.3.27 (화) 13 : 30

2. 장소 : 서울용산 미8군내
SOFA Conference Room,
Bldg 2370 Yongsan Reservation

3. 의제 : (1) 한미 쌍방 인사소개

(2) 유엔군 급수사용요율 갱신

(군산비행장, 춘천시, 인천시, 군산시, 대구시, 부산시)

(3) 기타 상호 협조 사항

4. 참석범위

(1) 한국측 위원

경제기획원 (~~물가정책국장~~, 물가조정과장)

외무부 (북미 2과장)

내무부 (세정과장, 행정과장)

상공부 (전기과장, [illegible]과장)

건설부 (상하수도 과장)

발송 No. 1973 3 17 경제기획원

184

(82)

체신부 (국내업무과장)

철도청 (화물과장)

(2) 관계기관

각지업무과장 (춘천, 인천, 군산, 대구, 부산)

전북농지개량조합 (재무과장)

(3) 미측 공공용역분과위원회 위원

경 제 기 획 원

수신처 : 외무부장관, 내무부장관, 상공부장관, 건설부장관, 체신부장관, 철도청장, 춘천시장, 인천시장, 군산시장, 대구시장, 부산시장, 전북농지개량조합.

정부공문서 규정 제27조 제2항의 규정에 의하여	물가정책국장 강 경 식	전결

1887

체 신 부

체전내 1623.7- 12606 1973. 7. 21.

수신 한미합동위원회

제목 군사및 치안기관에 대한 통신회선 전용 요금

1. 체신부와 미육군성간의 전기통신 시설 사용 약정서 제16조 관련

2. 통신회선 전용요금 제도 개정 사항 (군사및 치안기관에 대한 통신회선 전용 요금제도 제정)을 별첨과 같이 통보 합니다.

첨부 : 군사및 치안기관에 대한 통신회선 전용 요금표 1부. 끝

보존 비고	공람	년 월 일	담당	과장	국장	참관보	차관	장관

체 신 부 장

184

외 무 부			
접수 일시	197 . . .		
	AUG '73 15 : 37		
접수 번호	제 1616		
주무과			
담당자			
위임 근거		197 . . . 까지 처리할것	

군사 및 치안기관에 대한 통신회선 전용 요금

1. 통신회선 전용료, 설비비 및 장치비

구분 요금의 종류	장기 종입 전용	단기 종입 전용	비 고
1. 시내전화 회선 전용료	100m까지 마다 2선식: 월액 25원 4선식: 월액 50원	1회선마다 일액 : 250원	
2. 시내전화 회선 전용료	1회선마다 월액 대시방식에 의하는 경우의 상당 보통 통화료의 1,500배	1회선마다 일액 대시방식에 의하는 경우의 상당 보통 통화료의 75배	
3. 설비비			
가. 전화기 설치	1개마다 6,000원		30일이상의 전용에 한 한다.
나. 인입선(전화기게 사진 또는 모사전신 장치와 교환설비 또는 전용자가 설치하는 전화기 설치)	1회선마다 6,000원		
4. 장치비			
가. 전화기 설치 또는 설치 장소 변경	1,600원	1,300원	
나. 인입주 이전	1,600원	1,300원	

185

다. 인입선(전신기계 사진 또는 모사전신 장치 교환설비(전용자가 설치하는 설비포함)또는 전용자가 설치하는 전화기의 설치(단기 종일 전용에 한함)또는 설치장소 변경)	1회선마다 1,600원	1회선마다 1,300원	

2. 집단시외 전화 회선 전용료

1의 전용자가 단일구간에 동일기간중 전용하는 시외전화 회선수	전 용 료	
	장기 종일 전용 (월액)	단기 종일 전용 (일액)
	1회선마다 대시통화방식에 의하는 경우의 상당 보통 통화료의	1회선마다 대시통화방식에 의하는 경우의 상당 보통 통화료의
3회선 이상	1,350배	70배
6회선 이상	1,275배	65배
12회선 이상	1,200배	60배
24회선 이상	1,125배	55배
48회선 이상	1,050배	50배

186

3. 대상기관

가. 군사기관

(1) 국방부와 육군 해군 공군본부 및 해병대 사령부와 그 예하 각급부대 및 병무청 단, 국립묘지 관리사무소는 제외

(2) 주한 유엔군 사령부(미8군 사령부 포함)

나. 치안기관

(1) 치안국과 솔하 각 경찰및 소방기관

4. 실시일자 : 73. 6. 1

187

경 제 기 획 원

물정331. 24-457 (70.3101) 1973. 10. 27.

수신 외무부 장관

제목 유엔군 소유 사유화차 수선비 개정에 따른 SOFA협의

미8군 구매처 계약관과 체결한 유엔군 철도군사 수송계약서 (DAJ B03 - 73 - D -3114, 73.6. 29) 중 사유화차 수선비에 대하여 별첨과 같이 개정코자 한미행정협정에 의한 협의를 미측 공공용역분과위원장에게 제의하였음을 통보합니다.

첨부 : 한국측 제의 공문 사본 1부. 끝.

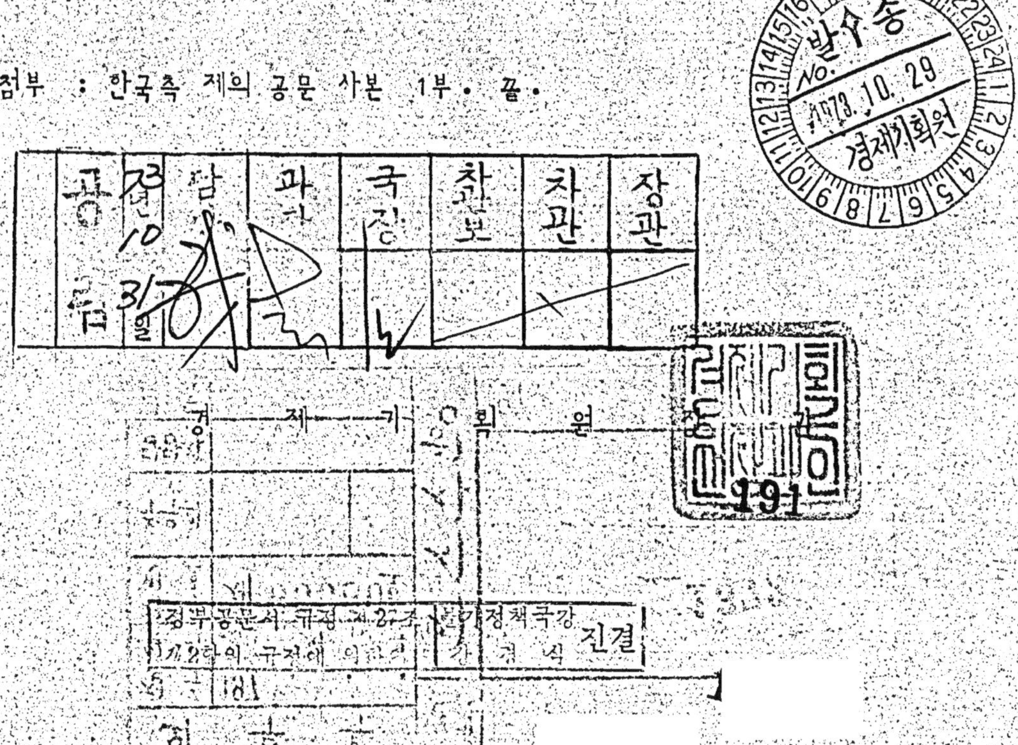

REPUBLIC OF KOREA-UNITED STATES

UTILITIES SUB COMMITTEE

October 27, 1973

Subject : Change in Maintenance Service Charge Applicable to the US-Owned Freight Cars

To : US Chairman, Utilities Sub Committee

1. References;

a. Paragraph 2 and Agreed Minute of Article VI of the Status of Forces of America

b. DAJ BO3-73-D-3114 (29 June 1973)

2. The Korean Government propose that the rates of maintenance service charges applicable to the U.S. owned freight cars are to be changed on and after 27 October, 1973.

3. Details of the Proposal are as follows

a. Effective date;

27 October, 1973, the date on which the proposal is initiated by ROKG for SOFA consultation.

b. Proposed rates to be changed (attached)

No tabulated rates are available applicable to Korean privately owned freight cars, ie they are charged on the basis of actual costs incurred.

c. Basis of calculation of old and new rates

Refer to item "b"

189

SUB- Change in Maintenance Service Charge Applicable to the US-Owned Freight Cars

d. Reason for revision of Rates

To cover the cost of KNR furnished materials and labor cost.

4. The Government of ROK advises the Government of the United States that priorities, conditions and rates being charged are no less favorable than those accorded any other user.

Your early review and concurrence will be appreciated.

Sincerely yours,

Kyong Shik, Kang
Director
Price Policy Bureau
Chairman, Republic of Korea
Utilities Sub-Committee

190

PROPOSAL OF THE REVISIONS

Existing contract:

24 months scheduled inspection excluding coating service for US Government owned ordinary freight cars:

₩38,000. Won

PROPOSED CHANGES IN THE EXISTING CONTRACT:

1. Change in the cost of present contract.

24 months scheduled inspection excluding coating service for US Government owned ordinary freight cars:

₩72,000. Won

2. Addition to the existing contract:
Temporary non-scheduled inspection excluding coating service, for US government owned freight cars:

₩49,000. Won

3. Addition to the existing contract:
24 months scheduled inspection excluding coating service, for US government owned Special type of freight cars:

₩144,000. Won

4. Addition to the existing contract:
Non-scheduled Temporary inspection excluding coating service, for US government owned Special type of freight cars:

₩99,000. Won

5. Addition to the existing contract:
Daily operation maintenance per car:

₩49.20 Won

191

5. 1974년

192.

체 신 부

체전내 1623.7 – 212 (70-3237) 1974. 1. 8.

수신 수신처 참조

제목 전화요금 개정 실시

1. 전화요금을 다음과 같이 개정 실시키로 되었아오니 양지 바랍니다.

가. 요금종목 : 자동전화 기본료

나. 요 금 액 : 1 가입전화마다 월액 390 원

다. 실시일자 : 74.1.1. 끝.

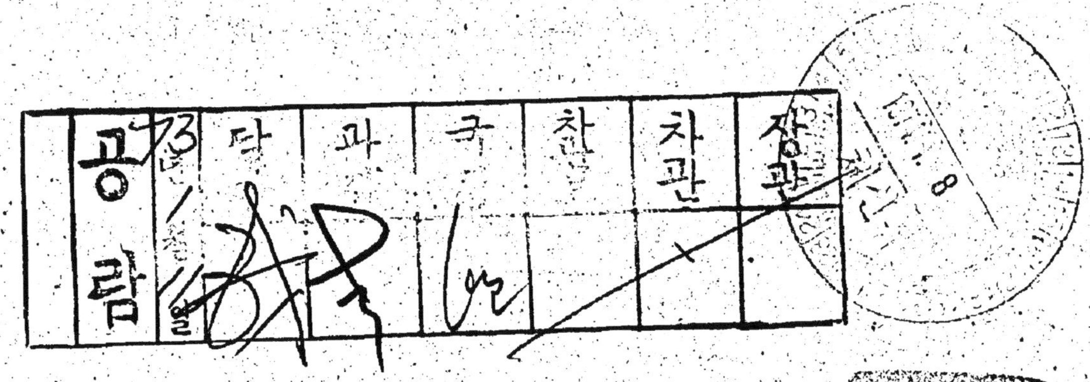

체 신 부 장

수신처 : 미 8 군 사령관, 한미합동 위원회.

193

외 무 부		번	
접 수 일 시	197 . . .		
	11 JAN 74 16 : 12		
접 수 번 호	1608		
주무과			시
담당자			
위 임 문 서			197 . . . 까지 처리할

196-1.E

경 제 기 획 원

물정331·24－27 (70·3001) 1974. 1. 16.

수신 외무부 장관

제목 한미합동 위원회 협의 요청

미 8군 구매처 계약관 과 체결한 유엔군 철도 수송계약서중 철도 화물 요금을 개정하고자 별첨과 같이 한미행정협정에 의한 협의를 미측 공공용역 분과 위원장에게 제의하였음을 통보합니다.

첨부 : 한국측 제의 공문 사본 1부. 끝.

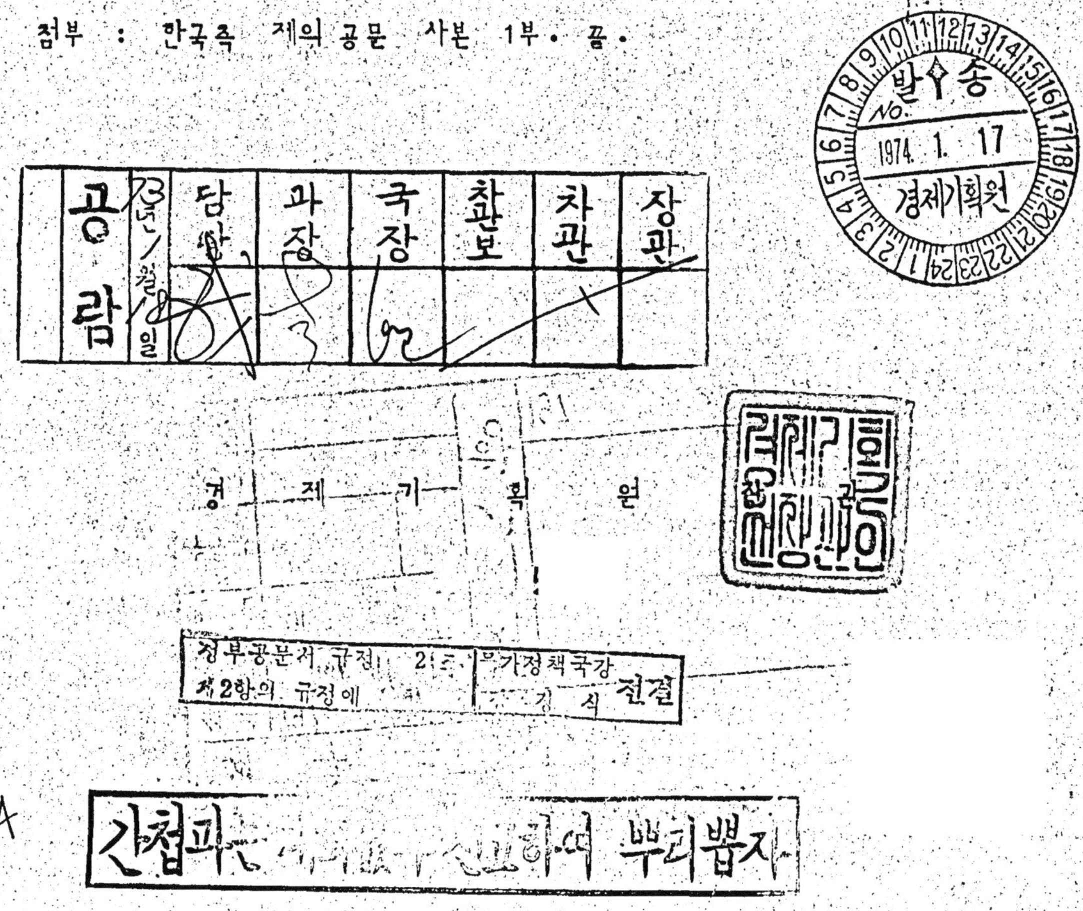

공람	73년 1월 18일	담당	과장	국장	참관보	차관	장관

발송 No. 1974. 1. 17 경제기획원

경 제 기 획 원

정부공문서 규정 제2항의 규정에 의 물가정책국장 강 식 전결

194

간첩피해 신고하여 뿌리뽑자

Republic of Korea-United States

Utilities Subcommittee

January 15, 1974

Subject : Change in Freight Rates of Railroad Applicable to the US Armed Forces under Article VI of the Status Forces' Agreement

To : Chairman, US Utilities Subcommittee

1. Reference : Paragraph 2 and Agreed Minute of Article VI of the Status of Forces Agreement.

2. The Government of the United States is informed through this written consultative process that the Republic of Korea proposes to change following rates/tariffs at locations indicated below;

Rate/Tariff	Location
Freight Rate schedule of railroad applicable to the US Armed Forces	The Whole country

3. The following data is provided ;

a. Effective date : 1 January 1974.

b. Rate Schedule showing rates that are charges all classes of users. (Attached)

c. Rate schedule of proposed change:Refer to item "b"

d. Calculation of old and new rate base:Refer to item "b"

e. Reasons for revision of rates

Decision of ROK Cabinet Council (dated 18 December 1973) to meet the conditions specified in Loan Agreement with IBRD and to secure transportation costs.

195

4. The Government of the ROK advises the Government of the United States that the priorities, conditions, and rates being charges are no less favorable than those accorded any other user.

You may be assured that your views will be greatly appreciated.

Sincerely yours,

K. S. Kang

Kyong Shik, Kang
Director
Price Policy Bureau
Chariman, Republic of Korea
Utilities Subcommittee

196

Freight Change Rates of Railroad

(Unit : Won)

	Description of rates	Unit	Present Rates	Change Rates KNR Proposed	ROKA	Remark
1.	Carload Freight					
	a. Basic Rate Using Carrier's Car	Per Car/ Km	70.00	77	77	10% increase
	b. Basic Rate Using US Owned Car	"	52.50	57.75	-	
	c. Minimum Charge for carload	per Car	4,120.00	4,532	4,532	
2.	Special Train Service Minimum Charge		150,000	165,000	165,000	
3.	Demurrage	6 hours/ per car	1,200	1,320	1,320	
4.	Diversion or Reconsignment	per car	2,400	2,640	2,640	
5.	Cancellation of Car Ordered	"	1,200	1,320	1,320	
6.	Switching Charge	"	623	686	686	
7.	Stopoff in transit		1,120	1,232	1,232	
8.	Equipment Rental	per car/ a day	950	1,045	1,045	
9.	Deadhead Monement of Rented or US Owned Car	Per Car/	18	20	20	
10.	Surcharge for Oversised Freight	"	51	57	57	

197

미 주 국

197 4 . 2 . 16 .

북미2과	담 당	과 장	국 장	차관보	차 관	장 관

제 목 주한미군당국에 대하여 전기, 철도요금 인상실시에 관한 협의

제의 통보(73. 2. 13. SOFA공공용역 분과위원회)

요 약

1. 전력요금

가. 시행시기 : 74. 2. 1.부터 시행되었으나, 주한미군당국에 대한 시행시기는 양측 합의에 따름.

나. 인상율 : 별첨 참조

다. 인상이유 : 유류 가격 인상에 따른 운영비 확보

2. 철도화물 운임

가. 시행시기 : 74. 2. 13.부터

나. 인상율 : 15%

다. 인상이유 : IBRD 차관 협정의 조건 이행 및 수송비확보

3. 철도 여객운임

조치사항

가. 시행시기 : 74. 2. 13.부터

나. 인상율 : 15%

198 다. 인상이유 : 유류가격 인상에 따른 수송비 확보

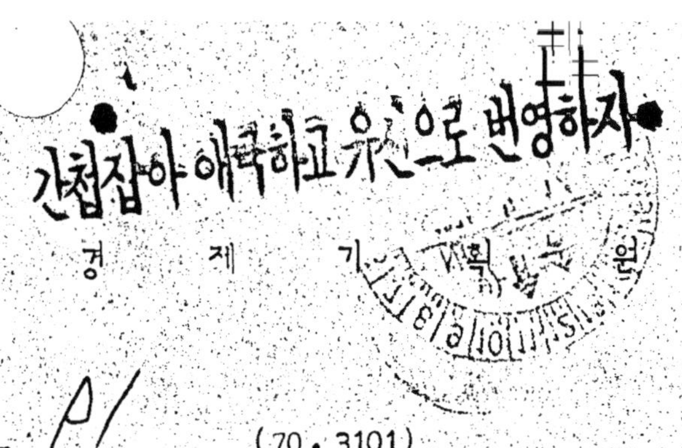

간첩잡아 애국하고 유신으로 번영하자

경 제 기 획 원

물정331. 24- (70.3101) 1974. 2. 14.

수신 외무부장관

제목 한미 합동 위원회 협의 요청

금번 전기, 철도요금의 인상 실시에 따라 미8군과 체결한 철도 군사수송 계약서중 철도화물운임, 여객운임 및 전력요금을 개정하고자 별첨과 같이 한미 행정 협정에 의한 협의를 미측 공공용역 분과위원장에게 제의하였음을 통보합니다.

점부 : 한국측 제의 공문 사본 3부. 끝.

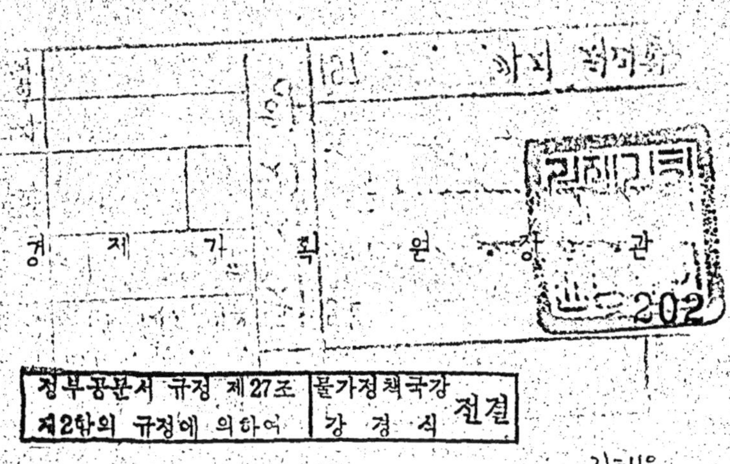

경 제 기 획 원 장 관

정부공문서 규정 제27조 제2항의 규정에 의하여	물가정책국장 강 경 식	전결

김태웅

199

REPUBLIC OF KOREA-UNITED STATES
UTILITIES SUBCOMMITTEE

February 13, 1974

Subject: Change in Electric Power Rates Applicable to the US Armed Forces under Article VI of the Status of Forces Agreement.

To : Chairman, US Utilities Subcommittee.

1. Reference: Paragraph 2 and Agreed Minute 1 of Article VI of the Status Forces Agreement.

2. The Government of the United States is informed through this written consultative process that the Republic of Korea proposes to change the following rates/tariffs at location indicated below;

Rate/Tariff	Location
Electric power rate schedule applicable to the US Armed Forces	the whole country

3. The following data is provided;

a. Effective date: Although the rate changes are effective from 1 February 1974, the new rates will be applied to the US Forces' use in accordance with the agreement set forth in the lettor dated 15 November 1969.

b. Rate schedule showing rates that are charged all classes of users. "Attached"

c. Rate schedule of proposed change. Refer to item "b"

d. Calculation of old and new rate base. "Attached"

e. Reason for revision of rates.

To secure operation costs according to increasing of oil price

4. The Government of ROK advises the Government of the United States that priorities, conditions and rates or tariffs being charged are no less favorable than those accorded any other user.

You may assured that your early views will be greatly appraciated.

Sincerely yours,

Kyong Shik Kang
Director, Price Policy Bureau
Chairman, Republic of Korea
Utilities Subcommittee

200

C O M P A R I S O N

Contents of Amendment

a. Rate category "High Tension Service" is deleted.
b. Energy charge rate in General Service A and B is reformed to single system.
c. Demand and energy charge rates are increased.

Old Rate Schedule	New Rate Schedule
1. GENERAL SERVICE A	1. GENERAL SERVICE A
Applicability: To residential service without limit and general service of 4kw demand or under	Applicability: Same as the old.
Type of supply: Single or three phase supply at any one of the Company's available standard voltages, 100v or 200v.	Type of supply: Same as the old.
Monthly bill: W163.88 for the first 3kwh. W 15.53 per kwh for the next 27kwh. W 11.79 per kwh for the next 180 kwh. * W 9.09 per kwh for each additional kwh. * Add 90 kwh at W11.79 block for each kw in excess of 3kw of demand. Minimum charge: W163.88.	Monthly bill: Basic charge: W213.00 per customer. Energy charge: W20.19 per kwh for all consumption

- 1 -

201

2. GENERAL SERVICE B

Applicability:
To general service of 4kw of contracted demand and over.

Type of supply:
Single or three phase at any one of the Company's available standard voltages, 20kv, 10kv, 6kv, 5.2kv, 3kv, 200v, 100v, or others.

Monthly bill:

Demand charge
W184.00 per kw for the first 50kw of the contracted demand.
W146.00 per kw for the next 450kw of the contracted demand.
W109.00 per kw for each additional kw of the contracted demand.

2. GENERAL SERVICE B

Applicability:
Same as the old.

Type of supply:
The company's available voltages of 150kv, 60kv are added to the old.

Monthly bill:

Demand charge
(a) For all contracted demands available less than 20kv, and the contracted demand under 500kw which are available at more than 20kv.
W240.00 per kw for the first 50kw of the contracted demand.
W190.00 per kw for the next 450kw of the contracted demand.
W142.00 per kw for each additional kw of the contracted demand.
(b) For the contracted demands of 500kw and over which are available at more than 20kv.
W198.00 per kw for the first 500kw of the contracted demand.
W132.00 per kw for each additional kw of the contracted demand.
(c) For the contracted demands of 1,000kw and over which are available at more than 150kv.
W132.00 per kw for the contracted demand.

202

Energy charge: W9.49 per kwh for the first 90kwh per kw of the contracted demand. W6.50 per kwh for the next 90kwh per kw of the contracted demand. W4.68 per kwh for the next 180kwh per kw of the contracted demand. W3.16 per kwh for each additional kwh.	Energy charge: W12.34 per kwh for all consumption.

203

3. HIGH TENSION SERVICE A

Applicability:
To service of 500kw of contracted demand and over, and 20kv and over.

Type of supply:
Three phase supply at any one of the Company's available standard voltages, 20kv and over.

Monthly bill:

Demand charge
W152.00 per kw for the first 500kw of the contracted demand.
W101.00 per kw of each additional kw of the contracted demand.

Energy charge
W9.49 per kwh for the first 90kwh per kw of the contracted demand.
W6.18 per kwh for the next 90kwh per kw of the contracted demand.
W4.30 per kwh for the next 180kwh per kw of the contracted demand.
W2.71 per kwh for each additional kwh.

High tension service A in old rate schedule is deleted and substituded to General Service B(b) in new rate schedule.

204

PROPOSED NEW ELECTRIC RATE SCHEDULE

KOREA ELECTRIC COMPANY

205

CONTENTS

Page

TARIFF 1 GENERAL SERVICE A 1

TARIFF 2 GENERAL SERVICE B 2

TARIFF 3 INDUSTRIAL SERVICE 5

TARIFF 4 FARMING SERVICE 15

TARIFF 5 STREET LIGHTING SERVICE 17

TARIFF 6 FLAT RATE LIGHTING SERVICE 18

TARIFF 7 FARMING LIGHTING SERVICE (LURING LAMP) 19

TARIFF 8 TEMPORARY LIGHTING SERVICE 20

TARIFF 9 TEMPORARY POWER SERVICE 21

SPECIAL PROVISIONS 22

COMMON PROVISIONS 24

SUPPLEMENTARY PROVISIONS 24

206

ELECTRIC RATE SCHEDULES

TARIFF 1

GENERAL SERVICE A

1. Applicability:

Applicable to residential service without any limit in the size of the contracted demand, and to general service with the contracted demand under 4 kilowatts.

2. Type of Service:

Alternating current, 60 cycles as nominal standard frequency, single or three phase, nominally at 100 volts or 200 volts.

3. Monthly Charge:

A. Basic Charge:

The basic charge shall be W213.00 per customer.

B. Energy Charge:

W20.19 per KWH for all energy usage.

- 1 -

207

TARIFF 2

GENERAL SERVICE B

1. Applicability:

Applicable to general service with contracted demand of 4KW and over, other than service for industrial or residential use (excluding apartment use).

2. Type of Service:

Alternating current, 60 cycles as nominal standard frequency, single or three phase, nominally at any one of the Company's available voltages of 150KV, 60KV, 20KV, 10KV, 6KV, 5.2KV, 3KV, 200 V, 100V, or others.

3. Monthly Charge:

A. Demand Charge

(1) For all contracted demands available less than 20KV, and the contract demands under 500KW which are available at more than 20KV.

W240.00 per KW for the first 50 KW of the contracted demand or less

W190.00 per KW for the next 450 KW of the contracted demand

W142.00 per KW for all over 500 KW of the contracted demand

208

(2) For the contracted demands of 500KW and over which are available at more than 20KV.

W198.00 per KW for the first 500KW of contracted demand or less

W132.00 per KW for all over 500KW of contracted demand

(3) For the contracted demands of 1,000KW and over which are available at more than 150KV,

W132.00 per KW for the contracted demand.

B. Energy Charge

W12.34 per KWH for all energy usage.

4. Determination of Contracted Demand:

A. The contracted demand for billing purposes each month will be determined by applying the following factors to the total input values of each input value of the customer's connected loads:

100% for the first 75 KW of the total input values
85% for the next 75 KW of the total input values
75% for the next 75 KW of the total input values
65% for the next 75 KW of the total input values
60% for all over 300 KW of the total input values

However,

(1) In computing the contracted demand, any fraction of 1 kilowatt will be taken as a full kilowatt.

(2) In case there is any unit or units of the customer's connected loads whose unit input value exceeds 75 kilowatts, the factors in the above table will be applied preferentially to such unit or units beginning with the largest unit in successive order from 100% to 60%.

(3) In case the contracted demand computed under the above table is recognized by the Company to be obviously unreasonable as compared with the real demand condition, the Company may install, at its own expense, a fifteen-minute maximum demand meter for determining the contracted demand for billing purposes each month. If the customer desires to do so, he also may install, at his own expense, the demand meter which is authorized by the Company for the same purposes.

B. When the service is supplied through the sole transformer which is exclusively used by one customer, the contracted demand for the customer shall not be more than the loading limit of such transformer's capability.

C. For the customer who installs the maximum demand meter, the contracted demand for billing purposes each month shall be the maximum integrated fifteen-minute demand in the previous three months, including the month for which the bill is rendered. If the period is less than three month after the installation of the demand meter, the contracted demand for such period shall be the maximum integrated fifteen-minute demand in such period. Notwithstanding the above provision, the contracted demand as the maximum integrated fifteen-minute demand measured by the maximum demand meter shall not be less than the minimum contracted demand which is computed by applying the following factors to the contracted demand computed on the basis of Clause "A & B" of this Article:

75% for the contracted demand from 100 KW to less than 10,000 KW
60% for the contracted demand of 10,000KW and over

TARIFF 3

INDUSTRIAL SERVICE

1. Small Power Service

A. Applicability:

Applicable to service for contracted demand with more than 4KW, other than the contracted demand of 500KW and over (only to the manufacturing industry specified in the attachment)

B. Type of Service:

Alternating current, 60 cycles as nominal stantard frequency, three phase, nominally at any one of the Company's available voltages of 20KV or over.

C. Ordinary Power Service:

The term "Ordinary Power Service" as used in this schedule means the power service to be supplied throughout the year without any limitation or restriction in time as season in power usage.

- 5 -

211

(1) Monthly Charge:

(a) Demand charge:

W240.00 per KW for the first 50 KW of the contracted demand or less

W190.00 per KW for the next 450 KW of the contracted demand

W142.00 per KW for all over 500 KW of the contracted demand

(b) Energy charge:

W12.34 per KWH for the first 90 KWH per KW of the contracted demand or less

W8.45 per KWH for the next 90 KWH per KW of the contracted demand

W6.09 per KWH for the next 180 KWH per KW of the contracted demand

W4.11 per KWH for all over 360 KWH per KW of the contracted demand

D. Combined Off-Peak Power Service Provision:

In case of supplying under the combined off-peak power service provision, it shall be treated as follows:

(1) The combined off-peak power service is applicable to a customer who, using ordinary power service, desires to use power in excess of his ordinary power service during the off-peak hours.

2/2

(2) The contracted demand for the off-peak power service customer shall be the excess demand of his ordinary power service, but not more than two times of the contracted demand under his ordinary power service. The minimum contracted demand under the off-peak power service shall be 50 kilowatts.

(3) The off-peak hours in which the off-peak power usage is available (daily off-peak period) shall be from 10:00 p.m. everyday through to 06:00 a.m. of the following day. The Company may increase, decrease or shift the time or duration of the daily off-peak period above when necessary due to the circumstances of demand and supply of power.

(4) The customer will furnish, install and maintain, at his own expense, a recording-type or other type fifteen-minute maximum demand meter and watthour meter (including their accessorial equipment) necessary for clarifying the condition of using off-peak power, which are authorized by the Company. The power and energy consumed by the customer will be measured by such meters.

(5) Monthly Charge:

(a) Demand charge:

The demand charge shall be computed by applying the basic rate of demand charge to the total of the contracted demand under the ordinary power service and that under the off-peak power service, and then of the total amount of the demand charge, the portion of the contracted demand under

- 7 -

213

the off-peak power service shall be discounted by 80%.

(b) Energy charge:

The energy charge shall be computed, on the basis of the contracted demand under the ordinary power service only, by applying the basic rate of energy charge to the total energy consumed under both the ordinary power service and the off-peak power service.

E. Independent Off-Peak Power Service Provision:

In case of supplying under the independent off-peak power service provision, it shall be treated as follows:

(1) The independent off-peak power service is applicable to a customer who desires to use power only during off-peak hours. The customer will furnish, install and maintain, at his own expense, the necessary private line from the Company's available substation which is exclusively used by him and the necessary metering equipment, both of which are authorized by the Company. The company will supply power service to separate connected loads through separate meters from the ordinary power service.

(2) The minimum contracted demand under the off-peak power service shall be 50 kilowatts.

(3) The off-peak hours in which the off-peak power usage is available (daily off-peak period) shall be from 10:00 p.m. everyday trough to 06:00 a.m. of the following day and 24 hours on Sunday. The Company may increase, decrease or shift the time or duration of the daily off-peak period above when necessary due to the circumstances of demand and supply of power.

(4) Monthly Charge:

(a) Demand charge:

The demand charge shall be discounted by 80% of the basic rate of demand charge under the ordinary power service.

(b) Energy charge

The energy charge shall be W5.49 per KWH for all energy consumed.

2. Large Power Service

A. Ordinary Power Service

(1) Large Power Service A

(a) Applicability:

Applicable to customers receiving service at 20 kilovolts and over where the contracted demand is 500 kilowatts and over (only to the manufacturing industry specified in the attachment).

215

(b) Type of Service:

Alternating current, 60 cycles as nominal standard frequency, three phase, nominally at any one of the Company's available voltages of 20 kilovolts or over.

(c) Monthly Charge:

1) Demand charge:

W198.00 per KW for the first 500 KW of the contracted demand or less

W132.00 per KW for all over 500 KW of the contracted demand

2) Energy charge:

W12.34 per KWH for the first 90 KWH per KW of the contracted demand or less

W8.05 per KWH for the next 90 KWH per KW of the contracted demand

W5.59 per KWH for the next 180 KWH per KW of the contracted demand

W3.53 per KWH for all over 360 KWH per KW of the contracted demand

3) Minimum Contracted Demand:

The minimum contracted demand shall be 500 kilowatts.

(d) Determination of Contracted Demand:

Same as "GENERAL SERVICE B".

(2) Large Power Service B

(a) Applicability:

Applicable to customers receiving service at 150 kilovolts and over where the contracted demand is 1,000 kilowatts or over (only to the manufacturing industry specified in the attachment).

(b) Type of Service:

Alternating current, 60 cycles as nominal standard frequency, three phase, nominally at any one of the Company's available voltages of 150 kilovolts or over.

(c) Monthly Charge:

Basic Rate

1) Demand charge:

W132.00 per KW for all of the contract demand

2) Energy charge:

W12.34 per KWH for the first 90 KWH per KW of the contracted demand or less

- 11 -

217

W 7.95 per KWH for the next 90 KWH per KW of the contracted demand

W 5.48 per KWH for the next 180 KWH per KW of the contracted demand

W3.51 per KWH for all over 360 KWH per KW of the contracted demand

(d) Determination of Contracted Demand:

Same as "GENERAL SERVICE B"

B. Combined Off-Peak Power Service Provision:

In case of supplying service under the off-peak power service provision, it shall be treated as follows:

(1) The combined off-peak power service is applicable to a customer who, using ordinary power service, desires to use power in excess of his ordinary power service during the off-peak hours.

(2) The contracted demand for the off-peak power service customer shall be the excess demand of his ordinary power service, but not more than two times of the contracted demand under the ordinary power service. The minimum contracted demand under the off-peak power service shall be 50 kilowatts.

(3) The off-peak hours in which the off-peak power usage is available shall be from 10.00 p.m. everyday through to 06:00 a.m. of the following day. The Company may increase, decrease or shift the time or duration of the daily off-peak

period above when necessary due to the circumstances of demand and supply of power.

(4) The customer will furnish, install and maintain, at his own expense, a recording-type or other type fifteen-minute maximum demand meter and watthour meter (including their accessorial equipment) necessary for clarifying the condition of using off-peak power, both of which are authorized by the Company. The Power and energy consumed by the customer will be measured by such meters.

(5) Monthly Charge:

(a) Demand charge:

The demand charge shall be computed by applying the basic rate of demand charge to the total of the contracted demand under the ordinary power service and that under the off-peak power service, and then of the total amount of the demand charge, the portion of the contracted demand under the off-peak power service shall be discounted by 80%.

(b) Energy charge:

The energy charge shall be computed, on the basis of the contracted demand under the ordinary power service only ,by applying the basic rate of energy charge to the total energy consumed under both the ordinary power service and the off-peak power service.

C. Independent Off-Peak Power Service Provision:

In case of supplying service under the independent off-peak power service provision, it shall be treated as follows:

(1) The independent off-peak power service is applicable to a customer who desires to use power only during off-peak hours. The customer will furnish, install and maintain, at his own expense, the necessary private line from the Company's available substation which is exclusively used by him and the necessary metering equipment, both of which are authorized by the Company.
The Company will supply power service to separate connected load through separate meters from the ordinary power service.

(2) The minimum contracted demand under the off-peak power service shall be 1,000 kilowatts.

(3) The off-peak hours in which the off-peak power usage is available shall be from 10:00 p.m. everyday through to 06:00 a.m. of the following day and 24 hours on Sunday. The Company may increase, decrease or shift the time or duration of the daily off-peak period above when necessary due to the circumstances of demand and supply of power.

(4) Monthly Charge:

(a) Demand charge:

The demand charge shall be discounted by 80% of the basic rate of demand charge under the ordinary power service.

(b) Energy charge:

The energy charge shall be ₩ 5.01per KWH for all energy consumed.

TARIFF 4

FARMING SERVICE

Farming Service A

1. Applicability:

Applicable to power service for the operation of pumps (incidental lighting inclusive) which are used to irrigate and drain for the purpose of cultivating and growing grain for food purpose only.

2. Type of Service:

Same as "GENERAL SERVICE B"

3. Monthly Charge:

Basic Rate

A. Demand charge:

₩71.00 per KW for all of the contracted demand

B. Energy charge:

₩ 4.57per KWH for all energy consumed

221

4. Determination of Contracted Demand:

Same as "GENERAL SERVICE B"

Farming Service B

1. Applicability:

Applicable to power service (incidental lighting inclusive) for the purpose of growing a seedling or cultivating crops with electric heating for the farming purpose.

2. Type of Service:

Same as "GENERAL SERVICE B"

3. Monthly Charge:

Basic Rate

A. Demand charge:

W195.00 per KW for all of the contracted demand

B. Energy charge:

W5.85 per KWH for all energy consumed

4. Determination of Contracted Demand:

Same as "GENERAL SERVICE B"

Farming Service C

1. Applicability:

Applicable to power service (incidental lighting inclusive) for farming and breeding purpose other than the power service of "Farming Service A & B".

2. Type of Service:

Same as "GENERAL SERVICE B"

3. Monthly Charge:

Basic Rate

A. Demand charge:

W195.00 per KW for all of the contracted demand

B. Energy charge:

W6.89 per KWH for all energy consumed

4. Determination of Contracted Demand:

Same as "GENERAL SERVICE B"

TARIFF 5

STREET LIGHTING SERVICE

1. Applicability:

Applicable to service for lighting purpose of streets, parks and other similar places for the benefit and convenience of the public.

2. Type of Service:

Alternating current, 60 cycles as nominal standard frequency, single phase, nominally at 100 volts or 200 volts.

3. Monthly Charge:

Basic Rate

A. Energy charge:

W3.59 per Watt for all of the connected load capacity

B. Minimum charge:

The minimum charge per month shall be W120.00

4. Service Time:

The service time under street lighting service shall be from sunset everyday through to sunrise of the following day.

TARIFF 6

FLAT RATE LIGHTING SERVICE

1. Applicability:

Applicable to lighting service (including radio substituted one set as one lamp), principally limited to 100 watts of the connected load with three lamps or under. One radio set shall be counted as 20 watts.

2. Type of Service.

Alternating current, 60 cycles as nominal standard frequency, single phase, nominally at 100 volts or 200 volts.

3. Monthly Charge:

Basic Rate

A. Energy charge:

W7.04 per Watt for the first 60 Watts of the connected load capacity or less

W4.79 per Watt for all over 60 Watts of the connected load capacity

B. Minimum charge:

The minimum charge per month shall be W120.00

TARIFF 7

FARMING LIGHTING SERVICE (LURING LAMP)

1. Applicability:

Applicable to service for the operation of luring lamps for the purpose of luring and exterminating noxious insects.

2. Type of Service:

Same as "GENERAL SERVICE A"

3. Monthly Charge:

Basic Rate

A. Energy charge:

W3.59 per Watt for all of the connected load capacity

B. Minimum charge:

The minimum charge per month shall be W120.00

TARIFF 8

TEMPORARY LIGHTING SERVICE

1. Applicability:

Applicable to such temporary demand for lighting for a certain given period as ceremony places, public perfomance places, etc.

2. Type of Service:

Same as "GENERAL SERVICE A"

3. Monthly Charge:

Basic Rate

A. Energy charge:

The energy charge shall be billed at the rates corresponding to 150% of the rates under "GENERAL

SERVICE A" for the first three months of using period or less, and to 110% of the rates under "GENERAL SERVICE A" for all over three months of using period.

B. Minimum charge:

The minimum charge per month shall be billed at the rates corresponding to 150% of the minimum charge under "GENERAL SERVICE A" for the first three months of using period or less, and to 110% of the minimum charge under "GENERAL SERVICE A" for all over three months.

TARIFF 9

TEMPORARY POWER SERVICE

1. Applicability:

Applicable to such temporary demand for power (incidental lighting inclusive) for a certain given period as construction works, etc., without requiring any permanent supplying facilities.

2. Type of Service:

Same as "GENERAL SERVICE B"

3. Monthly Charge:

Basic Rate

A. Demand charge:

The demand charge shall be billed at the rates

corresponding to 150% of the rates of the corresponding class of service for the first three months of using period or less, and to 110% of the rates of the corresponding class of service for all over three months of using period.

B. Energy charge:

The energy charge shall be billed at the rates corresponding to 150% of the rates of the corresponding class of service for the first three months of using period or less, and to 110% of the rates of the corresponding class of service forall over three months of using period.

SPECIAL PROVISIONS

Special Industry Tariff Discount

For the following special industry customers, their ordinary monthly electric charges shall be discounted by customer as provided below:

1. 30% discount: For the export industry customers whose contracted demand is 200 kilowatts or less, and for the P.V.C. manufacturing industry customers whose products are made by the Carbide-Acetylene Method and whose establishing fund is financed from the foreign loan for which reimbursement is guaranteed by the Government.

2. For the aluminium refinery industry, iron industry and steel industry customers (limited tothe production of pig-iron, iron-steel, ingot only) whose power charges occupy

10% and over of the total production cost, their monthly electric charge shall be discounted as follows:

The percentage of power charge of the total production cost is;

From 10% to less than 30% .... 20% discount
From 30% to less than 40% .... 25% discount
Over 40% .... 30% discount

3. For the manufacturing industry customers whose power charges occupy 20% and over of the total production cost, who are designated by the Minister of Commerce and Industry, their monthly electric charge shall be discounted as follows:

The percentage of power charge of the total Production cost is;

From 20% to less than 30% .... 15% discount
From 30% to less than 40% .... 20% discount
From 40% to less than 50% ....25% discount
Over 50%.......................... 30% discount

Municipal Water Service Tariff

The rate for municipal water service may be discounted by the instructions of the Minister of Commerce and Industry.

Island Tariff

A special tariff may be established for island areas which are isolated from mainland power system, subject to the approval of the Minister of Commerce and Industry.

COMMON PROVISIONS

1. Maintenance of Power Factor:

   The customer is requested to maintain the power factor of his power requirements at 85% or more and, when necessary, is requested to install an appropriate corrective equipment to maintain the power factor specified above. When the power factor is less than 85%, the Company will correct the contracted demand in kilowatts for billing purpose for that month by multiplying by 85% and dividing by the actually measured power factor in percent for that month.

2. Load Balance and Voltage Regulation:

   The customer is requested to always maintain a correlated balance of the electric loads carried by the respective phases of electricity at his service location. In case the customer's use of electricity causes or there is fear that it will cause irregular voltage fluctuations or interferences with the service to other customers, he shall install at his own expense an appropriate regulating equipment for screening from such effects. The maximum allowable difference of load balance in respective phases shall be 10% or under. When the difference is over 10%, the monthly electric charge shall be billed at three times of the power and energy of the heaviest phase instead of the power and energy supplied actually.

SUPPLEMENTARY PROVISIONS

1. Effective Date of the Rate Schedules:

   The rate schedules shall be effective on and after December 1, 1973.

230

(ATTACHMENT)

LIST OF SPECIFIED INDUSTRIAL CLASSIFICATION

Major Group	Group	Title of Category
Mining and Quarrying	Coal Mining	Mining of anthracite, lignite, peat, and bituminous coal.
	Metal Ore Mining	Iron ore mining. Non-ferrous ore mining.
	Other Mining	Quarrying or mining of Stone, clay and sand, Chemical and fertilizer mineral, salt, graphite, kaolin, talc, agalmatolite, asbestos, gypsum, mica, crystal, calcite, alumstone.
Manufacture of Food and Beverages	Grain Mill Products	Industries of husking, polishing and milling of grain.
	Ice Manu-facture	Industries of ice munufacturing and freezing.
	Beverage Industries	Soft drinks and wine manufacture.
	Other Manu-facture of Food and Beverages	Manufacture of canning, salting, sugar, malt, cake, seasoning, starch, noodle, ginseng, been-curd, vegetable gelatine, dairy products.

0022

231

Major Group	Group	Title of Category
Textile Industries	Manu-facture of Textiles	Spinning, weaving, bleaching and dyeing textiles, knitting mills. Manufacture of rope, net, carpets and rugs.
Manu-facture of Chemicals	Manu-facture of Fortilizers	Manufacture of fortilizers.
	Manu-facture of Oils and Paints	Manufacture of Vegetable and animal oils and fats, soap, glycerin, paints, varnishes, enamels and lacquers.
	Compressed and Liquified Gas	Manufacture of oxygen, hydrogen, carbon dioxide and other gas.
	Electric Heating Industries	Manufacture of carbide and artificial graphite by electric smelting.
	Manu-facture of Pulp and Paper	Manufacture of pulp, paper, paperboard and paper products.
	Manu-facture of Drugs and Medicines	Manufacture of drugs and medicines.

Major Group	Group	Title of Category
	Manufacture of Other Chemical Products	Manufacture of basic industrial chemicals, phosphoric acid, match, synthetic fibres.
Manufacture of Rubber products	Manufacture of Rubber Products	Manufacture of tyres, tubes, footwear and all kinds of rubber products from natural or synthetic rubber
Manufacture of Wood and Wood Products	Manufacture of Wood and Wood Products	Sawmills. Manufacture of wooden containers, veneer, plywood, furniture and cork products.
Ceramics	Manufacture of Cement	Manufacture of cement
	Manufacture of Glass and Glass Products	Manufacture of glass, glass fibres and other glass products.
	Manufacture of Other Earthenware	Manufacture of pottery, earthenware, bricks, tile, earthen pipe, concrete products, graphite, white bead, slate, limestone and gypsum.

- 27 -

237

Major Group	Group	Title of Category
Metal Industries	Basic Metal Industries	Manufacture of ferrous and non-ferrous metal products, consisting of all processes from smelting, alloying and refining, rolling and drawing and founding and casting.
	Manu-facture of Febricat-ed Metal Products	Manufacture of iron plate, hand tools, farming tools, hardware and other metal products.
Manu-facture of Machinery and Apparatus	Manu-facture of Machinery	Manufacture of motor, agricutural machinery and equipment, machinery used by construction and mining industries, metal working machinery, and precision machine.
	Manu-facture of Electrical Machinery and Apparatus	Manufacture of electrical industrial machinery and apparatus. Manufacture of radio, tolevision and communication equipment and apparatus. Manufacture of electrical appliances and house-ware.
	Manu-facture of Transport Equipment	Ship building and repairing. Manufacture of railroad equipment, motor vehicles and specialized parts, and other transport equipment.

Major Group	Grcup	Title of Category
Other Manufacturing Industries	Manufacture of Coal and Petroleum Products	Manufacture of coal products. Petroleum refineries.
	Printing and Publishing Industries	Printing and Publishing newspapers, periodicals and books. Bookbinding.
	Manufacture of Leather and Products of Leather	Manufacture of leather and products of leather.
	Manufacturing Industries not elsewhere classified	Manufactur of toys, office materials, sport goods, wigs, personal ornamental, musical instruments, tobacco products, animal feeds.
Other Industries		Water-service and other manufacture not elsewhere classified which is specified by the Minister of Economic Planning Board in accordance with the Code of Statistics.

REPUBLIC OF KOREA-UNITED STATES
UTILITIES SUBCOMMITTEE

February 13, 1974

Subject: Change in Freight Rates of Railroad Applicable to the US Armed Forces under Article VI of the Status of Forces Agreement.

To : Chairman, US Utilities Subcommittee.

1. Reference: Paragraph 2 and Agreed Minute of Article VI of the Status of Forces Agreement.

2. The Government of the United States is informed through this written consultative process that the Republic of Korea proposes to change following rates/tariffs at location indicated below:

Rate/Tariff	Location
Freight rate schedule of railroad applicable to the US Armed Forces	the whole country

3. The following data is provided:

a. Effective date: 13 February 1974

b. Rate schedule of proposed change. "Attached"

c. Rate schedule showing rates that are charged all classes of users. Refer to item "b"

d. Calculation of old and new rate base. Refer to item "b"

e. Reason for revision of rates.
To meet the conditions specified in Loan Agreement with IBRD and to secure transportation costs.

4. The Government of ROK advises the Government of the United States that the priorities, conditions, and rates being charges are no less favorable than those accorded any other user.

You may be assured that your views will be greatly appreciated.

Sincerely yours,

Kyong Shik Kang
Director, Price Policy Bureau
Chairman, Republic of Korea
Utilities Subcommittee

Freight Change Rates of Railroad

(Unit : Won)

A. US Army

	Description of rates	Unit	Present Rates	Change Rates KNR Proposed ROKA (74.1.1-74.2.12)	Change Rates KNR Proposed ROKA (74. 2.13-)	Remark
1.	Carload Freight					
	a. Basic Rate Using Carrier's Car	Per Car/Km	70.00	77	81	1) 10% increase
	b. Basic Rate Using US Owned Car	"	52.50	57.75	60.64	2) 5% increase Total 15%
	c. Minimum Charge for carload	Per Car	4,120.00	4,532	4,759	
2.	Special Train Service Minimum Charge		150,000	165,000	173,250	
3.	Demurrage	6 hours/ per car	1,200	1,320	1,386	
4.	Diversion or Reconsignment	per car	2,400	2,640	2,772	
5.	Cancellation of Car Ordered	"	1,200	1,320	1,386	
6.	Switching Charge	"	625	686	721	
7.	Stopoff in transit		1,120	1,232	1,294	
8.	Equipment Rental	per car/ a day	950	1,045	[illegible]	

	Description of rates	Unit	Present Rates	Change Rates KNR Proposed ROK.	Change Rates KNR Proposed [illegible]	Remark
9.	Deadhead Movement of Rented or US Owned Car	per car/ Km	18	20	21	
10.	Surcharge for Oversized Freight	"	51	57	60	
19.	US Government Owned car Scheduled General Inspection and Repair Excluding Painting (every 24 months)	per car	58,100	41,900	44,000	
B.	Pacen					
	Carload Freight Basic Rate	"	81	90	95	

238

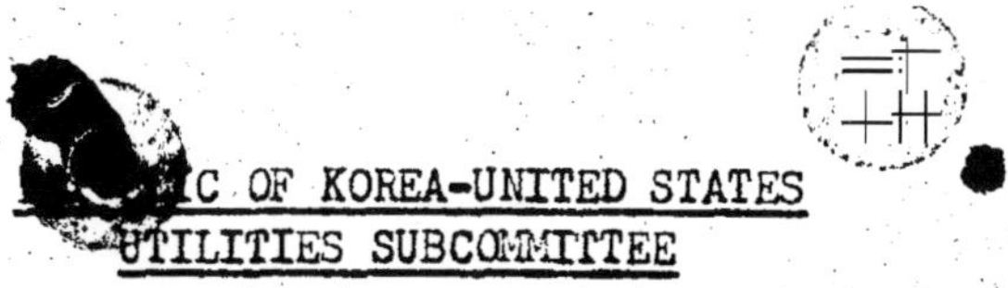

February 13, 1974

Subject: Change in Passenger Fares of Railroad Applicable to the US Armed Forces under Article VI of the Status Forces Agreement.

To : Chairman, US Utilities Subcommittee.

1. Reference: Paragraph 2 and Agreed Minute of Article VI of Status Forces Agreement.

2. The Government of the United States is informed through this written consultative process that the Republic of Korea proposes to change following rates/tariffs at location indicated below:

Rate/Tariff	Location
Passenger Fare schedule of railroad applicable to the US Armed Forces	The whole country

3. The following data is provided;

a. Effective date: 13 February 1974

b. Rate schedule showing rates that are charged all classes of users."Attached"

c. Rate schedule of proposed change. Refer to item "b"

d. Calculation of old and new rate base. Refer to item "b"

e. Reason for revision of rates.

To secure transportation costs according to increasing of oil price

4. The Government of the ROK advises the Government of the United States that the priorities, conditions, and rates being charges are no less favorable than those accorded any other user.

Your may be assured that your views will greatly appreciated.

Sincerely yours,

Kyong Shik Kang
Director, Price Policy Bureau
Chairman, Republic of Korea
Utilities Subcommittee

239

Revision Contents of Schedule of Rates, Fares and Charges

Item No	Description of Service	Unit	Rates(Won) old	new	Remarks
	Passenger service				
11. a	Basic Rate for transportation of charter coach, baggagecar	per car/Km	118.80	136.62	15% Inclease
b	Surcharge for Exclusive use of passenger accommodation	Up to 200Km	400Km	more than400Km	1)15% Inclease
	Category #1	35,040	52,320	65,280	2)Data in
	(Super express special car)	(40,300)	(60,170)	(75,070)	paranthesis are
	Category #2	25,200	40,880	50,960	new Rates.
	(Super express ordinary car)	(28,980)	(47,010)	(58,600)	
	Category #3	15,120	25,200	30,800	
	(Special express special car)	(17,390)	(28,980)	(35,420)	
	Category #4	6,480	6,480	6,480	
	(Special express ordinary car)	(7,450)	(7,450)	(7,450)	
12	Minimum charge for passenger special train service	per train	118,580	136,370	15% Inclease
13	Motor coach service				
	a. Basic rate	per car/Km	118.80	136.62	15% Inclease
	b. Surcharge	Per car	25,810	29,810	"
	c. Minimum charge for motor coach	per car	36,460	41,930	"

240

Item No	Description of Service	Unit	Rates(Won) old	Rates(Won) new	Remarks
14	Surcharge for Express Service				
	a. Common express	per car			15% Inclease
		1-200Km	7,200	8,280	
		201-400Km	14,400	16,560	
		more than 401Km	21,600	24,840	
	b. Special express	per car			
		1-200Km	10,800	12,420	"
		201-400Km	21,600	24,840	
		401 or more	43,200	49,680	
	c. Super express	per car			
		1-200Km	11,200	12,880	
		201-400Km	22,400	25,760	
		401 or more	44,800	51,520	
16	Equipment Rental				
	a. passenger car	per car/per day	1,620	1,860	15% Inclease
	b. Baggage, mail car	"	1,290	16,70	"
	c. passenger-mail combination car	"	1,450	1,480	"

241

Item No	Description of Service	Unit	Reateu (Won)		Remarks
			old	new	
17	Deadhead movement	per car/Km	28	32	15% Inclease
18	Movement of Sentry dog				
	a. Less than 100Km	per dog	369	424	
	b. 101-200Km	"	621	714	
	c. 201-500Km	"	834	959	
	d. more than 501Km	"	1,071	1,232	

242

REPUBLIC OF KOREA - UNITED STATES
UTILITIES SUBCOMMITTEE

4 April 1974

MEMORANDUM TO: The Joint Committee

SUBJECT: Consultation on Water Rates Applicable to Seoul and Taegu Rental Guarantee Housing Sites

1. Subcommittee Members:

Republic of Korea	United States
Mr. KANG Kyong Shik, Chairman	COL Jack L. McClaran, Chairman
Mr. LEE Hak Sung, Secretary	COL James E. Hilmar, Alt.Chairman
Mr. SOHN Tai Yum, Member	MAJ Earl E. Carr, Secretary
Mr. LEE Sang Kook, Member	LTC Franklin W. Reese, Member
Mr. LEE Sang Hee, Member	Mr. William E. Woodford, Member
Mr. KIM Jong Ho, Member	MAJ J. Galbreith, Member
Mr. KIM Chang Yun, Member	Mr. Samuel Pollack, Member
Mr. KIM Gi Dug, Member	Mr. Don Leland, Member
Mr. JU Woel Dong, Member	Mr. Francis K. Cook, Member
Mr. CHUNG Eui Yong, Member	LTC Morris W. Pearson, Member

2. Subject of Recommendation: Agreed Minute 1 to Article VI, ROK-US SOFA, provides that any changes determined by the authorities of the Republic of Korea in priorities, conditions, rates or tariffs applicable to the United States Armed Forces shall be the subject of consultation in the Joint Committee prior to their effective date.

3. The US Chairman initiated consultation concerning a change in water rates applicable to Seoul and Taegu Rental Guarantee Housing Sites under contract DAJB03-71-C-6064 (See Inclosure 1).

4. The ROK Component of the Utilities Subcommittee response included new proposed water rates (Inclosure 2).

5. The United States component of the Utilities Subcommittee has reviewed the ROK proposed new water rates and has determined that the requested change in rate or tariff (Inclosure 2) is no less favorable than those accorded any other comparable user.

243

6. It is recommended that the two Inclosures referenced in paragraphs 3 and 4 be accepted by the Joint Committee as evidence of consultation contemplated by Article VI of the Status of Forces Agreement.

KANG KYONG SHIK	JAMES E. HILMAR
Republic of Korea Chairman	Colonel, U. S. Army
Utilities Subcommittee	United States Alternate Chairman
	Utilities Subcommittee

2 Incl

2

244

REPUBLIC OF KOREA-UNITED STATES
UTILITIES SUBCOMMITTEE

SUBJECT: Water Rates Applicable to Seoul and Taegu Rental Guarantee Housing Sites

TO: ROK Chairman, Utilities Subcommittee 16 Nov. 1973

1. References:

a. Paragraph 2 and Agreed Minute 1 of Article VI of the Status of Forces Agreement.

b. Memorandum to the Joint Committee, dated 20 Apr 71, subject: Change in Taegu Water Rate under Article VI of the Status of Forces Agreement.

c. Memorandum to the Joint Committee, dated 11 May 72, subject: Consultation on Rate/Tariff Changes.

2. The USFK have been advised of a proposed water rate charge for USFK personnel occupying the Rental Guarantee Housing Projects at Seoul and Taegu, Korea (incl 1).

3. In accordance with references 1b and 1c, above, the established rates for United States Armed Forces are 20 won per m^3 for the city of Seoul, and 25 won per m^3 for the city of Taegu.

4. Request your assistance in applying the approved water rates for United States Armed Forces occupying Rental Guarantee Housing Projects at Seoul and Taegu, Korea.

J. L. McClaran
J. L. McCLARAN
Colonel, US Army
Chairman, Utilities Subcommittee

245

SAMPOONG-FEMCO (A JOINT VENTURE)

SAM POONG CONSTRUCTION & INDUSTRIAL CO., LTD.
TEL; MAIN OFFICE; 26-0107
R.G.H. SITE; SEOUL, 69-5711 EXT 3073-4 TAEGU, 5-1973
I. P. O. BOX 4257

FISCHER ENGINEERING & MAINTENANCE CO., INC.
TEL; 54-8673 YONGSAN 404-3137
APO SAN FRANCISCO 96301

Date : 26 Sept. 1973

Subject : Water Rate and Power Consumption for water
Contract NR DAJB03-71-C-6064
(Rental Guarantee Housing Project-Korea)

To : Contracting Officer
US Army Korea Procurement Agency
APO. 96301

Re : Your letter of 7 Sept. 1973

Dear Sirs,

In compliance with referenced letter above, the following is submitted.

1. Water Rate : Translated copy of the letter from Seoul City Government is enclosed.

2. Estimated Cost of electric power for water pumps :
The power consumption for water will be metered and the cost thereof will be billed as shown on the enclosure.

Sincerely Yours,

Kim Ok Keun
Executive Director
Sam Poong

246

ESTIMATED WATER CONSUMPTION CHARGE

The following is the proposed method of calculating water charges. The actual consumption will be measured by the meteres installed by Sponsor as listed below

	LOCATION			
WATER METER	PUMP HOUSE	DUPLEX	APARTMENTS SEOUL	APARTMENTS TAEGU
	Main Meter (Seoul & Taegu)	One for each bld (One for two family units)	One for each family unit	Two for each family unit (One for hot water and one for cold water)
Elec Meter for Water Pumps	One for Seoul & Taegu			

1. ESTIMATED QUANTITY OF WATER :

500 GL X 30 day X 300 unit = 4,500,000 GL/Mon/Total (For Seoul)
500 GL X 30 day X 70 unit = 1,050,000 GL/Mon/Total (For Taegu)

4,500,000 GL ÷ 264.19 GL = 17,033 M^3 .... (For Seoul)
1,050,000 GL ÷ 264.19 GL = 3,974 M^3 .... (For Taegu)
(M^3 of water = 264.19 GL)

2. CHLORINATION COST : 10% of the water cost for Seoul and Taegu. Labor cost for the chlorination will not be included in the water bill as it will be paid by Sam Poong.

3. POWER COST FOR WATER PUMPS : An electric meter will be installed in the pump house at both Seoul and Taegu. The charge to be paid by each family unit will be determined as follows:

a. For Seoul :

Meter reading X 80% ÷ 300 unit X General service B Rate = Amount per unit per mon
Meter reading X 20% = Will be paid by Sam Poong because approximately 20% of the water will be consumed by persons other than tenants.

b. For Taegu :

Meter reading ÷ 70 unit X General service B rate = Amount per unit per month.

249

4. CONCLUSION :

Water cost consists of water charge paid to City Government, cost for chlorination and power for pumps. Billing for the water charge will be made in accordance with the following table.

FOR SEOUL :

$$\frac{\text{(Meter reading X 40 won)}}{\text{Part A : Cost of water}} + \frac{\text{(Part A x 10\%)}}{\text{Part B : Chlorination}} + \frac{\text{(Meter reading X 80\% ÷ 300 unit X General Service B)}}{\text{Part C = Power Cost}}$$

= Amount per month per unit

FOR TAEGU :

Same as Seoul except power cost is meter reading (100%) ÷ 70 unit X general service B rate.

248

TRANSLATION COPY

SEOUL SPECIAL CITY

18 Sept. 1973

Rc : 1201

To : Sam Poong Const. & Ind. Co., Ltd.
#310, 4-ka, Ulchi-Ro, Chung-ku, Seoul

Atten. : President Lee Joon

Subject : Water rate for rental guarantee housing project for the family of US military personnel in Korea

1. Reference is made to your letter of 15 Sept. 1973, letter NR Sam Poong 82.

2. Please be notified that the military special rate can not be applied to the residential houses for the family of the military personnel as informed you on 5 Sept. 1973 by information number 1201-377.

OFFICIAL SEAL
MAYOR OF SEOUL CITY

249

서 울 특 별 시

업무 1201 — 398   73. 9. 18.

수 신   시내 중구 을지로 4가 310

참 조   삼풍건설 (주) 대표 이 준

제 목   주한 미군 가족주택 수도

1. 삼풍 총 제 82호 (73.9.15.) 에 관련 입니다.

2. 업무 1201— 377 (73.9.5.) 에 의거 조처 하시기 바라며 군가족용 주택으로 특수용 적용은 불가능하니 양지 하시기 바랍니다.

끝.

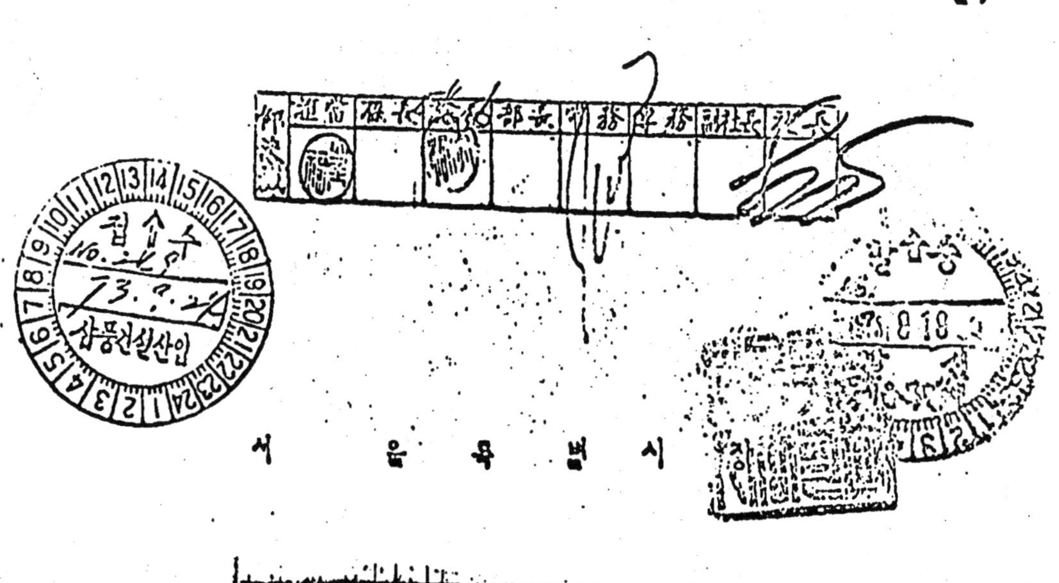

서 울 특 별 시

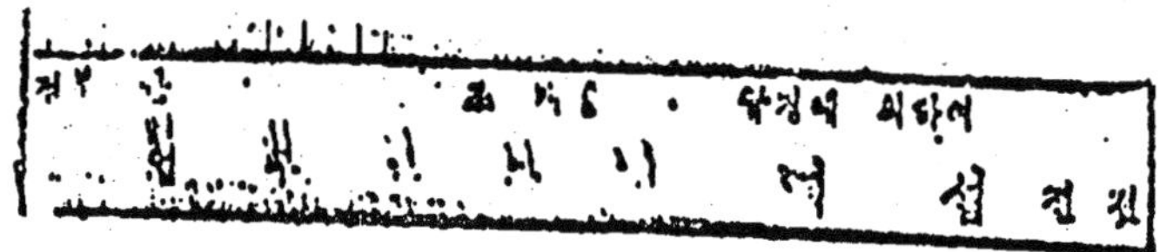

250

OCTOBER 1973

TABLE OF WATER CHARGE ON MONTHLY BASE

SEOUL CITY		TAEGU CITY	
Domestic	United Nations Military	Domestic	United Nations Military
Basic Charge UP to 10 ton ₩150	₩20/m3	Basic Charge UP to 10 ton ₩150	₩25/m3
Excessive Ton 11-20 15		Excessive Ton 10-30 ₩23	
Ton 21-30 ₩20		Ton 31-50 ₩28	
Ton 31-40 ₩30		Ton 51-100 ₩36	
Over 40 ₩40		Ton Over 100 ₩48	
R.G.H (300 unit) 17,033 m3	17,033 m3	(70 unit) 3,974 m3	3,974 m3
17,033 ÷ 300 = 56.7 ton 10 ton ------ ₩150 46.7 ton --- ₩40 × 46.7 = ₩1,868 (₩150 + ₩1,868) × 300 = ₩605,400.	₩20 × 17,033 = ₩340,660	3,974 ÷ 70 = 56.7 ton 10 ton ----- ₩150 46.7 ton ---- ₩28 × 46.7 = ₩1,307.60 (₩150 + ₩1,307.60) × 70 = ₩102,032	₩25 × 3,974 = ₩99,350.

NOTE: Obtained above information from Mr. Kim Young Hwan, MOC ROK Gov't (Tel: 70-4029) and Mr. Kim, Utility Br. EAEN on 16 October 1973.

1 GAL = 8.33 lbs

1 m3 = 264.17 Gal

8.33 lbs × 264.17 = 2,200.5 lbs

2200.5 ÷ 2204 ≒ Approx. 1 ton

Say 1 m3 (by volume) = 1 ton (by weight)

※ THE HIGHEST DOMESTIC WATER RATE FOR RGH

In discussions with Sampoong-FEMCO this Agency has been advised the cities of Seoul and Taegu take the position that each site is the same as one (1) house and therefore the highest domestic water rate applies due to the large consumption as follows:

SEOUL	TAEGU
₩40 × 17,033 m3 = ₩681,320	₩48 × 3,974 = ₩190,752

251

REPUBLIC OF KOREA-UNITED STATES
UTILITIES SUBCOMMITTEE

March 20, 1974

Subject : Water Rates Applicable to Seoul and Taegu Rental Guarantee Housing Sites

To : Chairman, US Utilities Subcommittee

1. References

a. Paragraph 1 of Article VI of the Status of Forces Agreements

b. US Chairman, Utilities Subcommittee letter dated 16 November 1973.

2. The letter from you, as stated in reference 1 b, has been reviewed in detail by the ROK government with the consultation of the local Governments, the ROK Utilities Subcommittee reached a conclusion that it is impossible to apply the approved water rates for United States Armed Forces occupying Rantal Guarantee Housing Project at Seoul and Taegu. The family of the US military personnel in the rental houses may not be included in the US Armed Forces in accordance with Paragraph 1 of Article VI of the Status of Forces Agreement. In case of water meter being installed at each family unit, the water charge will be billed on its actual consumption of as exampled on Attachment.

Your understanding will be greatly appreciated.

Sincerely yours,

K. S. Kang

Kyong Shik Kang
Director, Price Policy Bureau
Chairman, Republic of Korea
Utilities Subcommittee

252
Incl 2

Attachment

	Q'ty used in Feb'74	Method of calculating water charge	
		Present	Meter installed
Seoul	22,633m³	10m³ : 15won x10m³=150 11-20 : 15x10=150 21-30 : 20x10=200 31-40 : 30x10=300 over 41m³ 40x22593=903,720 Total : 904,500	22633m³+300 family= 76m³ 10m³ : 15won x10m³ =150 11-20: 15x10= 150 21-30: 20x10= 200 31-40: 30x10= 300 36m³ : 40x36= 1,440 Total : 2,240won x300 = 672,000
Taegu	2,303m³	10m³ : 20won x10m³=200 11-30 : 30x20=600 31-50 : 40x20=800 51-100 : 50x50=2,500 ever 101m³=:60x2203= 132,180 Total : 136,280	2303m³+68 family=34m³ 10m³ : 20won x10=200 11-30: 30x20=600 4m³ : 40x40=160 Total : 960won x68=65,280

257

기 안 용 지

분류기호 문서번호	미이 723 -	(전화번호)	전결규정 조 항 국장 전결사항
처리기간			
시행일자	74. 6. 8.		
보존년한		국 장	
보조기관	과 장		협조
기안책임자	양세훈	북미2과	

경 유	
수 신	경제기획원장관
참 조	물가정책국장
제 목	철도 요율 변경에 대한 SOFA 합동위 승인 통보

발송 1974. 6. 8 외무부

통제 검열 1974. 6. 8 통제관

74. 4. 12.자 철도요율 변경에 관한 SOFA 공익사업 용역 분과 위원회의 건의에 대하여 5. 2. 개최된 SOFA 제 94차 합동위원회가 별첨 회의록 제 13항과 같이 이를 원안대로 승인하였음을 알려드리오니 시행에 필요한 조치를 취하시기 바랍니다.

첨부 : SOFA 제 94차 합동위 회의록 1부. 끝.

정서

관인

발송

254

0201-1-8A (갑)
1969. 11. 10. 승인

190mm×268mm(특급인쇄용지40g/m²)
조 달 청 (5,500,000매 인 쇄)

AGENDA ITEM VI ROK Presentation

(1. FOR YOUR INFORMATION: The ROK Representative will present and request acceptance of two memoranda received from the Utilities Subcommittee, concerning a total of five changes in utility rates. The first memorandum, dated 4 April 1974, relates to a change in water rates applicable to the Seoul and Taegu Rental Guarantee Housing sites. The second memorandum, dated 12 April 1974, concerns a change in four rates for Korean National Railroad services, involving two freight rates, one rate for maintenance service charges, and one rate for passenger fares.)

(2. FOR YOUR INFORMATION: The US side has carefully reviewed the new rates as specified above, and has determined that the changes in these rates as applicable to the USFK are no less favorable than rates accorded other comparable users of these services, as required by paragraph 2 of Article VI of the SOFA. Hence, there is no obstacle to acceptance by the USFK of the new rates.)

3. The United States Representative is happy to concur in the acceptance of the two memoranda of the Utilities Subcommittee that you have just presented, involving changes in water and railroad services rates respectively. These two memoranda evidence the completion of the consultations required under Article VI of the Status of Forces Agreement for these rate changes.

94th J.C (74.5.2.)

74.4.30. 경기원 물가정책국 (70-3101) 김태웅씨. 확인필

255

REPUBLIC OF KOREA - UNITED STATES
UTILITIES SUBCOMMITTEE

12 April 1974

MEMORANDUM TO: The Joint Committee

SUBJECT: Consultation on Increase in Rates and Charges of Korean National Railroad Applicable to the US Armed Forces

1. Subcommittee Members:

Republic of Korea	United States
Mr. KANG Kyong Shik, Chairman	COL Jack L. McClaran, Chairman
Mr. LEE Hak Sung, Secretary	COL James E. Hilmar, Alt Chairman
Mr. SOHN Tai Yum, Member	MAJ Earl E. Carr, Secretary
Mr. LEE Sang Kook, Member	Mr. William E. Woodford, Member
Mr. LEE Sang Hee, Member ✓	Mr. Samuel Pollack, Member
Mr. KIM Jong Ho, Member	Mr. Don Leland, Member
Mr. KIM Chang Yun, Member	Mr. Francis K. Cook, Member
Mr. KIM Gi Dug, Member	
Mr. JU Woel Dong, Member	
Mr. CHUNG Eui Yong, Member ✓	

2. Subject of Recommendation: Agreed Minute 1 to Article VI, ROK-US SOFA, provides that any changes determined by the authorities of the Republic of Korea in priorities, conditions, rates or tariffs applicable to the United States Armed Forces shall be the subject of consultation in the Joint Committee prior to their effective date.

3. The Republic of Korea has initiated consultation concerning freight rate increases, maintenance service charges and passenger fares furnished by the Korean National Railroad under contract DAJB 03-73-D-3114 in accordance with the four letters identified at Inclosure 1.

4. The United States component of the Utilities Subcommittee has reviewed the ROK requests for consultation and submits at Inclosure 2 an approved schedule of rates, fares and charges with applicable effective dates.

12 April 1974

SUBJECT: Consultation on Increase in Rates and Charges of Korean National Railroad Applicable to the US Armed Forces

5. The US and ROK components of the Utilities Subcommittee concur that the approved changes in rates or tariffs as submitted in Inclosure 2 are no less favorable than those accorded any other comparable user.

6. It is recommended that the two inclosures referenced in paragraphs 3 and 4 be accepted by the Joint Committee as evidence of consultation contemplated by Article VI of the Status of Forces Agreement.

KANG KYONG SHIK
Republic of Korea Chairman
Utilities Subcommittee

J. L. McCLARAN, COL, USA
United States Chairman
Utilities Subcommittee

2

257-1. E

259

REPUBLIC OF KOREA-UNITED STATES

UTILITIES SUB COMMITTEE

October 27, 1973

Subject : Change in Maintenance Service Charge Applicable to the US-Owned Freight Cars

To : US Chairman, Utilities Sub Committee

1. References;

a. Paragraph 2 and Agreed Minute 1 of Article VI of the Status of Forces of America

b. DAJ B03-73-D-3114 (29 June 1973)

2. The Korean Government propose that the rates of maintenance service charges applicable to the U.S. owned freight cars are to be changed on and after 27 October, 1973.

3. Details of the Proposal are as follows

a. Effective date;

27 October 1973, the date on which the proposal is initiated by ROKG for SOFA consultation.

b. Proposed rates to be changed (attached)

No tabulated rates are available applicable to Korean privately owned freight cars, i.e. they are charged on the basis of actual costs incurred.

c. Basis of calculation of old and new rates

Refer to item "b"

SUB- Change in Maintenance Service Charge Applicable to the US-Owned Freight Cars

d. Reason for revision of Rates

To cover the cost of KNR furnished materials and labor cost.

4. The Government of ROK advises the Government of the United States that priorities, conditions and rates being charged are no less favorable than those accorded any other user.

Your early review and concurrence will be appreciated.

Sincerely yours,

K. S. Kang

Kyong Shik, Kang
Director
Price Policy Bureau
Chairman, Republic of Korea
Utilities Sub-Committee

749

PROPOSAL OF THE REVISIONS

Existing contract:

24 months scheduled inspection excluding coating service for US Government owned ordinary freight cars:

₩38,000. Won

PROPOSED CHANGES IN THE EXISTING CONTRACT:

1. Change in the cost of present contract.

   24 months scheduled inspection excluding coating service for US Government owned ordinary freight cars:

   ₩72,000. Won

2. Addition to the existing contract:
   Temporary non-scheduled inspection excluding coating service, for US government owned freight cars:

   ₩49,000. Won

3. Addition to the existing contract:
   24 months scheduled inspection excluding coating service, for US government owned Special type of freight cars:

   ₩144,000. Won

4. Addition to the existing contract:
   Non-scheduled Temporary inspection excluding coating service, for US government owned Special type of freight cars:

   ₩99,000. Won

5. Addition to the existing contract:
   Daily operation maintenance per car:

   ₩49.20 Won

260

Republic of Korea-United States
Utilities Subcommittee

January 15, 1974

Subject : Change in Freight Rates of Railroad Applicable to the US Armed Forces under Article VI of the Status Forces Agreement

To : Chairman, US Utilities Subcommittee

1. Reference : Paragraph 2 and Agreed Minute of Article VI of the Status of Forces Agreement.

2. The Government of the United States is informed through this written consultative process that the Republic of Korea proposes to change following rates/tariffs at locations indicated below;

Rate/Tariff	Location
Freight Rate schedule of railroad applicable to the US Armed Forces	The Whole country

3. The following data is provided ;

a. Effective date : 1 January 1974.

b. Rate Schedule showing rates that are charges all classes of users. (Attached)

c. Rate schedule of proposed change:Refer to item "b"

d. Calculation of old and new rate base:Refer to item "b"

e. Reasons for revision of rates
Decision of ROK Cabinet Council (dated 18 December 1973) to meet the conditions specified in Loan Agreement with IBRD and to secure transportation costs.

261

4. The Government of the ROK advises the Government of the United States that the priorities, conditions, and rates being charges are no less favorable than those accorded any other user.

You may be assured that your views will be greatly appreciated.

Sincerely yours,

K. S. Kang

Kyong Shik, Kang
Director
Price Policy Bureau
Chariman, Republic of Korea
Utilities Subcommittee

262

Freight Change Rates of Railroad

(Unit : Won)

	Description of rates	Unit	Present Rates	Change Rates KNR Proposed	Change Rates ROKA	Remark
1.	Carload Freight					
	a. Basic Rate Using Carrier's Car	Per Car/ Km	70^{00}	77	77	10% increase
	b. Basic Rate Using US Owned Car	"	52^{50}	57^{75}	-	
	c. Minimum Charge for carload	per Car	$4,120^{00}$	4,532	4,532	
2.	Special Train Service Minimum Charge		150,000	165,000	165,000	
3.	Demurrage	6 hours/ per car	1,200	1,320	1,320	
4.	Diversion or Reconsignment	per car	2,400	2,640	2,640	
5.	Cancellation of Car Ordered	"	1,200	1,320	1,320	
6.	Switching Charge	"	623	686	686	
7.	Stopoff in transit		1,120	1,232	1,232	
8.	Equipment Rental	per car/ a day	950	1,045	1,045	
9.	Deadhead Monement of Rented or US Owned Car	Per Car/	18	20	20	
10.	Surcharge for Oversised Freight	"	51	57	57	

263

REPUBLIC OF KOREA-UNITED STATES
UTILITIES SUBCOMMITTEE

February 13, 1974

Subject: Change in Freight Rates of Railroad Applicable to the US Armed Forces under Article VI of the Status of Forces Agreement.

To : Chairman, US Utilities Subcommittee.

1. Reference: Paragraph 2 and Agreed Minute of Article VI of the Status of Forces Agreement.

2. The Government of the United States is informed through this written consultative process that the Republic of Korea proposes to change following rates/tariffs at location indicated below;

Rate/Tariff	Location
Freight rate schedule of railroad applicable to the US Armed Forces	the whole country

3. The following data is provided;

a. Effective date: 13 February 1974

b. Rate schedule of proposed change. "Attached"

c. Rate schedule showing rates that are charged all classes of users. Refer to item "b"

d. Calculation of old and new rate base. Refer to item "b"

e. Reason for revision of rates.
To meet the conditions specified in Loan Agreement with IBRD and to secure transportation costs.

4. The Government of ROK advises the Government of the United States that the priorities, conditions, and rates being charges are no less favorable than those accorded any other user.

You may be assured that your views will be greatly appreciated.

Sincerely yours,

K. S. Kang

Kyong Shik Kang
Director, Price Policy Bureau
Chairman, Republic of Korea
Utilities Subcommittee

264

Freight Change Rates of Railroad

(Unit : Won)

A. US Army

	Description of rates	Unit	Present Rates	Change Rates KNR Proposed ROKA (74.1.1-74.2.12)	Change Rates KNR Proposed ROKA (74. 2.13-)	Remark
1.	Carload Freight					
	a. Basic Rate Using Carrier's Car	Per Car/Km	70.00	77	81	1) 10% increase
	b. Basic Rate Using US Owned Car	"	52.50	57.75	60.64	2) 5% increase Total 15%
	c. Minimum Charge for carload	Per Car	4,120.00	4,532	4,759	
2.	Special Train Service Minimum Charge		150,000	165,000	173,250	
3.	Demurrage	6 hours/per car	1,200	1,320	1,386	
4.	Diversion or Reconsignment	per car	2,400	2,640	2,772	
5.	Cancellation of Car Ordered	"	1,200	1,320	1,386	
6.	Switching Charge	"	623	686	721	
7.	Stopoff in transit		1,120	1,232	1,294	
8.	Equipment Rental	per car/a day	950	1,045	1,098	

	Description of rates	Unit	Present Rages	Change Rates KNR Proposed ROKA	Change Rates KNR Proposed ROKA	Remark
9.	Deadhead Monement of Rented or US Owned Car	per car/Km	18	20	21	
10.	Surcharge for Oversised Freight	"	51	57	60	
19.	US Government Owned car Scheduled General Inspection and Repair Excluding Painting (every 24 months)	per car	38,100	41,900	44,006	
B.	Pacex					
	Carload Freight Basic Rate	"	81	90	95	

266

REPUBLIC OF KOREA-UNITED STATES
UTILITIES SUBCOMMITTEE

February 13, 1974

Subject: Change in Passenger Fares of Railroad Applicable to the US Armed Forces under Article VI of the Status Forces Agreement.

To : Chairman, US Utilities Subcommittee.

1. Reference: Paragraph 2 and Agreed Minute of Article VI of Status Forces Agreement.

2. The Government of the United States is informed through this written consultative process that the Republic of Korea proposes to change following rates/tariffs at location indicated below;

Rate/Tariff	Location
Passenger Fare schedule of railroad applicable to the US Armed Forces	The whole country

3. The following data is provided;

a. Effective date: 13 February 1974

b. Rate schedule showing rates that are charged all classes of users."Attached"

c. Rate schedule of proposed change. Refer to item "b"

d. Calculation of old and new rate base. Refer to item "b"

e. Reason for revision of rates.

To secure transportation costs according to increasing of oil price

4. The Government of the ROK advises the Government of the United States that the priorities, conditions, and rates being charges are no less favorable than those accorded any other user.

Your may be assured that your views will greatly appreciated.

Sincerely yours,

K. S. Kang

Kyong Shik Kang
Director, Price Policy Bureau
Chairman, Republic of Korea
Utilities Subcommittee

267

Revision Contents of Schedule of Rates, Fares and Charges

Item No	Description of Service	Unit	Rates(Won) old	Rates(Won) new	Remarks
	Passenger service				
11. a	Basic Rate for transportation of charter coach, baggagecar	per car/Km	118.80	136.62	15% Inclease
b	Surcharge for Exclusive use of passenger accommodation	Up to 200Km	400Km	more than400Km	1)15% Inclease
	Category #1	35,040	52,320	65,280	2)Data in
	(Super express special car)	(40,300)	(60,170)	(75,070)	paranthesis are
	Category #2	25,200	40,880	50,960	new Rates.
	(Super express ordinary car)	(28,980)	(47,010)	(58,600)	
	Category #3	15,120	25,200	30,800	
	(Special express special car)	(17,390)	(28,980)	(35,420)	
	Category #4	6,480	6,480	6,480	
	(Special express ordinary car)	(7,450)	(7,450)	(7,450)	
12	Minimum charge for passenger special train service	per train	118,580	136,370	15% Inclease
13	Motor coach service				
	a. Basic rate	per car/Km	118.80	136.62	15% Inclease
	b. Surcharge	per car	725,920	29,810	"
	c. Minimum charge for motor coach	per car	36,460	41,930	"

Item No	Description of Service	Unit	Rates(Won)		Remarks
			old	new	
14	Surcharge for Express Service				
	a. Common express	per car			15% Inclease
		1-200Km	7,200	8,280	
		201-400Km	14,400	16,560	
		more than 401Km	21,600	24,840	
	b. Special express	per car			
		1-200Km	10,800	12,420	"
		201-400Km	21,600	24,840	
		401 or more	43,200	49,680	
	c. Super express	per car			1454
		1-200Km	11,200	12,880	
		201-400Km	22,400	25,760	
		401 or more	44,800	51,520	
15	Equipment Rental				
	a. passenger car	per car/per day	1,630	1,860	15% Inclease
	b. Baggage,mail car	"	1,290	16,50	"
	c. passenger-mail combination car	"	1,450	1,480	"

269

Item No	Description of Service	Unit	Reatew (Won)		Remarks
			old	new	
17	Deadhead movement	per car/Km	28	32	15% Inolease
18	Movement of Sentry dog				
	a. Less than 100Km	per dog	369	424	
	b. 101-200Km	"	621	714	
	c. 201-500Km	"	834	959	
	d. more than 501Km	"	1,071	1,232	

240

SCHEDULE OF RATES, FARES AND CHARGES

ITEM NO.		DESCRIPTION OF SERVICE	APPLICABLE TECH SPEC	UNIT	RATE (WON)	REMARKS
A.	Freight Service					
1.		Car load Freight				
	a.	Basic Rate using KNR owned car	3.1.2. & 3.1.3.13.	Per Car/KM	₩ 70	All types of car
	b.	Basic rate using US owned car	3.1.2. & 3.1.3.13.	Per Car/KM	25 % less than 1a, above	All types of car
	c.	Minimum charge for carload freight	6.3.14.	Per car	₩ 4,120	US owned, leased and KNR car
2.		Special Freight Train Service Minimum Charge	3.1.3.3. & 6.3.36.	Per Train	₩ 150,000	
3.		Demurrage	3.1.3.9.	Per car Per unit of 6 hrs.	₩ 1,200	6 hours or fraction thereof beyond the free time.

Free Time Table (Tch Spec 3.1.3.9.)

Cars Placed	Expiration of Free Time
Between 0001 hours & 0600 hours	By 1200 hours the same day
Between 0601 hours & 0900 hours	By 1400 hours the same day
Between 0901 hours & 1200 hours	By 1700 hours the same day
Between 1201 hours & 2400 hours	By 1200 hours the following day

ITEM NO.	DESCRIPTION OF SERVICE	APPLICABLE TECH SPEC	UNIT	RATE (WON)	REMARKS
4.	Diversion or Re-consignment	3.1.3.8.	Per car	₩ 2,400	
5.	Cancellation of Car (Movement) Ordered	3.1.3.10.	Per car	₩ 1,200	
6.	Switching Charge	3.1.3.5.	Per car	₩ 623	Loaded car only and removing from installation for car movement and spotting into installation for unloading.

271

ITEM NO.	DESCRIPTION OF SERVICE	APPLICABLE TECH SPEC	UNIT	RATE (WON)	REMARK
7.	Stop-off In-transit	3.1.3.7.	Per car per stop	₩ 1,120	
8.	Equipment Rental	3.1.3.2.	Per car per day	₩ 950	Only when the car is in serviceable condition.
9.	Deadhead Movement	3.1.3.6.	Per car/KM	₩ 18	US owned or leased car only
10.	Oversize Freight Surcharge	3.1.3.4.	Per car/KM	₩ 51	

B. Passenger Service

11. a.	Basic Rate for transportation of charter coach/ baggage car	3.2.1.4.	Per car/KM	₩ 11,880	All type of car minimum movement distance shall be 50KM.
b.	Surcharge for exclusive use of passenger accommodation				

		Up to 200 KM	400 KM	More than 400 KM
Category #1	(Super Express) (Special car)	₩ 35,040	₩ 52,320	₩ 65,280
Category #2	(Super Express) (Ordinary car)	₩ 25,200	₩ 40,880	₩ 50,960
Category #3	(Special Express) (Special car)	₩ 15,120	₩ 25,200	₩ 30,800
Category #4	(Special Express) (Ordinary car)	₩ 6,480	₩ 6,480	₩ 6,480

Remarks: The surcharge if not applicable to common express.

ITEM NO.		DESCRIPTION OF SERVICE	APPLICABLE TECH SPEC	UNIT	RATE (WON)	REMARKS
12.		Minimum charge for Passenger Special train service	3.2.2.	Per train	₩ 118,580	
13.		Motor Coach service	3.2.1. & 3.2.1.4.			
	a.	Basic rate		Per car/KM	₩ 118.80	See remarks under item 11
	b.	Surcharge		Per car	₩ 25,920	Paid in addition to basic rate
	c.	Minimum charge for motor coach		Per car (train)	₩ 36,460	
14.		Surcharge for Express Service				
	a.	Common Express	3.2.3.4.	Per car		Applicable to charter service only
				Rate: 0.1 - 200 KM	₩ 7,200	
				200.1 - 400 KM	₩ 14,400	
				400.1 or more	₩ 21,600	
	b.	Special Express	3.2.3.4.	Per car		Applicable to charter service only
				Rate: 0.1 - 200 KM	₩ 10,800	
				200.1 - 400 KM	₩ 21,600	
				400.1 or more	₩ 43,200	
	c.	Super Express	3.2.3.4.	Per car		Applicable to charter service only
				Rate: 0.1 - 200 KM	₩ 11,200	
				200.1 - 400 KM	₩ 22,400	
				400.1 or more	₩ 44,800	
15.	a.	Individual or Group Travel via KN scheduled regular train	3.2.1.1.	Rate: Rates prescribed in the officially published KN passenger tariff effective on the date of travel, excluding transportation tax.		

3

293

ITEM NO.	DESCRIPTION OF SERVICE	APPLICABLE TECH SPEC	UNIT	RATE (WON)	REMARKS
b.	Unused tickets	3.2.1.1.6.		Refund for unused tickets shall be handled in accordance with rules and regulation of KNR as provided in officially published KNR passenger tariff and in effect on the date of tickets.	
16.	Equipment Rental	3.2.3.1.			
a.	Passenger car		Per car per day	W 1,620	
b.	Baggage/mail car		"	W 1,290	
c.	Passenger-mail combination car		"	W 1,450	
17.	Deadhead Movement	3.2.3.2.	Per car/KM	W 28	All type of cars US owned or leased car only
18.	Movement of Sentry Dog	3.2.1.3.		Less than 100 KM Per Dog W 369 100.1-200 Km Per Dog W 621 200.1-500 KM Per Dog W 834 More than 500 KM Per Dog W 1,071	

C. Maintenance Service

ITEM NO.	DESCRIPTION OF SERVICE	APPLICABLE TECH SPEC	UNIT	RATE (WON)	REMARKS
19.	24 month Maintenance of US-owned freight car	3.3.3.5.	Per car	W 38,100	
20.	Component Parts	6.2.2.1.			

In the event the following parts and material are required to be furnished by the KNR in lieu of GFM as per para 6.2.2.1., cost for the material shall be paid by the US Government at prices indicated below:

a. Wheel set, chilled steel (an axle and two wheels) W 167,000

b. Wheel, chilled steel W 61,047

c. Axle W 43,890

d. Coupler W 46,284

e. Draft Gear W 35,910

f. Triple valve W 27,930

g. Bolster Spring (inner & outer) W 37,107

h. Side Frame W 43,890

i. Brake Beam W 16,359

j. Bolster W 57,700

5

295

REVISION I TO

SCHEDULE OF RATES, FARES AND CHARGES

ITEM NO.	DESCRIPTION OF SERVICE	APPLICABLE TECH SPEC	UNIT	RATE (WON)	REMARKS
A.	Freight Service (EFFECTIVE 1 JAN 74 thru 12 FEB 74)				
1.	Car load Freight				
a.	Basic Rate using KNR owned car	3.1.2. & 3.1.3.13.	Per Car/KM	₩ 77	All types of car
b.	Basic rate using US Owned car	3.1.2. & 3.1.3.13.	Per Car/KM	25% less than 1a, above	All types of car
c.	Minimum charge for carload freight	6.3.14.	Per car	₩ 4,532	US owned, leased and KNR car
2.	Special Freight Train Service Minimum Charge	3.1.3.3. & 6.3.36.	Per Train	₩165,000	
3.	Demurrage	3.1.3.9.	Per car Per unit of 6 hrs.	₩ 1,320	6 hours or fraction thereof beyond the free time.

Free Time Table (Tech Spec 3.1.3.9.)

Cars Placed	Expiration of Free Time
Between 0001 hours & 0600 hours	By 1200 hours the same day
Between 0601 hours & 0900 hours	By 1400 hours the same day
Between 0901 hours & 1200 hours	By 1700 hours the same day
Between 1201 hours & 2400 hours	By 1200 hours the following day

ITEM NO.	DESCRIPTION OF SERVICE	APPLICABLE TECH SPEC	UNIT	RATE (WON)	REMARKS
4.	Diversion of Re-consignment	3.1.3.8.	Per car	₩ 2,640	
5.	Cancellation of Car (Movement) Ordered	3.1.3.10.	Per car	₩ 1,320	
6.	Switching Charge	3.1.3.5.	Per car	₩ 686	Loaded car only and removing from installation for onward movement and spotting into installation for unloading.

1

216

ITEM NO.	DESCRIPTION OF SERVICE	APPLICABLE TECH SPEC	UNIT	RATE (WON)	REMARKS
7.	Stop-off In-transit	3.1.3.7.	Per car per stop	₩ 1,232	
8.	Equipment Rental	3.1.3.2.	Per car per day	₩ 1,045	Only when the car is in serviceable condition.
9.	Deadhead Movement	3.1.3.6.	Per car/KM	₩ 20	US owned or leased car only
10.	Oversize Freight Surcharge	3.1.3.4.	Per car/KM	₩ 57	

B. Freight Service (EFFECTIVE 13 February 1974 thru 30 June 1974)

1.	Car load Freight				
a.	Basic Rate using KNR owned car	3.1.2. & 3.1.3.13.	Per Car/KM	₩ 81	All types of car
b.	Basic rate using US Owned car	3.1.2. & 3.1.3.13.	Per Car/KM	25% less than 1a, above	All types of car
c.	Minimum charge for carload freight	6.3.14.	Per car	₩ 4,759	US owned, leased and KNR car
2.	Special Freight Train Service Minimum Charge	3.1.3.3. & 6.3.36.	Per Train	₩173,250	
3.	Demurrage	3.1.3.9.	Per car Per unit of 6 hrs.	₩ 1,386	6 hours or fraction thereof beyond the free time.

Free Time Table (Tech Spec 3.1.3.9.)

Cars Placed	Expiration of Free Time
Between 0001 hours & 0600 hours	By 1200 hours the same day
Between 0601 hours & 0900 hours	By 1400 hours the same day
Between 0901 hours & 1200 hours	By 1700 hours the same day
Between 1201 hours & 2400 hours	By 1200 hours the following day

ITEM NO.	DESCRIPTION OF SERVICE	APPLICABLE TECH SPEC	UNIT	RATE (WON)	REMARKS
4.	Diversion or Re-consignment	3.1.3.8.	Per car	₩ 2,772	
5.	Cancellation of Car (Movement) Ordered	3.1.3.10.	Per car	₩ 1,386	
6.	Switching Charge	3.1.3.5.	Per car	₩ 721	Loaded car only and removing from installation for onward movement and spotting into installation for unloading.
7.	Stop-off In-transit	3.1.3.7.	Per car per stop	₩ 1,294	
8.	Equipment Rental	3.1.3.2.	Per car per day	₩ 1,098	Only when the car is in serviceable condition.
9.	Deadhead Movement	3.1.3.6.	Per car/KM	₩ 21	US owned or leased car only
10.	Oversize Freight Surcharge	3.1.3.4.	Per car/KM	₩ 60	

C. Passenger Service (EFFECTIVE 13 February 1974 thru 30 June 1974)

11.	a. Basic Rate for transportation of charter coach/ baggage car	3.2.1.4.	Per car/KM	₩ 136.62	All type of car minimum movement distance shall be 50 KM

b. Surcharge for exclusive use of passenger accommodation.

		Up to 200 KM	400 KM	More than 400 KM
Category #1	(Super Express) (Special car)	₩40,300	₩60,170	₩75,070
Category #2	(Super Express) (Ordinary car)	₩28,980	₩47,010	₩58,600
Category #3	(Special Express) (Special car)	₩17,390	₩28,980	₩35,420
Category #4	(Special Express) (Ordinary car)	₩7,450	₩ 7,450	₩ 7,450

The surcharge is not applicable to common express and troop main.

278

ITEM NO.	DESCRIPTION OF SERVICE	APPLICABLE TECH SPEC	UNIT	RATE (WON)	REMARKS
12.	Minimum charge for Passenger Special train service	3.2.2.	Per train	₩136,370	
13.	Motor Coach service	3.2.1. & 3.2.1.4.			
a.	Basic rate		Per car/KM	₩ 136.62	See remarks under item 11
b.	Surcharge		Per car	₩ 29,810	Paid in addition to basic rate
c.	Minimum charge for motor coach		Per car (train)	₩ 41,930	
14.	Surcharge for Express service				
a.	Common Express	3.2.3.4.	Per car		Applicable to charter service only
			Rate: 0.1 - 200 KM	₩ 8,280	
			200.1 - 400 KM	₩16,560	
			400.1 or more	₩24,840	
b.	Special Express	3.2.3.4.	Per car		Applicable to charter service only
			Rate: 0.1 - 200 KM	₩12,420	
			200.1 - 400 KM	₩24,840	
			400.1 or more	₩49,680	
c.	Super Express	3.2.3.4.	Per Car		Applicable to Charter Service only
			Rate: 0.1 - 200 KM	₩12,880	
			200.1 - 400 KM	₩25,760	
			400.1 or more	₩51,520	
15.a.	Individual or Group Travel via KNR scheduled regular train	3.2.1.1.	Rate:	Rates prescribed in the officially published KNR passenger tariff effective on the date of travel, excluding transportation tax.	
b.	Unused tickets	3.2.1.1.6.		Refund for unused tickets shall be handled in accordance with rules and regulation of KNR as provided in officially published KNR passenger tariff and in effect on the date of tickets.	

279

4

ITEM NO.	DESCRIPTION OF SERVICE	APPLICABLE TECH SPEC	UNIT	RATE (WON)	REMARKS
16.	Equipment Rental	3.2.3.1.			
a.	Passenger car		Per car per day	₩1,860	
b.	Baggage/mail car		"	₩1,480	
c.	Passenger-mail combination car		"	₩1,670	
17.	Deadhead Movement	3.2.3.2.	Per car/KM	₩ 32	All type of cars US owned or leased car only
18.	Movement of Sentry Dog	3.2.1.3.	Less than 100 KM Per Dog	₩ 424	
			100.1-200 KM Per Dog	₩ 714	
			200.1-500 KM Per Dog	₩ 959	
			More than 500 KM Per Dog	₩1,232	

D. Maintenance Service:

(Effective 27 October 1973 thru 30 June 1974)

ITEM NO.	DESCRIPTION OF SERVICE	APPLICABLE TECH SPEC	UNIT	RATE (WON)	REMARKS
19. a.	24 month Maintenance of US-owned freight car	3.3.3.5.	Per car	₩ 72,000	
b.	Non-Scheduled Maintenance of US-owned freight car		Per car	₩ 49,000	
c.	24 month maintenance of US-owned heavy duty freight car	3.3.3.5.	Per car	₩108,000	
d.	Non-Scheduled Maintenance of US-owned heavy duty freight car		Per car	₩ 73,500	
e.	Maintenance Operating Charges (other than Back Shop Maintenance)	3.3.2.1. 3.3.2.2. 3.3.3.2. 3.3.3.3. 3.3.3.4.	Car/day	₩ 10.75	

ITEM NO.	DESCRIPTION OF SERVICE	APPLICABLE TECH SPEC	UNIT	RATE(WON)	REMARKS
	(Effective 1 July 1973 thru 30 June 1974)				
20.	Component Parts	6.2.2.1.			

In the event the following parts and material are required to be furnished by the KNR in liew of GFM as per para 6.2.2.1., cost for the material shall be paid by the US Government at prices indicated below:

a.	Wheel set, chilled steel (an axle and two wheels)	₩167,000
b.	Wheel, chilled steel	₩61,047
c.	Axle	₩43,890
d.	Coupler	₩46,284
e.	Draft Gear	₩35,910
f.	Triple valve	₩27,930
g.	Bolster Spring (inner & Outer)	₩37,107
h.	Side Frame	₩43,890
i.	Brake Beam	₩16,359
j.	Bolster	₩57,700

6

281

공공용역.

선로하여 예독하고 자수하여 (???) 찾자

경 제 기 획 원

물정331. 24 - 271 (70. 3101) 1974. 9. 19.

수신 외무부장관

제목 전화요금및 도선요금 한미합동위원회 협의요청

미군측에 적용되는 전화요금 및 도선요금을 개정하고자 별첨 공문 사본과 같이 한미행정협정에 의한 협의를 미측 공공용역분과위원장에게 제의하였음을 통보합니다.

첨부 : 한국측 제의공문 사본 2부. 끝.

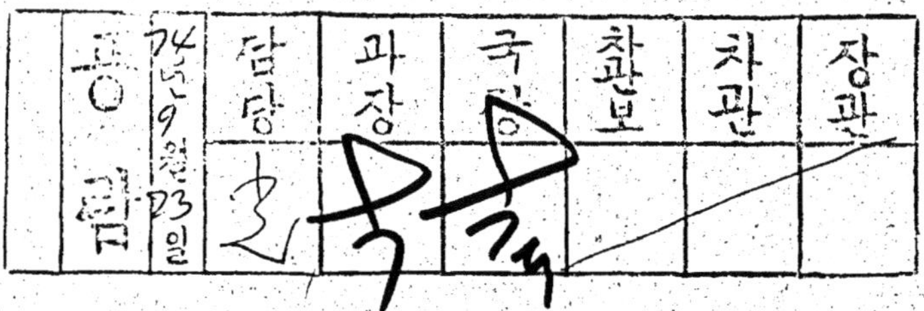

공 람	74년 9월 23일	담당	과장	국장	차관보	차관	장관

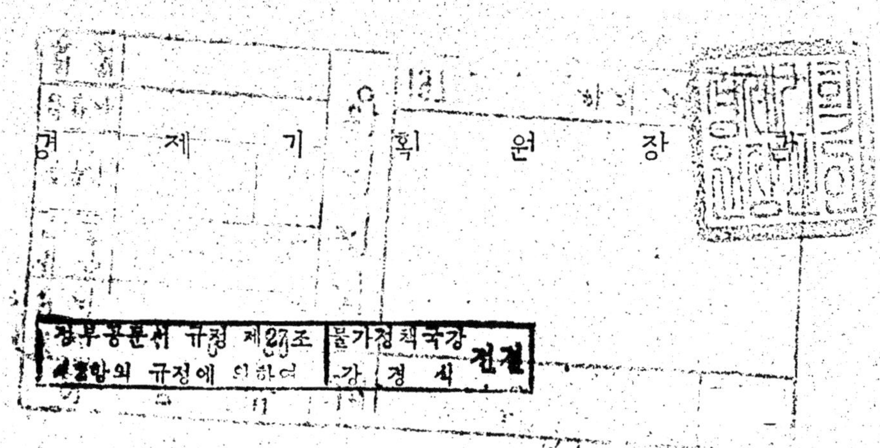

282

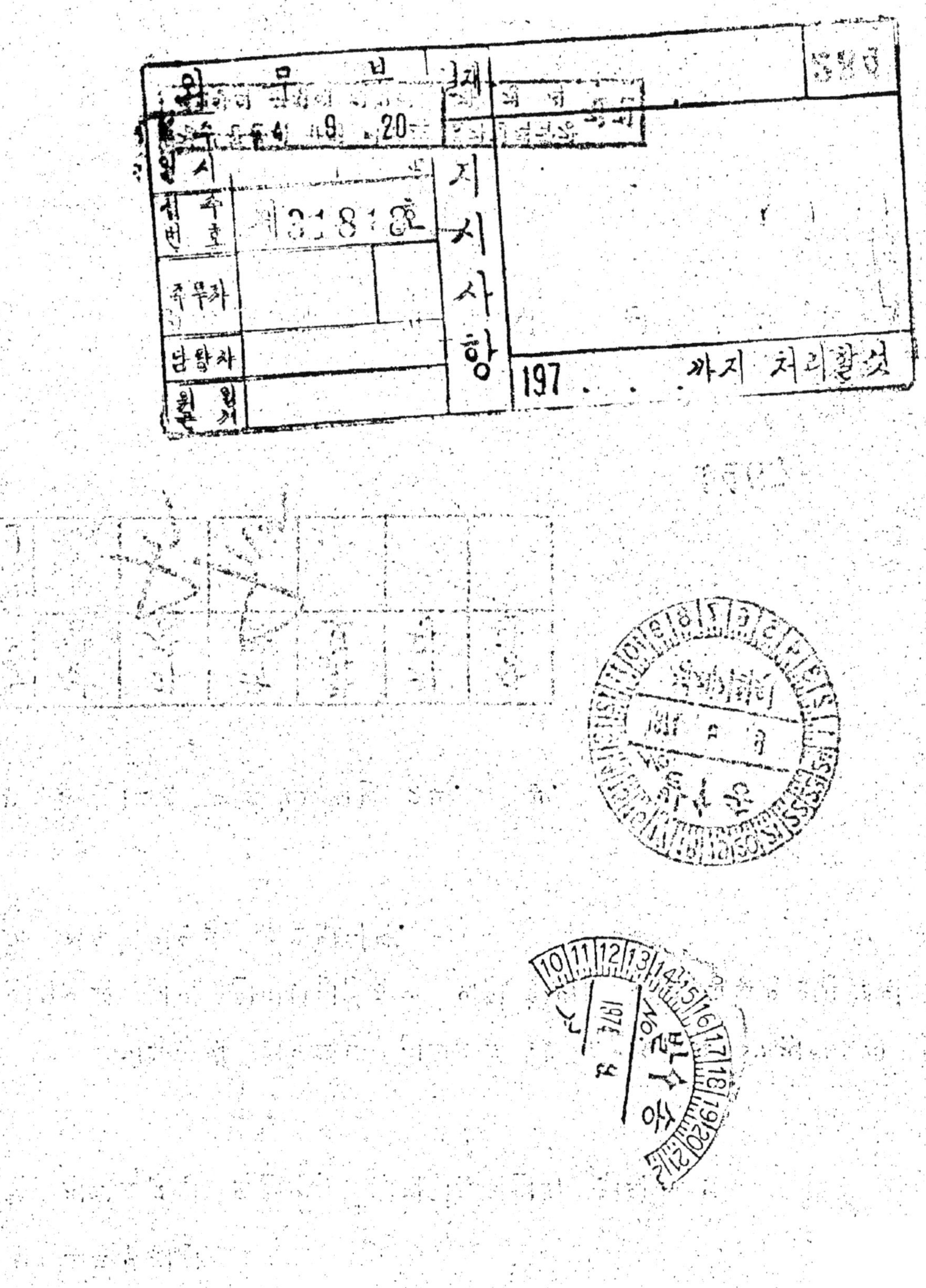

197 . . . 까지 처리할것
지시사항

REPUBLIC OF KOREA - UNITES STATES

UTILITIES SUBCOMMITTEE

Subject : Change in Rates of Communication Service applicable to USFK under Article VI of the Status of Forces Agreement

To : Chairman, US Utilities Subcommittee

1. Reference :

a. Paragraph 2 and Agreed Minute 1 of Article VI of Status of Forces Agreement.

b. US Chairman, Utilities Subcommittee letter dated 19 July 1974.

2. The Government of the United States is informed through this written consultative process that the Republic of Korea proposes to change following rates/tariffs at location indicated below;

RATE/TARIFF	LOCATION
Rates of communication service applicable to USFK	The whole country

3. The following data is provided;

a. Effective date : Remarked effective date at attached rate schedule.
b. Rate schedule showing rate that are charged all classes of user.
"Attached"
c. Rate schedule of proposed change. Refer to item b
d. Reason for revision of rates
- Adjustment of communication charges applicable to military and police lines.
- To cover the increased operation cost.

4. The Government of the ROK advises the Government of the United States that the priorities, conditions and rates being charged are no less favorable than those accorded any other user.

You may be assured that your views will greatly appreciated.

Sincerely yours,

Kyong Shik Kang
Director, Price Policy Bureau
Chairman, Republic of Korea
Utilities Subcommittee

286

283

A. Ordinary Telephone Rental Charges

1.142 Call Rate

1.1421 Basic Monthly Charge per Station

Present Rates	Change Rates	Effective Date
5th Class: ₩3000	1st - 13th: ₩390	January 1, 1974
6th Class: ₩300		
Beyond 7th Class: ₩300		

B. Installation Charges

1.161 Ordinary Telephone per station

Class		Present Rates	Change Rates	Effective Date
1st	Manual	₩9,000	₩9,000	Nov. 1, 1974
	Automatic		₩37,500	
2nd	Manual	₩12,000	₩12,000	
	Automatic		₩37,500	
3rd	Manual	₩12,000	₩12,000	
	Automatic		₩37,500	
4th	Manual	₩15,000	₩15,000	
	Automatic		₩37,500	
5th	Manual	₩21,000	₩21,000	
	Automatic	₩37,500	₩37,500	

284

6th	Manual	₩31,500	₩31,500
	Automatic	₩60,000	₩60,000
7th	Automatic	₩75,000	₩75,000
8th	"	₩90,000	₩90,000
9th	"	₩105,000	₩105,000
10th	"	₩120,000	₩120,000
11th	"	₩135,000	₩135,000
12th	"	₩150,000	₩150,000
13th	"	₩165,000	₩165,000

C. Temporary Main Line Station

Present Rates	Change Rates	Effective Date
₩2.000	1st - 3rd Class: ₩2,000	January 1, 1973
	4th - 5th Class: ₩4,000	
	Beyond 6th Class: ₩6,000	

D. Leased Local Circuits(only military affairs)

1.31 Long term lease, for each 100 meters of circuit, per month

Present Rates	Change Rates	Effective Date
₩30	₩25	June 1, 1973

1.32 Short term lease, per circuit per day

Present rate	Change Rate	Effective Date
₩300	₩250	June 1, 1973

1.331 Installation Charge (Long Term)

	Present Rates	Change Rates	Effective date
Installation of telephone	₩8,000	₩6,000	June 1, 1973
Installation of drop wire	₩8,000	₩6,000	

1.332 Equipment Charge

	Present Rates		Change Rates		Effec.
	Long Term	Short Term	Long Term	Short Term	Date
Retermination of Telephone	₩3,200	₩2,600	₩1,600	₩1,300	June 1, 1973
Additional Charge when telephone pole erection is required	"	"	"	"	
Reterminationa of drop wire or telephone which are installed by user	"	"	"	"	

286

2.0 Leased Long Distance Service

2.11 Lease Charge (per circuits)

(Present Rates)

Distance	Long Term Monthly	Short Term Daily	Per 3 Minutes
10Km	₩ 21,000	₩ 1,000	₩ 20
30	52,000	2,500	50
50	84,000	4,000	80
100	147,000	7,000	140
200	210,000	10,000	200
300	252,000	12,000	240
400	294,000	14,000	280
500	336,000	16,000	320
600	318,000	18,000	360
over 600	420,000	40,000	400

(Changed Rates)

No. of Ckt	1 to 2 Circuits		3 thru 5 Circuits		6 thru 11 Circuits	
	Long T.	Short T.	Long T.	Short T.	Long T.	Short T.
Distance	Monthly	Daily	Monthly	Daily	Monthly	Daily
10KM	15,000	750	13,500	700	12,750	650
30	37,500	11,875	33,750	1,750	31,875	1,625

289

50	60,000	3,000	54,000	2,800	51,000	2,600
100	105,000	5,250	94,000	4,900	89,250	4,550
200	150,000	7,500	135,000	7,000	127,500	6,500
300	180,000	9,000	162,000	8,400	153,000	7,8000
400	210,000	10,500	189,000	9,800	178,500	9,100
500	240,000	12,000	216,000	11,200	204,000	10,400
600	270,000	13,500	243,000	12,6000	229,500	11,700
Over 600	300,000	15,000	270,000	14,000	255,000	13,000

No. of Ckt	12 thru 23 Ckts		24 thru 47 Ckts		Over 48 Ckts		
	Long T.	Short T.	Long T.	Short T.	Long T.	Short T.	
Distance	Monthly	Daily	Monthly	Daily	Monthly	Daily	3 Min.
10KM	12,000	600	11,250	550	10,500	500	20
30	30,000	1,500	28,125	1,375	26,250	1,250	50
50	48,000	2,400	45,000	2,200	42,000	2,000	80
100	84,000	4,200	78,750	3,850	73,500	3,500	140
200	120,000	6,000	112,500	5,500	105,000	5,000	200
300	144,000	7,200	135,000	6,600	126,000	6,000	240
400	168,000	8,400	157,500	7,700	147,000	7,000	280
500	192,000	9,600	180,000	8,800	168,000	8,000	320
600	216,000	10,800	202,500	9,9000	189,000	9,000	360
Over 600	240,000	12,000	225,000	11,000	210,000	10,000	400

* **Effective Date:** June 1, 1973

288

1.14 Ordinary Telephone Rental Charges

1.141 Flat Rate (per month)

Class	Present rate	New rate	Effective date
1st Class	250 won	400 won	Sep. 1, 1974
2nd Class	330 won	500 won	
3rd Class	500 won	750 won	
4th Class	730 won	1,100 won	
th Class	1,250 won	1,900 won	
6th Class	2,000 won	3,000won	
Beyond 7th Class	2,400 won	3,600 won	

1.142 Call rate

1.1422 Call fee per outgoing call

Present rate	New Rate	Effective Date
4 won	6 won	Sep. 1, 1974

289

1.16 Installation charges

1.1611 Ordinary telephone, per station

Class		P. A.	N. A.	Effec. date
1st class	automatic	37,500 won	56,300 won	Sep. 1, 1974
	manual	9,000 won	13,500 won	
2nd calss	automatic	37,500 won	56,300 won	
	manual	12,000 won	18,000 won	
3rd class	automatic	37,500 won	56,300 won	
	manual	12,000 won	18,000 won	
4th class	automatic	37,500 won	5 6,300 won	
	manual	15,000 won	22, 00 won	
5th class	automatic	37,500 won	56,300 won	
	manual	21,000 won	31,500 won	
6th class	automatic	60,000 won	90,000 won	
	manual	31,500 won	47,300 won	
7th class		75,000 won	112,500 won	
8th class		90,000 won	135,000 won	
9th class		105,000 won	157,500 won	
10th class		120,000 won	180,000 won	
11th class		135,000 won	202,500 won	
12th class		150,000 won	225,000 won	
13th class		165,000 won	247,500 won	

* P. A. = Present Amount

N. A. = New Amount

290

2. 1.1. Lease Charges, per circuits

Distance (km)	1 - 2 circuits				3 - 5 circuits				6-11 circuits				Affects date
	Long Term		Short Term		Long Term		Short Term		Long Term		Short Term		
	Monthly charges		Daily charges		Monthly charges		Daily charges		Monthly charges		Daily charges		
	Present charges	New charges	Present charges	New charges	Present charges	New charges	Present charges	New charges	Present charges	New charges	Present charges	New charges	
10	15,000 won	22,500 won	750 won	1,125 won	13,500 won	20,250 won	700 won	1,050 won	12,750 won	19,125 won	650 won	975 won	Sep. 1, 1974
30	37,500 won	60,000 won	1,875 won	3,000 won	33,750 won	54,000 won	1,750 won	2,800 won	31,875 won	51,000 won	1,625 won	2,600 won	
50	60,000 won	90,000 won	3,000 won	4,500 won	54,000 won	81,000 won	2,800 won	4,200 won	51,000 won	76,500 won	2,600 won	3,900 won	
100	105,000 won	157,500 won	5,250 won	7,875 won	74,500 Won	141,750 won	4,900 won	7,350 won	89,250 won	133,875 won	4,550 won	6,825 won	
200	150,000 won	225,000 won	7,500 won	11,250 won	135,000 won	202,500 won	7,000 won	10,500 won	127,500 won	191,250 won	6,500 won	9,750 won	
300	180,000 won	270,000 won	9,000 won	13,500 won	162,000 won	243,000 won	8,400 won	12,600 won	153,999 won	229,500 won	7,800 won	11,700 won	
400	210,000 won	315,000 won	10,500 won	15,750 won	189,000 won	283,500 won	9,800 won	14,700 won	178,500 won	267,750 won	9,100 won	13,650 won	
500	240,000 won	360,000 won	12,000 won	18,000 won	216,000 won	324,000 won	11,200 won	16,800 won	204,000 won	306,000 won	10,400 won	15,600 won	
600	270,000 won	405,000 won	13,500 won	20,250 won	243,000 won	364,500 won	12,600 won	18,900 won	229,500 won	344,250 won	11,700 won	17,550 won	
Beyond 600	300,000 won	450,000 won	15,000 won	22,500 won	270,000 won	405,000 won	14,000 won	21,000 won	255,000 won	382,500 won	13,000 won	19,500 won	

Distance (km)	12-23 circuits				24-47 circuits				Beyond 48 circuits				Time Term		Affect date
	Long Term		Short Term		Long Term		Short Term		Long Term		Short Term		(Every 3-Minutes)		
	Monthly charges		Daily charges		Monthly charges		Daily charges		Monthly charges		Daily charges				
	Present charges	New charges	Present charges	New charges	Present charges	New charges	Present charges	New charges	Present charges	New charges	Present charges	New charges	Present charges	New charges	
	won	won	won	won	won	won	won	won	won	won	won	won	won	won	
10	12,000	18,000	600	900	11,250	16,875	550	825	10,500	15,750	500	750	20	30	Sep. 1, 1974
30	30,000	48,000	1,500	2,400	28,125	45,000	1,375	2,200	26,250	42,000	1,250	2,000	50	80	
50	48,000	72,000	2,400	3,600	45,000	67,500	2,200	3,300	42,000	63,000	2,000	3,000	80	120	
100	84,000	126,000	4,200	6,300	78,750	118,125	3,850	5,775	73,500	110,250	3,500	5,250	140	210	
200	120,000	180,000	6,000	9,000	112,500	168,750	5,500	8,250	105,000	157,500	5,000	7,500	200	300	
300	144,000	216,000	7,200	10,800	135,000	202,500	6,600	9,900	126,000	189,000	6,000	9,000	240	360	
400	168,000	252,000	8,400	12,600	157,500	236,250	7,700	11,550	147,000	220,500	7,000	10,500	280	420	
500	192,000	288,000	9,600	14,400	180,000	270,000	8,800	13,200	168,000	252,000	8,000	12,000	320	480	
600	216,000	324,000	10,800	16,200	202,500	303,750	9,900	14,850	189,000	283,500	9,000	13,500	360	540	
Beyond 600	240,000	360,000	12,000	18,000	225,000	337,500	11,000	16,500	210,000	315,000	10,000	15,000	400	600	

2.2. Long Distance Toll charges (with in Korea)

2.2.1. within the same city, up (a town) or Myon (a division of a country) : per call

Present Rate	New Rate	Affects date
10 won	15 won	Sep. 1, 1974

2. 2. 2. Beyond the same city, up or Myon, per call

Distance (km)	Services by C.L.R. System		Services by delay System						Affects date
			Ordinary		Urgent		Emergency		
	Present Rate	New Rate	Present Rate	New Rate	Present Rate	New Rate	Present Rate	New Rate	
10	10 won	15 won	10 won	15 won	20 won	30 won	30 won	45 won	Sep. 1, 1974
30	30 won	45 won	25 won	40 won	50 won	80 won	75 won	120 won	
50	50 won	75 won	40 won	60 won	80 won	120 won	120 won	180won	
100	100 won	150 won	70 won	105 won	140 won	210 won	210 won	315 won	
200	150 won	225 won	100 won	150 won	200 won	300 won	300 won	450 won	
300	190 won	285 won	120 won	180 won	240 won	360 won	360 won	540 won	
400	230 won	345 won	140 wo n	210 won	280 won	420 won	420 won	630 won	
500	260 won	390 won	160 won	240 won	320 won	480 won	480 won	720 won	
600	290 won	435 won	180 won	270 won	360 won	540 won	540 won	810 won	
Beyond 600	320 won	480 won	200 won	300 won	400 won	600 won	600 won	900 won	

REPUBLIC OF KOREA - UNITED STATES
UTILITIES SUBCOMMITTEE

Subject : Change in rates of ferriage for the vehicles ferry applicable to USFK under Article VI of the Status of Forces Agreement

To : Chairman, US Utilities Subcommittee

1. Reference:
   a. Paragraph 2 and Agreed Minute 1 of Article VI of Status of Forces Agreement

2. The Government of the United States is informed through this written consultative process that the Republic of Korea proposes to change following rates/tariffs at location indicated below;

RATE/TARIFF	LOCATION
Rates of ferriage services applicable to USFK	Kunsan area

3. The following data is provided;
   a. Effective date : 19 September 1974.
   b. Rate schedule showing rates that are charged all classes of user. "Attached"
   c. Rate schedule of proposed change. Refer to item b
   d. Reason for revision of rates
      Increase of maintenance and operation costs.

4. The Government of the ROK advises the Government of the United States that the priorities, conditions and rates being charged are no less favorable than those accorded any other user.

You may be assured that your views will greatly appreciated.

Sincerely yours,

Kyung Shik Kang
Director, Price Policy Bureau
Chairman, Republic of Korea
Utilites Subcommittee

294

Rate Schedule of Ferriage

Unit : Won

No	Name of Vehicle	Present Rates General Vehicle	Present Rates USFK	Change Rates General Vehicle	Change Rates USFK
1	Joop 1/4 Ton	300	230	450	390
2	Truck 3/4 Ton	400	370	670	630
3	Truck 2 1/2 Ton	900	600	1,300	1,100
4	Truck 5 Ton & Over	1,500	900	1,500	1,400
5	" " (Loaded)	1,800	1,500	2,500	2,400
6	Trailer 1/4 Ton	300	150	300	260
7	" 3/4 "	-	200	-	300
8	" 2 "	-	200	-	300
9	" 2 1/2 "	-	200	-	300

Remark : Effective date of Change Rates for general Vehicle is August 1, 1974.

295

의제 4

공공 용역 분과 위원회는 군산 지역 미군 차량 도선 요금 변경에 관한 각서를 합동 위원회에 제출 하였읍니다.

주둔군 지위협정 6조에 규정된 협의를 하였다는 증거로서 공공 용역 분과 위원회의 동 각서를 합동 위원회가 수락할 것을 제의 합니다.

(미 측 동 의)

머피 장군, 동의해 주셔서 감사 합니다.

다음 의제로 넘어 가겠읍니다.

98次 合同委 ('74. 10. 17)

296

AGENDA ITEM IV

The Utilities Subcommittee submitted to the Joint Committee a memorandum concerning a change in utility rates for the ferriage of USFK vehicles in the Kunsan areas.

It is proposed that the memorandum of the Utilities Subcommittee be accepted by this Joint Committee as evidence of consultation contemplated by Article VI of the SOFA.

(US Concurrence)

Thank you, General Murphy, for your concurrence.

Please turn to the next Agenda Item.

(1. FOR YOUR INFORMATION: The ROK Representative will present and request acceptance of one memorandum from the Utilities Subcommittee, concerning a change in utility rates for the ferriage of USFK vehicles in the Kunsan ares.)

(2. FOR YOUR INFORMATION: The US side has carefully reviewed the new rates for this service, and has determined that the change in these rates as applicable to the USFK is no less favorable than rates accorded to other comparable users of this service, as required by paragraph 2 of Article VI of the SOFA. Hence, there is no obstacle to acceptance by the USFK of the new rates.)

3. The United States Representative is happy to concur in the acceptance of the memorandum of the Utilities Subcommittee that you have just presented, involving changes in rates for ferriage service in the Kunsan area. This memorandum evidences the completion of the consultations required under Article VI of the Status of Forces Agreement for this rate change.

REPUBLIC OF KOREA - UNITED STATES
UTILITIES SUBCOMMITTEE

10 October 1974

MEMORANDUM TO: The Joint Committee

SUBJECT: Consultation on Increase in Rates and Charges of Ferriage for Vehicles Ferry Applicable to USFK Under Article VI of the Status of Forces Agreement

1. Subcommittee Members:

Republic of Korea	United States
Mr. Kang Kyong Shik, Chairman	COL F. A. Frech, Chairman
Mr. Min Tai Hyung, Secretary	COL Jack L. McClaran, Alt Chairman
Mr. Sohn Tai Yum, Member	MAJ Earl E. Carr, Secretary
Mr. Lee Sang Kook, Member	LCDR Jerry F. Woolett, Member
Mr. Lee Byong Hae, Member	MAJ Charles Carter, Member
Mr. Lee Sang Hee, Member	Mr. Samuel Pollack, Member
Mr. Kim Chang Yun, Member	MAJ T. M. Willis, Member
Mr. Kim Gi Dug, Member	Mr. Francis K. Cook, Member
Mr. Shin Young Chul, Member	COL Elo Mussetto, Member
Mr. Lew Kwang Suck, Member	

2. Subject of Recommendation: Agreed Minute 1 to Article VI, ROK-US SOFA, provides that any changes determined by the authorities of the Republic of Korea in priorities, conditions, rates or tariffs applicable to the United States Armed Forces shall be the subject of consultation in the Joint Committee prior to their effective date.

3. The Republic of Korea initiated consultation concerning a change in rates of ferriage for the vehicles ferry under Contract DAJB03-73-C-3184, by letter included at Inclosure 1.

4. The United States component of the Utilities Subcommittee has reviewed the ROK requests for consultation and submits at Inclosure 2 an approved schedule of rates of ferriage with an effective date of 19 September 1974.

5. The US and ROK components of the Utilities Subcommittee concur that the approved change in rates as submitted at Inclosure 2 are no less favorable than those accorded any other comparable user.

6. It is recommended that the two inclosures referenced in paragraphs 3 and 4 be accepted by the Joint Committee as evidence of consultation contemplated by Article VI of the Status of Forces Agreement.

2 Incl
as

K. S. Kang
KANG KYONG SHIK
Republic of Korea Chairman
Utilities Subcommittee

Frederic A. Frech
FREDERIC A. FRECH
Colonel, US Army
United States Chairman
Utilities Subcommittee

2

300

REPUBLIC OF KOREA - UNITED STATES
UTILITIES SUBCOMMITTEE

Subject : Change in rates of ferriage for the vehicles ferry applicable to USFK under Article VI of the Status of Forces Agreement

To : Chairman, US Utilities Subcommittee

1. Reference:
   a. Paragraph 2 and Agreed Minute 1 of Article VI of Status of Forces Agreement

2. The Government of the United States is informed through this written consultative process that the Republic of Korea proposes to change following rates/tariffs at location indicated below;

RATE/TARIFF	LOCATION
Rates of ferriage services applicable to USFK	Kunsan area

3. The following data is provided;
   a. Effective date : 19 September 1974.
   b. Rate schedule showing rates that are charged all classes of user. "attached"
   c. Rate schedule of proposed change. Refer to item b
   d. Reason for revision of rates
      Increase of maintenance and operation costs.

4. The Government of the ROK advises the Government of the United States that the priorities, conditions and rates being charged are no less favorable than those accorded any other user.

You may be assured that your views will greatly appreciated.

Sincerely yours,

K. S. Kang

Kyung Shik Kang
Director, Price Policy Bureau
Chairman, Republic of Korea
Utilites Subcommittee

Incl 1

301

RATES OF FERRIAGE

Effective 19 September 1974

Item No.	Description	Price
1	Jeep, 1/4 ton	W390
2	Truck, 3/4 ton	630
3	Truck, 2 1/2 ton	670
4	Truck, 5 ton and over	1,400
5	Truck, 5 ton and over (loaded)	2,150
6	Trailer, 1/4 ton	260
7	Trailer, 3/4 ton	300
8	Trailer, 1 1/2 ton	300
9	Trailer, 2 ton	300

Incl 2

302

Rate Schedule of Ferriage

Unit : Won

No	Name of Vehicle	Present Rates General Vehicle	Present Rates USFK	Change Rates General Vehicle	Change Rates USFK
1	Jeep 1/4 Ton	300	230	450	390
2	Truck 3/4 Ton	400	370	670	630
3	Truck 2 1/2 Ton	900	600	1,300	1,100
4	Truck 5 Ton & Over	1,500	900	1,500	1,400
5	" " (Loaded)	1,800	1,500	2,500	2,100
6	Trailer 1/4 Ton	300	150	300	260
7	" 3/4 "	-	200	-	300
8	" 2 "	-	200	-	300
9	" 2 1/2 "	-	200	-	300

Remark : Effective date of Change Rates for general Vehicle is August 1, 1974.

303

미 주 국

197 4 . 11 . 4 .

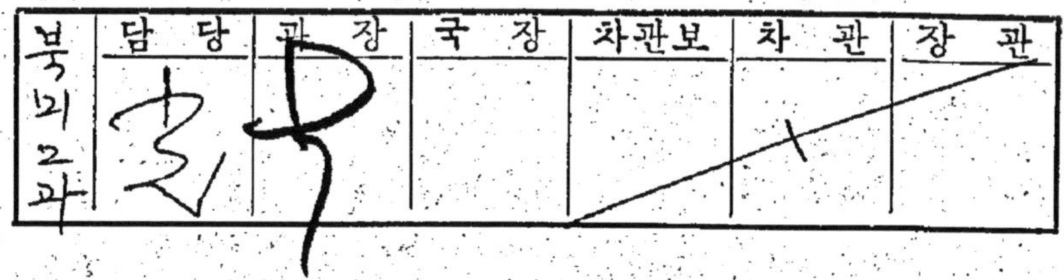

북미2과	담 당	과 장	국 장	차관보	차 관	장 관

제 목 : 공공용역 분과위원회의 미측에 대한 상수도요금 인상 협의요청

요 약

경제기획원은 74.10.30. SOFA 6조의 규정에따라, 원가상승으로 인한 부산및 대구의 상수도요금 인상을 협의할 것을 미측에 요청함.

조치사항

304

간첩잡아 애국하고 유신으로 번영하자

경 제 기 획 원

물정331.24 - 711 (70.3101) 1974. 11. 1.

수신 외무부장관

제목 부산및 대구시 상수도요금 한미합동위원회 협의요청

미군측에 적용되는 부산및 대구시의 상수도요금을 개정하고자 별첨 공문사본과 같이 한미행정협정에 의한 협의를 미측 공공용역분과위원장에게 제의하였음을 통보합니다.

첨부 : 한국측 제의공문 사본 1부. 끝.

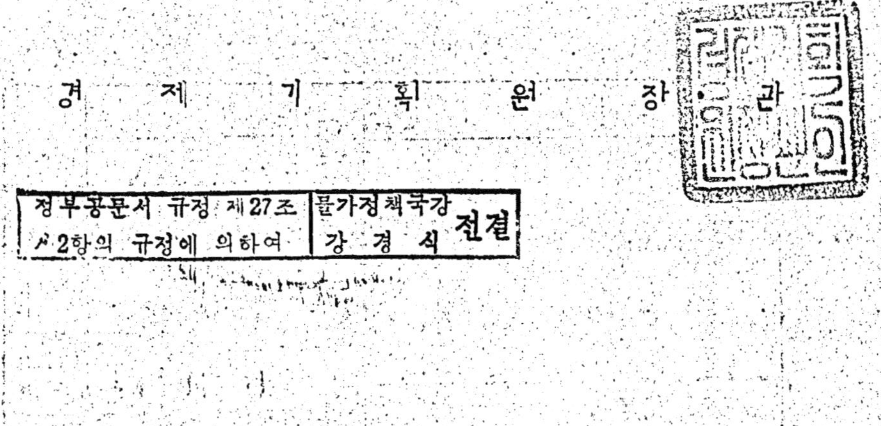
경 제 기 획 원 장 관

정부공문서 규정 제27조 2항의 규정에 의하여	물가정책국장 강경식 전결

121(1)

305

외 무 부		결재	
접수일시	74 11. 1		
접수번호	제 [illegible]		
[illegible]	[illegible]	[illegible]	[illegible]
[illegible]		항	
회문일자			197 . . 까지 처리할것

REPUBLIC OF KOREA - UNITED STATES
UTILITIES SUBCOMMITTEE

October 30, 1974

Subject : Change in Water Supply Rates applicable to the US Armed Forces under Article VI of Status of Forces Agreement
To : US Chairman, Utilities Subcommittee

1. Reference :

Paragraph 2 and Agreed Minute 1 of Article VI of the Status of Forces Agreement.

2. The Government of the United States is informed through this written consultative process that the ROK proposes to change the following rate/tariff at location indicated below;

Rate/Tariff	Location
Water Supply rate schedule applicable to the US Armed Forces	The City of Busan and the City of Daegu

3. The following data is provided

a. Effective date : October 30, 1974.
b. Rate schedule showing rates that are charged all classes of user.
"Attached"
c. Rate schedule of proposed change. Refer to item "b"
d. Calculation of old and new rate base.

Name of City	Description	Old rate(won)	New rate(won)
Busan	Basic rate for first 30 m^3	-	1,000
	Excess charge per m^3	30	35
Daegu	Basic rate for first 30m^3	-	750
	Excess charge per m^3	25	30

e. Reason for revision of rate.

To cover the rising prime cost.

306

4. The Government of ROK advises the Government of the United States that priorities, conditions, and rates or tariffs being charged are no less favorable than those accorded any other user.

You may be assured that your early views will be greatly appreciated.

Sincerely yours,

K. S. Kang

Kyong Shik Kang
Director, Price Policy Bureau
Chairman, Republic of Korea
Utilities Subcommittee

309

경 제 기 획 원

문정 331.24-3317 (70-3101) 1974. 11. 19.

수신 수신처참조

제목 공공용역분과위원회 한.미합동회의 개최 통보 (74年 첫회의)

한미행정협정에 의한 공공용역분과위원회의 한.미 합동회의를 다음과 같이 개최하기로 하였는바 각 위원은 필히 참석하시기 바랍니다.

다 음

1. 회의 개최일시: 1974. 11. 26.(화) 13:30
2. 회의 장소: 미8군 SOFA 회의실(건물번호2370)
3. 회의 순서:
   1) 한.미 각 위원 소개.
   2) 한.미 위원장의 개회사.
   3) 토의 내용: 통신요금, 전력요금, 부산 및 대구시의 상수도 요금.
   4) 차기회의 개최.
   5) 폐회.
4. 한국측 위원
   가. 위원장: 경제기획원 물가정책국장.
   나. 간사: 경제기획원 물가조정과장.
   다. 위원:
      1) 상공부 동력개발국 전력과장.
      2) " 상역국 수출 3과장.
      3) 내무부 지방국 세정과장.
      4) " " 재정과장.
      5) 체신부 전무국 국내업무과장.
      6) 건설부 도시국 상하수도 과장.

308

의심나면 다시보고 수상하면 신고하자

품정 331.24-　　　　　　　　　　　　　　　　　　1974. 11.

7) 외무부 미주국 북미 2과장.

8) 철도청 운수국 화물과장.

첨부: 회의자료 1부. 끝.

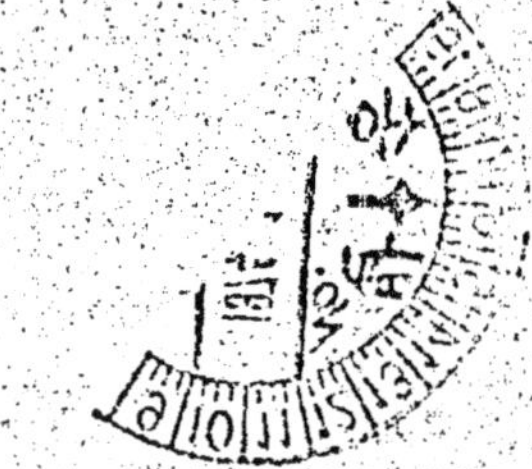

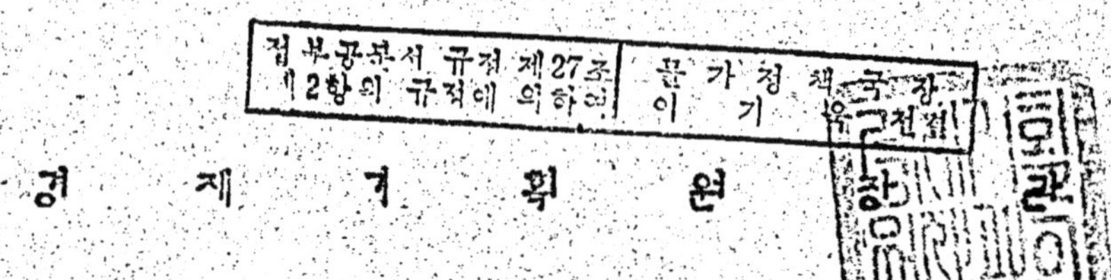

경 제 기 획 원

수신처: 외무부 장관, 내무부 장관, 상공부 장관, 건설부 장관, 체신부 장관, 철도청장.

309

한.미 합동공공용역분과위원회

회의자료

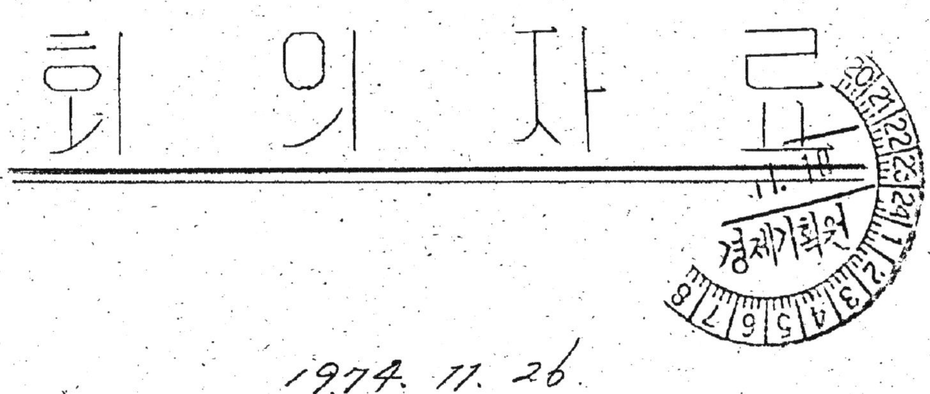

1974. 11. 26

경제기획원
물가정책국

310

一、회 의 일 정

1. 회의개최일시 ; 1974. 11. 26 (화) 13:30

2. 회의장소 ; 미8군 SOFA 회의실 (Bldg 2370).

3. 회의순서 ;

1) 한·미 각위원 소개

2) 한·미 위원장의 개회사

3) 토의 내용 ; 통신요금, 전력요금, 부산 및 대구시 상수도요금.

4) 차기회의 계획

5) 폐회

(1)

311

二 한국측 공공용역분과위원

Utilities Subcommittee-ROK Component

순번	직 명	성 명	위 원 직 명	전화번호
1	위원장 (chairman)	이 기 욱 (Lee Kie Wook)	경제기획원 물가정책국장 (Director, Bureau of price policy Economic planning Board)	70-3020
2	간 사 (Secretary)	민 태 형 (Min Tai Hyung)	경제기획원 물가정책국 물가조정과장 (chief, price control Division price policy Bureau, E.P.B)	70-3101
3	위 원 (Member)	유 광 석 (Lew Kwang Suck)	외무부 미주국 북미2과 (North America Section Ⅱ. Bureau of American Affairs. Ministry of Foreig Affairs)	70-2324

312

4	〃	이 상 희 (Lee Sang Hee)	내무부 지방국 재정과장 (Chief, Finance Section Bureau of Local Administration Ministry of Home Affairs)	70-2482
5	〃	이 병 내 (Lee Byong Nae)	내무부 지방국 세정과장 (Chief, Tax Administration Section Bureau of Local Administration Ministry of Home Affairs)	70-2479
6	〃	손 태 엽 (Sohn Tai Yum)	상공부 동력개발국 전력과장 (Chief, Electric Administration Section Bureau of Power Development Ministry of Commerce and Industry)	70-3526

(3)

317

(4)

순번	직 명	성 명	위 원 직 명	전화번호
7	위 원 (member)	이 상 국 (Lee Sang Kook)	상공부 상역국 수출3과장 (Chief, Export Division III Bureau of Trade Ministry of Commerce and Industry)	70-3511
8	〃	신 영 철 (Shin Young chul)	건설부 주택도시국 상하수도과장 (Chief, Water and Sewage Works Section Bureau of Housing and Municipal Engineering, Ministry of Construction	70-4029

314

9	〃	양 한 모 (Yang Han Mo)	체신부 전무국 국내업무과장 (Chief, Home Affairs Section I Bureau of Tele-Communications Ministry of Communication)	70-2229
10	〃	김 기 덕 (Kim Ki Duk)	철도청 운수국 화물과장 (Chief, Freight Section Bureau of Transportation Office of Korean National Railroads)	23-5741

(6)

三. 협의 내용

1. 통신요금 조정

1) 전화기본료

(단위 : 원)

현 행		개 정 요 구		시 행 일
구 분	요 금	구 분	요 금	
5 급 지	300	1~13 급지	390	74. 1. 1
6 급 지	300			
7급지 이상	300			

2) 설 비 비

(단위 : 원)

구 분		현 행	개 정 요 구			
급지	방 식 별	요 금	1차 변경	시 행 일	2차 변경	시 행 일
1급	공전및자석식	9,000	9,000	73.11.1	13,500	74.9.1
	자 동 식		37,500		56,300	
2급	공전및자석식	12,000	12,000		18,000	
	자 동 식		37,500		56,300	

316

3급	공전및자석식	12,000	12,000		18,000	
	자 동 식		37,500		56,300	
4급	공전및자석식	15,000	15,000		22,500	
	자 동 식		37,500		56,300	
5급	공전및자석식	21,000	21,000		31,500	
	자 동 식	37,500	37,500		56,300	
6급	공전및자석식	31,500	31,500		47,300	
	자 동 식	60,000	60,000		90,000	
7급	자 동 식	75,000	75,000		112,500	
8급	"	90,000	90,000		135,000	
9급	"	105,000	105,000		157,500	
10급	"	120,000	120,000		180,000	
11급	"	135,000	135,000		202,500	
12급	"	150,000	150,000		225,000	
13급	"	165,000	165,000		247,500	

(7)

317

3) 전화사용료

가. 정액요금 (월액)

(단위 : 원)

급 지	현 행	개 정 요 구	
	요 금	요 금	시행일
1 급 지	250	400	74. 9. 1
2 〃	330	500	
3 〃	500	750	
4 〃	730	1,100	
5 〃	1,250	1,900	
6 〃	2,000	3,000	
7 급이상	2,400	3,600	

318

나 도수료

단위 : 원

구 분	현행	개정요구	
	요금	요금	시행일
1도수마다	4	6	74. 9. 1

다 임시가입전화(월액)

단위 : 원

구 분	현행	개정요구	
	요금	요금	시행일
1~3급지	2,000	2,000	73. 1. 1
4~5 〃		4,000	
6급지 이상		6,000	

(9)

319

(4) 전용료(군사 및 치안기관에 한함)

가. 시내전용회선

(단위; 원)

구분	현행	개정요구	
	요금	요금	실시일자
장기전용	30	25	73. 6. 1
단기전용	300	250	〃

나. 설비비(장기전용에 한함)

구분	현행	개정요구	
	요금	요금	실시일자
전화기설치	8,000	6,000	73. 6. 1
인입선의 설치	8,000	6,000	

다. 장치비

구분	현행		개정요구		
	장기	단기	장기	단기	실시일자
전화기설치장소변경	3,200	2,600	1,600	1,300	73. 6. 1
전주를 요할 때 가산액	3,200	2,600	1,600	1,300	
인입선의 설치장소변경	3,200	2,600	1,600	1,300	

3

320

라. 시외전용료

거리	현행 (1회선마다)			가정요구 1~2회선				3~5회선				6~11회선				12~23회선				24~47회선				48회선 이상			
	장기 (월액)	단기 (1월액)	시간 (매3분마다)	장기 1次	장기 2次	단기 1次	단기 2次	장기 1次	장기 2次	단기 1次	단기 2次	장기 1次	장기 2次	단기 1次	단기 2次	장기 1次	장기 2次	단기 1次	단기 2次	장기 1次	장기 2次	단기 1次	단기 2次	장기 1次	장기 2次	단기 1次	단기 2次
10Km	21.000	1.000	20	15.000	22.500	750	1.125	13.500	20.250	700	1.050	12.750	19.125	650	975	12.000	18.000	600	900	11.250	16.875	550	825	10.500	15.750	500	750
30"	52.000	2.500	50	37.500	60.000	1.875	3.000	33.750	54.000	1.750	2.800	31.875	51.000	1.625	2.600	30.000	48.000	1.500	2.400	28.125	45.000	1.375	2.200	26.250	42.000	1.250	2.000
50"	84.000	4.000	80	60.000	90.000	3.000	4.500	54.000	81.000	2.800	4.200	51.000	76.500	2.600	3.900	48.000	72.000	2.400	3.600	45.000	67.500	2.200	3.300	42.000	63.000	2.000	3.000
100"	147.000	7.000	140	105.000	157.500	5.250	7.875	94.500	141.750	4.900	7.350	89.250	133.875	4.550	6.825	84.000	126.000	4.200	6.300	78.750	118.125	3.850	5.775	73.500	110.250	3.500	5.250
200"	210.000	10.000	200	150.000	225.000	7.500	11.250	135.000	202.500	7.000	10.500	127.500	191.250	6.500	9.750	120.000	180.000	6.000	9.000	112.500	168.750	5.500	8.250	105.000	157.500	5.000	7.500
300"	252.000	12.000	240	180.000	270.000	9.000	13.500	162.000	243.000	8.400	12.600	153.000	229.500	7.800	11.700	144.000	216.000	7.200	10.800	135.000	202.500	6.600	9.900	126.000	189.000	6.000	9.000
400"	294.000	14.000	280	210.000	315.000	10.500	15.750	189.000	283.500	9.800	14.700	178.500	267.750	9.100	13.650	168.000	252.000	8.400	12.600	157.500	236.250	7.700	11.550	147.000	220.500	7.000	10.500
500"	336.000	16.000	320	240.000	360.000	12.000	18.000	216.000	324.000	11.200	16.800	204.000	306.000	10.400	15.600	192.000	288.000	9.600	14.400	180.000	270.000	8.800	13.200	168.000	252.000	8.000	12.000
600"	378.000	18.000	360	270.000	405.000	13.500	20.250	243.000	364.500	12.600	18.900	229.500	344.250	11.700	17.550	216.000	324.000	10.800	16.200	202.500	303.750	9.900	14.850	189.000	283.500	9.000	13.500
600이상	420.000	40.000	400	300.000	450.000	15.000	22.500	270.000	405.000	14.000	21.000	255.000	382.500	13.000	19.500	240.000	360.000	12.000	18.000	225.000	337.500	11.000	16.500	210.000	315.000	10.000	15.000

(11)

321

가 정 요 우																									비 고
1~2회선			3~5회선				6~11회선				12~23회선				24~47회선				48회선 이상				시간 (매3분마다)		
기	단기		장기		단기		장기		단기		장기		단기		장기		단기		장기		단기				
2次	1次	2次	1次	2次	1次	2次	1次	2次	1次	2次	1次	2次	1次	2次	1次	2次	1次	2次	1次	2次	1次	2次	1次	2次	
22.500	750	1.125	13.500	20.250	700	1.050	12.750	19.125	650	975	12.000	18.000	600	900	11.250	16.875	550	825	10.500	15.750	500	750	20	30	1차개정시행 ;
60.000	1.875	3.000	33.750	54.000	1.750	2.800	31.875	51.000	1.625	2.600	30.000	48.000	1.500	2.400	28.125	45.000	1.375	2.200	26.250	42.000	1.250	2.000	50	80	73. 6. 1
90.000	3.000	4.500	54.000	81.000	2.800	4.200	51.000	76.500	2.600	3.900	48.000	72.000	2.400	3.600	45.000	67.500	2.200	3.300	42.000	63.000	2.000	3.000	80	120	2차개정시행 ; 74. 9. 1
157.500	5.250	7.875	94.500	141.750	4.900	7.350	89.250	133.875	4.550	6.825	84.000	126.000	4.200	6.300	78.750	118.125	3.850	5.775	73.500	110.250	3.500	5.250	140	210	
225.000	7.500	11.250	135.000	202.500	7.000	10.500	127.500	191.250	6.500	9.750	120.000	180.000	6.000	9.000	112.500	168.750	5.500	8.250	105.000	157.500	5.000	7.500	200	300	
270.000	9.000	13.500	162.000	243.000	8.400	12.600	153.000	229.500	7.800	11.700	144.000	216.000	7.200	10.800	135.000	202.500	6.600	9.900	126.000	189.000	6.000	9.000	240	360	
315.000	10.500	15.750	189.000	283.500	9.800	14.700	178.500	267.750	9.100	13.650	168.000	252.000	8.400	12.600	157.500	236.250	7.700	11.550	147.000	220.500	7.000	10.500	280	420	
360.000	12.000	18.000	216.000	324.000	11.200	16.800	204.000	306.000	10.400	15.600	192.000	288.000	9.600	14.400	180.000	270.000	8.800	13.200	168.000	252.000	8.000	12.000	320	480	
405.000	13.500	20.250	243.000	364.500	12.600	18.900	229.500	344.250	11.700	17.550	216.000	324.000	10.800	16.200	202.500	303.750	9.900	14.850	189.000	283.500	9.000	13.500	360	540	
450.000	15.000	22.500	270.000	405.000	14.000	21.000	255.000	382.500	13.000	19.500	240.000	360.000	12.000	18.000	225.000	337.500	11.000	16.500	210.000	315.000	10.000	15.000	400	600	

(11)

5) 시외통화료

가. 동일 시읍면 내 (1통화)

(단위 : 원)

현행	개정요구	시행일
10	15	74. 9. 1

나. 동일 시읍면 외 (1통화)

(단위 : 원)

거리	현행		개정요구		시행일
	수동즉시통화	대시통화	수동즉시	대시통화	
10 Km	10	10	15	15	74. 9. 1
30 〃	30	25	45	40	
50 〃	50	40	75	60	
100 〃	100	70	150	105	
200 〃	150	100	225	150	
300 〃	190	120	285	180	
400 〃	240	140	345	210	
500 〃	260	160	390	240	
600 〃	290	180	435	270	
600 〃 이상	320	200	480	300	

(13)

322

6) 통신요금의 예상문제점

미측 주장 가능	한국측 의견
효력발생일 이후 협의 제의하여 합의가 이루어 진 경우 협의 제의일 부터 효력이 발생하게 된다는 제47차 회의 의사록 3항에 따라 통신요금의 적용시기를 협의제의일로 할 것을 주장	1. 요금조정후 빠른시일내 SOFA 제의를 못한것은 전적으로 체신부 실무진의 잘못임을 시과한다 2. 대한민국 체신부와 미육군성 간의 "전기통신시설 사용약정서" (약정서번호 DAJB03-69-D-0154)

326-1.E

329

구 분	실시일	체신부 요구	당원 SOFA 제의일
기본료	74. 1. 1	74. 7. 29	74. 9. 19
설비비	1차: 73. 11. 1 2차: 74. 9. 1	74. 7. 29 74. 9. 12	〃
청약료	74. 9. 1	74. 9. 12	〃
수도료	74. 9. 1	〃	〃
임시가입료	73. 1. 1	74. 7. 29	〃
군사 및 처한 기관 전용료	73. 6. 1	74. 7. 29	〃
시외전용료	1차: 73. 6. 1 2차: 74. 9. 1	74. 7. 29 74. 9. 12	〃 〃
시외통화료	74. 9. 1	〃	〃

제16조에 체신부는 개정요금표를 계약관에게 통보하고 SOFA 협의완료로 미족은 개정 발효일에 소급하여 그 개정된 요금을 지불한다는 조문에 따라 SOFA 협의가 지연되었어도 적용시기에는 문제가 없으며

3 체신부는 SOFA 협의가 지연되었어도 개정된 요금표에 의거 요금을 받고 있음

(25)

329

(16)

2. 전력요금조정

1) 협의제의 내용

종류	구분	개정전 요금	한국측제의(안) 요금	한국측제의(안) 상승율	미군요구(안) 요금	미군요구(안) 상승율
가 일반전력 (乙)	수용요금				(산업용소동력)	
	50KW 까지	184.00	240.00	30.4%	좌 동	%
	450 "	146.00	190.00	30.1		
	500 "	109.00	142.00	30.3		
	전력량요금					
	처음 90시간	9.42	12.24	30.0	12.24	30.0
	다음 90 "	6.50		89.8	8.45	30.0
	" 180 "	4.68		163.7	6.09	30.1
	360시간 초과	3.16		290.5	4.11	30.1
나 특고압 전력 A	수용요금				(산업용대동력A)	
	처음 500KW	152.00	198.00	30.3	좌 동	
	500KW 초과	101.00	132.00	30.7		
	전력량요금					
	처음 90시간	9.42	12.24	30.0	12.24	30.0
	다음 90 "	6.18		99.7	8.05	30.3
	" 180 "	4.30		187.0	5.59	30.0
	360시간 초과	2.21		355.0	3.53	30.3

0078

325

(참고)

요금구조 변경내용 (73.12.1)

종별		변경전	변경후
일반전력 갑		1. 주택용 수용 2. 4KW 미만의 기타 수용 3. 전압: 저압(100, 200, 380V)	전과 동
일반전력 을		1. 4KW 이상 수용 2. 전압: 제한없음	1. 비산업용의 4KW이상 수용 2. 전압: 제한없음 3. 산업용은 신요율 산업용 소동력으로 분류
특고압	A	전압 20KV급 이상으로서 계약전력 500KW 이상수용	제조용은 산업용으로 비산업용은 일반전력 을로 각각 분류
	B	전압 154KV급 이상으로서 계약전력 1,000KW 이상수용	〃

(17)

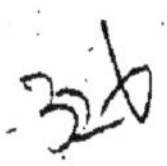

종	별	변 경 전	변 경 후
산 업 용			변경전 일반전력 을 및 특고압중에서 별도 산업분류표에 정한 업종에 해당하는 4KW 이상 수용
	소동력		계약전력에 관계없이 전압 20KV급 미만의 수용
	대동력 A		전압 20KV급 이상으로서 계약전력 500KW 이상수용
	〃 B		전압 154KV급 이상으로서 계약전력 1,000KW 이상 수용

0301

2). 금회 협의 경위

가. 전력요금 구조개선 및 요금인상

- 73.12.1. 전력량 기준에서 용도별 기준으로 요금구조를 전환함

- 산업용 전력은 산업분류에 기재된 산업군에 한정하고 비산업사용자는 일반전력(乙)을 적용.

- 74.2.1 요금구조 변경당시 요금에 일률적으로 30% 인상.

나. 미측에 SOFA 제의

- 요금구조 개선에 따른 협의요청을 74년 1월 23일 상공부로부터 접수, 요금인상분 2월12일 접수하여 74.2.13일 요금인상내용으로 함께 제의

(19)

338

현 행	변 경	비 고
특고압 (A)(B)의 적용을 받되 수출산업에 준하여 200KW 이하의 경우 30% 할인을 하여줌.	용도별 기준으로 바뀜에 따라 종전의 특고압전력 사용처도 개정후 일반전력(乙)을 적용함으로 미군도 일반전력(乙)의 요금을 적용함.	관공서, 미대사관, 한국군도 현재 일반전력(乙) 적용.

329

다. 미측의 이의 제기

(1) 한미행정협정 제6조 2항의 해석상 "어느 타 이용자보다 불리하지 아니한 요율" (no less favorable than those accorded any other user)은 "어느 다른 모든 이용자보다 불리하지 아니한 요율" (no less favorable than those accorded to any other generally comparable user)로 해석되므로 산업용의 적용을 받는 것이 타당하다.

(2) 합리적인 요금계산을 할 수 있도록 Demand Meter기를 설치하여 줄 것

(21)

330

라. 한국측의 견해 회신

(1) 신요금구조에서 산업용 요율은 산업분류기준상에 포함되는 산업용에 한하여 적용을 받는다.

(2) 과거에 특고압 요율을 적용받던 한국군, 한국정부기관, 미국정부기관도 신요금구조에서 일반전력(을)의 적용을 받으며 어느 타 이용자보다 불리한 것이 아니다.

(3) 전기공급규정상 *Demand meter*기 부설은 부설이 유리하다고 판단되면 수용가의 부담으로 설치할 수 있다.

마. 한전측의 견해.

(1) 한미행정협정 제6조 2항의 해석은 동일 대상 수용범위내에서 불리하지 아니한 조건을 보장하

331

는 것이므로 일반전력(을)의 요금 적용이 타당함(한국정부 견해와 동)

(2) 67. 11. 1. 전기요금 인상시에도 미측에서 수출산업(200kW 이하 수용에 대하여 30% 할인) 및 상수도요금의 할인(46.7%)에 준한 할인 혜택 부여를 주장을 하였으나 한국측은 공급 여건 및 사용목적이 다르다는 이유로 반대하여 합의를 못보다가 69. 4. 22 한·미 합동 공공용역 분과위원회에서 한국측의 수출산업에 준한(200kW 이하 수용에 대하여 30% 할인) 할인혜택만을 부여하겠다는 제안에 대하여 미측이 동의하여 현재에 이르고 있음.

(3) 그러나 200kW 초과수용에 대하여 특고압(A)(B)

(23)

777

의 적용을 동의한 것은 한국내에 있어서 공급 조건 및 사용목적이 동일한 수용의 요율적용을 실질적으로 인정한 것임.

(4) 당시 더 유리한 요금(상수도용, 농사용)이 있었음에도 불구하고 미측이 한국측 제안을 수락한 예로 보아 공급여건 및 사용목적에 관계치 않고 산업용 요금 혜택 부여 주장은 타당치 않음.

(5) 협의가 안되는 경우 종래와 같이 200kW 이하의 수용은 30% 할인제를 양보할 수 있음.

바. 당원의견

(1) 한미행정협정 제6조제2항의 "어느 타 이용자보다 불리하지 아니한 요율" (no less

3337

favorable than those accorded any other user)에 대한 해석을 미측은 "어느 다른 모든 이용자 보다 불리하지 아니한 요율" (no less favorable than those accorded to any other generally comparable user)로 해석하여 모든 요금을 전 요금표중 제일 싼 요금이 타당하다고 주장하고 한국측은 "동일 대상 범위의 어느 다른 이용자 보다 불리하지 아니한 요율"(no less favorable than those accorded any other comparable user)로 해석하여 한국정부기관이나 한국군에 적용되는 요율이 미군측에도 적용되어야 한다고 주장하여

(25)

334

현재까지 이 조문 해석의 문제가 타결되지 않고 있음.

(2) 한미행정협정 제6조제2항의 조문 해석에 대한 견해차가 선행되지 않는 한 전력요금의 타결은 어려울 것임.

(3) 미국정부가 타국정부간에 체결된 공공요금 적용에 관한 조문예로 보더라도 미군측이 주장하고 있는 견해는 한국측에 불리한 해석으로 판단됨.

335

(참고자료 1)

미군수용현황및요금비교표

가. 미군수용현황

200KW 이하	56 개소	3,221 KW	(30% 할인대상)
200-500이하미만	19 개소	6,019 "	(")
500 " 이상	21 개소	56,839 "	(")
계	96 개소	66,079 "	(")

나. 요금비교

(단위; 1,000원)

월별	판매량 (M.W.H)	실수금액 73.12.1	한국측주장 (일"월"적용)	미측주장 (산업용적용)	차액
74.1	24.244	149.776	230.655	149.776	80.879
2	23.241	146.898	242.382	168.933	73.449
3	20.204	134.777	268.206	175.210	92.996
4	22.612	149.627	297.758	194.515	103.243
5	20.967	138.988	276.586	180.684	95.902
6	22.356	145.273	289.093	188.854	100.239
7	23.068	147.995	294.510	192.394	102.116
計	156.692	1.013.334	1.899.190	1.250.366	648.824

(주) ; 미측주장대로 한다면 월 약 1 억원의 손해를 보게됨.

(27)

336

(참고자료 2)

주둔미군과 타외국간에 체결된 공공요금 적용에 대한 조문대비

국 명	영 문	국 문
Korea	Any other user	어떠한 타이용자보다 불리하지 아니한 요금
Japan	The Ministries and agencies of the Government of Japan	일본정부기관 및 부속기관에 적용하는 것보다 불리하지 아니한 요금
Philippines	The military forces of the philippines.	필리핀 군대에 적용하는 것보다 불리하지 아니한 요금
Australia	Other users in like	별도 협의가 없는 한

361

	circumstances unless otherwise agreed.	동일한 상태에 있는 타사용자보다 불리하지 아니한 요금
Dominican Republic	Under such terms and conditions as shall be mutually agreed upon by the two Govts.	양국간에 상호 협의된 조건으로 사용
West Indies	Those available to other user unless Otherwise agreed	별도 협의가 없는한 타 사용자보다 불리하지 아니한 조건으로 사용

(29)

338

국명	영문	국문
Ethiopia	At the most favorable rates obtained by other public users who employ and use such facilities	동일한 시설사용을 하는 타 공중 사용자에 적용하는 가장 유리한 요율로 지불
Germany	Accorded to the German Armed Forces	독일군대에 부여하는 것보다 불리하지 아니한 요금

339

3. 부산 및 대구시 상수도요금개정

1) 부산시

(단위: 원)

	현행				개정요구				비고
	기본요금		초과요금		기본요금		초과요금		
	수량	금액	수량	금액	수량	금액	수량	금액	
가정1종	10톤	156	톤	26	15톤	330	16~30톤	30	
가정2종	20	480	21~50	36			31~50	35	
			51이상	60			51이상	45	
영업1종	20	720	톤	42	30	1,500	31~50	90	
							51~100	120	
							101이상	160	
영업2종	30	1,440	31~100	75	20	800	21~50	50	
			101이상	150			51~100	60	
							101이상	80	
욕탕1종	500	12,500	톤	35	500	40,000	501~700	200	
							701~1,000	250	
							1,001이상	300	
욕탕2종	500	38,000	501~1,000	200	500	15,000	501~700	40	
			1,001이상	300			701~1,000	50	
							1,001이상	60	
공업용	200	5,000	톤	32	200	6,000	톤	40	
공공용			〃	30	30	1,000	〃	35	미군에적용
철도용							〃	40	
업무용			톤		30	1,000	〃	40	
선박용			〃	50			〃	60	
전용공업			〃	30			〃	6	
임시용			〃	63			〃	70	
공사설공용			〃	13			〃	15	
소화용			1회10분	345			1회10분	500	

(31)

340

2) 대구시

(단위; 원)

	현행				개정요구				비고
	기본요금		초과요금		기본요금		초과요금		
	수량	금액	수량	금액	수량	금액	수량	금액	
가정용	10톤	200	11~30톤	30	15톤	360	16~30톤	40	
			31-50	40			31~50	50	
			51~100	50			51이상	70	
			101이상	60					
영업1종	10	320	11~50톤	45	30	1,350	31~50	60	
			51~100	80			51~100	100	
			101이상	100			101이상	130	
영업2종	10	320	11~50	45	20	800	21~50	55	
			51이상	50			51~100	70	
							101이상	80	
욕탕1종	100	3,000	101~300	35	500	30.000	501~700	120	
			301-500	65			701~1,000	140	
			501~1,000	100			1,001이상	240	
			1,001~1,500	150					
			1,501이상	230					
욕탕2종	100	2,000	101~1,000	30	500	15,000	501~700	35	
			1,001이상	40			701~1,000	40	
							1,001이상	55	
공업용	100	1,800	101~1,000	23	200	4,800	201이상	30	
			1,000이상	25					
공공용			톤	25	30	750	31이상	30	미군에 적용
업무용					30	780	31 〃	35	
임시용							톤	200	
시설공용	10	170	톤	25	15	300	16이상	30	
공설공용	100	1,400	톤	22	100	1,600	101이상	25	
소화용			1회1전	200			1회1전	300	

341

3) 상수도 요금의 예상되는 문제점

시 별	미측 주장 가능		한국측의 의견
부산시	공업용이 관공용보다 비싸므로 이의 없을 것임		
	관공용 (요구)	기본 : 30m³ 1,000 (33.33) 초과 : m³ ~ 35	현행 요금도 관공서용 요금적용으로 합의 된것임
	공업용	기본 : 200m³ 6,000 (30-) 초과 : m³ ~ 40	

(35)

342

<table>
<tr><th>시 별</th><th>미측 주장 가능</th><th>한국측의 의견</th></tr>
<tr><td>대구시</td><td>공업용이 관공서용보다 싼결과가 되므로 공업요금을 주장할 가능성이 있음

<table><tr><td>관공용 (요 구)</td><td>기본: 30m³~750
초과: m³~30</td></tr><tr><td>공업용</td><td>기본: 200m³~4,800
초과: m³~30</td></tr></table></td><td>1) 미군은 여타 한국정부 한국군과 같은 성격의 공공기관이므로 비교할수 있는 타사용자와 같은 요율적용은 타당함.
2) 전시(全市)의 요금구조를 통일하였으므로 대구시에 공업용수 요율을 적용하겠다면 부산시도 공업용수 요율을 적용하여야 할것임.</td></tr>
</table>

34

347

4) 과거상수도 요금 협의 경위

시 별	한국측제의			미측적용요율			비 고
	협의요청일	적용대상	요 금	협의완료	적용대상	요 금	
인천시	72.2.16	한국군.공업용	기본 100 m^3 ~3,300 초과 m^3 ~35	73.5.24 (84차)	한국군.공업용	기본 100 m^3 ~3,300 초과 m^3 ~35	원안의결 : 원가계산상 환율차손과 대손상각의 계산에 대한 의견이 있었음
춘천시	72.8.1	병영	기본 30 m^3 ~600 초과 m^3 ~30	73.5.24 (84차)	공공용	기본 20 m^3 ~450 초과 m^3 ~30	수정의결 : 미측은 기본요금은 관공서용을 주장하고 초과요금은 관공서용이 m^3당 36인데 비하여 16원 주장하였으나 기본요금은 관공서용으로 초과요금은 병영용으로 합의 함.
대전시	71.9.27	특수용	기본 30 m^3 ~700 초과 m^3 ~40	72.3.28 (72차)	특수용	기본 30 m^3 ~700 초과 m^3 ~40	원안의결 :
부산시	72.9.11	관공서용	m^3 ~30	73.5.24 (84차)	관공서용	m^3 ~30	원안의결 :
서울시	72.2.17	특수용(관공서)	m^3 ~20	72.5.31 (74차)	특수용	m^3 ~20	원안의결 :

(37)

344

시 별	한국측 제의			미측 적용요율			비 고
	협의요청일	적용대상	요 금	협의완료	적용대상	요 금	
군산시	72.10.27	유엔군용	m^3 ~27	73.5.24 (84차)	유엔군용	m^3 ~27	원안의결 :
전북 농지 개량 조합	72.5.27		71 : 24^{50}/1,000 개론 72 : 33^{90}/1,000 개론	〃		71 : 18^{35}/ 1,000 72 : 20^{24}/ 1,000	수정의결 : 73.3.27 자 한미합동공공용역 분과위원회에서 군산비행장의 원수사용요율은 향후 정부추곡수매가격 인상율을 자동적으로 적용토록하고 SOFA 협의를 거치지 않기로 협의
대구시	72.9.11	군 용	m^3 ~35 (현행 25)	73.12.21 (현행대로 두기로 합의)	공업용	기본료 : m^3 100 ~1,800 초 과 : 101-1,000 ~23 1,001이상 ~25	미측의 주장 : (1) 71.4.22 제61차 합동위원회에서 공업요율과 동일요율을 적용토록한 선례가 있음 (2) 한미행정협정 제6조 제2항의 어느 타 이용자보다 불리하지 않아야 한다 (— no less faborable than those accorded any other user)는 조문해석을 모든 어떤 타사용자 (any other generally comparable user)로 해석하여 제일 싼요금인 공업용수요금 적용을 주장 함. (3) 장기간 합의가 이루어지지 않으므로 73.12.21 미측 주장대로 공업용수요율 톤당 25원을 적용한다는데 합의하여 요율인상이 보류됨

(39)

345

참 고 자 료

(41)

376

一. 공공용역 분과위원회 운영요강

1. 법적근거

ㅇ 한미행정협정 제6조 및 제6조에 대한 합의의사록
(발효 66. 7. 8)

2. 협의 절차.

ㅇ 공공용역분과위원회 운영절차(68. 3. 14 제22차 회의)

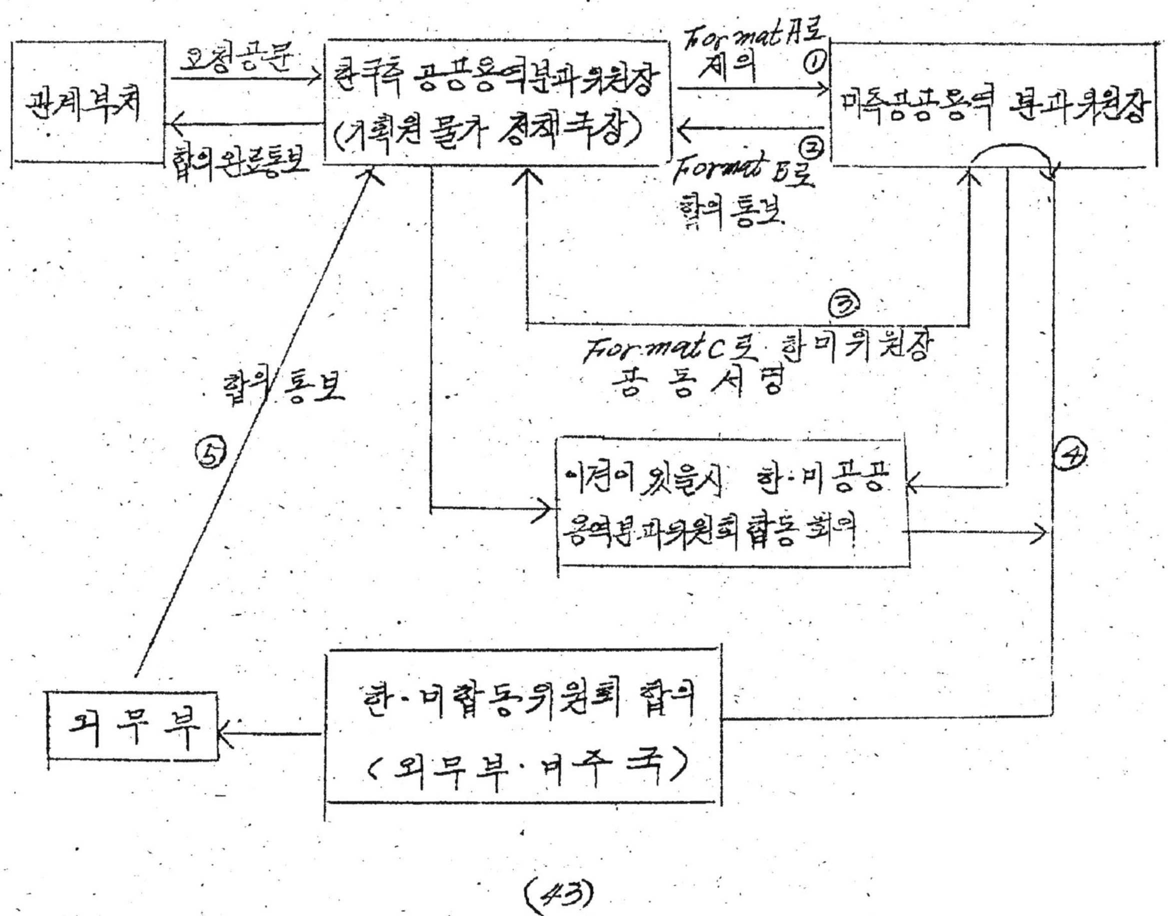

(43)

347

3. 효력 발생일

1) 효력 발생일 이전 협의 제의 → 합의 → 효력발생일

효력 발생일부터 적용 (합의 의사록 6조 1항)

Agreed Minutes Article VI

1. It is understood that any changes determined by the authorities of the Republic of Korea in priorities, conditions and rates or tariffs, applicable to the United States armed forces shall be the subject of consultation in the Joint Committee prior to their effective data.

2) 효력발생일 이전 협의 제의 → 효력 발생일 → 합의

효력 발생일 부터 소급 적용

(제 22차 회의 의사록 4)

Minutes of the Twenty-Second Meeting(14 March 1968)

4.e. If the consultation process extends past the effective date of the change, payment by the United States armed forces will be at the prior rates. After the consultation process is completed by the Joint Committee, the United States armed forces will retroactively pay the new rates from the effective date set by the Republic of Korea Government by prior communication in Format A.

- 45 -

248

3) 효력발생일 이후 협의 제의 → 합의
협의 제의일부터 효력 발생
(제47차 회의 의사록 3)

Minutes of the Forty-Seventh Meeting(19 February 1970)

3.---------------. Accordingly, any change, the consultation of which is initiated past the effective date, will be effective from the initial date of consultation.

4. However, we would like to make our understanding clear that retroactive payments would be made, if the consultation initiated prior to the effective date extends past the effective date, This, we believe, is in full concert with paragraph 4.e. of consultation procedures agreed to by the Joint Committee.

5. Let us make one thing more clear that the principle set forth in paragraph 3 should not apply to the rate change, consultation of which was completed prior to the effective date. You will agree to me that the consultation for rate changes of, for example, electricity and rail transportation was initiated after the effective date because of the delay in working out the consultation procedures. This problem has already been fully discussed at the stage of drafting the consultation procedures present in force.

349

二 한미행정협정(국문)

제6조

공익사업과 용역

1. 합중국 군대는 대한민국 정부 또는 그 지방 행정기관이 소유, 관리 또는 규제하는 모든 공익사업과 용역을 이용한다. "공익사업과 용역"이라 함은 수송과 통신의 시설 및 기관, 전기, 「까스」, 수도, 「스팀」, 전열, 전등, 동력 및 하수 오물 처리를 포함하되, 이것에만 한정하는것은 아니다. 본항에 규정된 공익사업과 용역의 이용은 합중국이 군용시설, 통신, 동력 및 합중국 군대의 운영에 필요한 기타 공익사업과 용역을 운영하는 권리를 침해하는 것은 아니다. 전기 권리는 대한민국 정부에 의한 동정부의 공익사 3

(47)

350

업과 용역의 운영과 합치하지 아니하는 방법으로 행사되어서는 아니된다.

2. 합중국에 의한 이러한 공익사업과 용역의 이용은 어느 타이용자에게 부여된것보다 불리하지 아니한 우선권, 조건 및 사용료나 요금에 따라야 한다.

제6조에 대한 합의의사록

1. 합중국 군대에 적용할 수 있는 우선권, 조건 및 사용료나 요금에 있어서 대한민국 당국이 결정한 변경은 그 효력 발생일전에 합동위원회의 협의대상이 될것임을 양해한다.

2. 본조는 1958년 12월 18일자 공익물에 관한 청구권 청산을 위한 협정을 어느 의미로나 폐지하는 것

351

으로 해석하지 아니하며 동 협정은 양정부가 달리 합의하지 아니하는 한 계속 유효하다.

3. 비상시에는 대한민국은 합중국군대의 수요를 충족시키는데 필요한 공익사업과 용역의 제공을 보장하기 위하여 적절한 조치를 취할 것에 합의한다.

(49)

352

三 한·미 행정협정 (英文)

ARTICLE VI

Utilities and Services

1. The United States armed forces shall have the use of all utilities and services which are owned, controlled or regulated by the Government of the Republic of Korea or Local administrative subdivisions thereof. The term utilities and services shall include, but not be limited to, transportation and communications facilities and systems, electricity, gas, water, steam, heat, light, power, and sewage disposal. The use of utilities and services as provided herein shall not prejudice the right of the United States to operate military transportation, communication, power and such other utilities and services deemed necessary for the operations of the United States armed forces. This right shall not be exercised in a manner inconsistent with the operation by the Government of the Republic of Korea of its utilities and services.

2. The use of such utilities and services by the United States shall be in accordance with priorities, conditions, and rates or tariffs no less favorable than those accorded any other user.

(Agreed Minutes) ARTICLE VI

1. It is understood that any changes determined by the authorities of the Republic of Korea in priorities, conditions and rates or tariffs, applicable to the United States armed forces shall be the subject of consultation in the Joint Committee prior to their effective date.

2. This Article will not be construed as in any way abrogating the Utilities Claims Settlement Agreement of December 18, 1958 which continues in full force and effect unless otherwise agreed by the two Governments.

3. In an emergency the Republic of Korea agrees to take appropriate measures to assure provision of utilities and services necessary to meet the needs of the United States armed forces.

四. 공공용역분과위원회운영절차
(68. 3. 14 제22차 회의)

Procedures for Utilities Subcommittee Consultation Process between ROK and US.

1. Paragraph 2 and Agreed Minute of Article VI requires that any changes determined by the Authorities of the Republic of Korea in priorities, conditions and rates or tariffs, applicable to the United States Armed forces shall be the subject of consultation in Joint Committee prior to their effective date. It is hereby confirmed that all types of services, utilities and supplies based on private contracts, on which the Government authorities have no control, cannot be the subject of consultation. In addition garbage disposal services, which are controlled by local adm. bodies, will be exempted from the formal consultation process. In order to accomplish this consultation in an orderly manner, the following steps will be taken:

a. The two chairmen of the respective components of the Subcommittee will maintain close liaison, and exchange information and views on prospective changes in priorities, conditions, and rates or tariffs on confidential basis even at policy formulating stages.

354

b. In the event of formal decision of the ROK for a change, the chairman of the Korean component will notify at the earliest possible date the chairman of the US component, furnishing in writing, using Format A, detailed information on the change and its effective date. If the consultation process extends past the effective date of rate change, billings to the US Armed forces will be at the prior rates. After the consultation process is completed, US Armed forces will retroactively pay the new rates from the effective date set by the ROKG by prior communication in Format A.

c. The US side will respond in writing, using Format B, at earliest possible date. After the US side has determined that the change in rates or tariffs is no less favorable than those accorded any other user, a memorandum to the Joint Committee will be prepared and signed by the ROK & US chairmen of the Utilities Subcommittee, using Format C.
This memorandum will include as inclosures the letters referenced in subparagraph b. & c. above and will recommend these be accepted by the Joint Committee as evidence of consultation contemplated by Article VI of SOFA.

d. In case of a disagreement, the matter will be brought to the Subcommittee, and the Subcommittee may bring the matter

355

to the Joint Committee for its decision. Both ROK and US sides, however, reserve the right to bring independently the matter relating to Article VI of the SOFA, to the Joint Committee at any time.

A - Format for Memorandum of Consultation

SUBJECT: Change in ______________________________
Under Article VI of the Status of Forces Agreement

TO: Chairman, US Utilities Subcommittee

1. Reference: Paragraph 2 and Agreed Minute of Article VI of the Status of Forces Agreement.

2. The Government of the United States is informed through this written consultative process that the Republic of Korea proposes to change following rates/tariffs at locations indicated below:

3. The following data is provided:

a. Effective date

b. Rate schedule of proposed change.

c. Rate schedule showing rates that are charged all classes of users (attached).

d. Calculation of old and new rate base.

e. Reasons for revision of rates.

4. The Government of the ROK advises the Government of the United States that the priorities, conditions, and rates or tariffs being changed are no less favorable than those accorded any other user. The view of the Government of the

United States is sollicited prior to the effective date of the rate changes. You may be assured that your views will be greatly appreciated.

Chairman
ROK Utilities Subcommittee

358

B - Format for US Ready to ROK Memorandum of Consultation

SUBJECT: Change in ______________________________
under Article VI of the Status of Forces Agreement

TO: Chairman, ROK Utilities Subcommittee

1. References:

a. Paragraph 2 and Agreed Minute 1 of Article VI of the States of Forces Agreement.

b. ROK Utilities Subcommittee Memorandum of Consultation, dated __________, subject as above, pertaining to a rate/tariff change for ____________________________.

2. The ROK memorandum, reference 1b above, has been reviewed and the United States Utilities Subcommittee fully understands the requirement for change in the __________________ in this instance and will join with the ROK Utilities Subcommittee in presenting a memorandum on the rates to the Joint Committee.

- or -

2. The ROK memorandum, reference 1b above, has been reviewed and while the requirement for ____________________ is understood, the United States Utilities Subcommittee taken this opportunity to express its views.

3. (Further comments).

Chairman
US Utilities Subcommittee

359

C. Format for Recommendation to Joint Committee

Republic of Korea - United States
Utilities Subcommittee

MEMORANDUM TO: The Joint Committee

SUBJECT:

1. Subcommittee Menbers:

Republic of Korea United States

2. Subject of Recommendation: Article VI of the Status of Forces Agreement requires "consultation" with the Government of the United States whenever the authorities of the Republic of Korea make any changes in priorities, conditions, and rates or tariffs applicable to the United States Armed forces.

3. The Republic of Korea has initiated the consultation process concerning a change in rates or tariffs for ______ ______ at ______________.
See Inclosure 1.

4. The United States Utilities Subcommittee has received the ROK request for consultation has determined that the requested change in rates or tariffs is no less favorable than those accorded any other user. See Inclosure 2.

5. It is recommended that the two inclosures referenced

360

in paragraph 3 & 4 be accepted by the Joint Committee as evidence of consultation contemplated by Article VI of the Status of Forces Agreement.

Chairman, ROK Utilities Subcommittee	Chairman, US Utilities Subcommittee

361

신고하여 애국하고 저축하여 행복찾자

경 제 기 획 원

물정331. 24 -750 (70. 3101) 1974. 12. 5.

수신 외무부장관

제목 서울시 상수도요금 한미합동 위원회 협의 요청

미군측에 적용되는 서울시 상수도요금을 개정하고자 별첨 공문 사본과 같이 한미행정 협정에 의한 협의를 미측공공용역분과위원장에게 제의하였음을 통보합니다.

첨부 : 한국측 제의 공문 사본 1부. 끝.

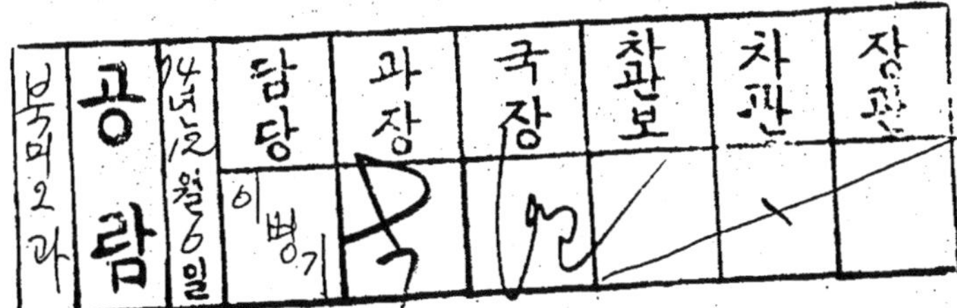

경 제 기 획 원

정부공문서 규정 제27조 제2항의 규정에 의하여 물가정책국장 이기욱 전결

6101

362

REPUBLIC OF KOREA-UNITED STATES
UTILITIES SUBCOMMITTEE

December 4, 1974

Subject : Change in Water Supply Rates applicable to the US Armed Forces under Article VI of Status of Forces Agreement

To : US Chairman, Utilities Subcommittee

1. Reference :

Paragraph 2 and Agreed Minute 1 of Article VI of the Status of Forces Agreement.

2. The Government of the United States is informed through this written consultative process that the ROK proposes to change the following rate/tariff at location indicated below;

Rate/Tariff	Location
Water Supply rate schedule applicable to the US Armed Forces	The City of Seoul

3. The following data is provided

a. Effective date : December 4, 1974.
b. Rate schedule showing rates that are charged all classes of user.
"Attached"
c. Rate schedule of proposed change. Refer to item "b"
d. Calculation of old and new base.

Classification	Description	Old rate(won)	New Rate(Won)
special use	per m^3	20	35

e. Reason for revision of rate.
To cover the rising prime cost.

The Government of ROK advises the Government of the United States that priorities, conditions, and rates or tariffs being charged are no less favorable than those accorded any other user.

366

367

You may be assured that your early views will be greatly appreciated.

Sincerely yours,

Kie Wook Lee
Director, Price Policy Bureau
Chairman, Republic of Korea
Utilities Subcommittee

364

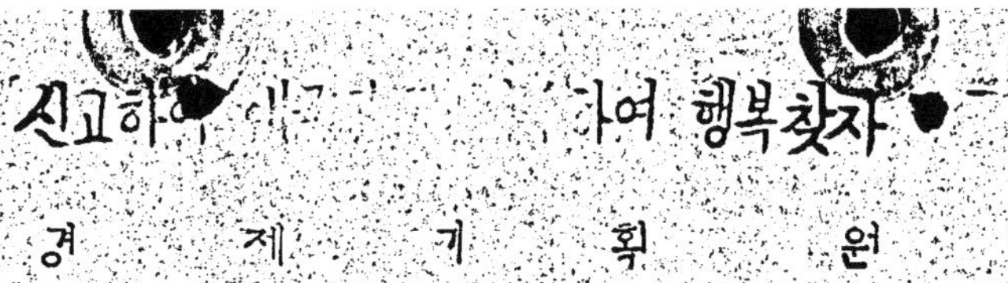

경 제 기 획 원

물정331. 24 - 761 (70. 3101) 1974. 12. 16.

수신 외무부장관

제목 전기및 철도화물 요금 한미합동위원회 협의 요청

금번 전기, 철도화물요금의 인상실시에 따라 미군에 적용되는 전기요금 및 철도화물요금을 개정하고자 별첨 영문과 같이 한미행정협정에 의한 협의를 미측공공용역분과위원장에게 제의 하였음을 통보합니다.

첨부 : 한국측 제의 공문 사본 2부. 끝.

북미2과	공람	74년 12월 18일	담당	과장	국장	참관보	차관	장관

발송 NO. 1974. 12. 16 경제기획원

경 제 기 획 원 장

정부공문서규정 제27조 제2항의 규정에 의거 ... 국장 전결

365

1222

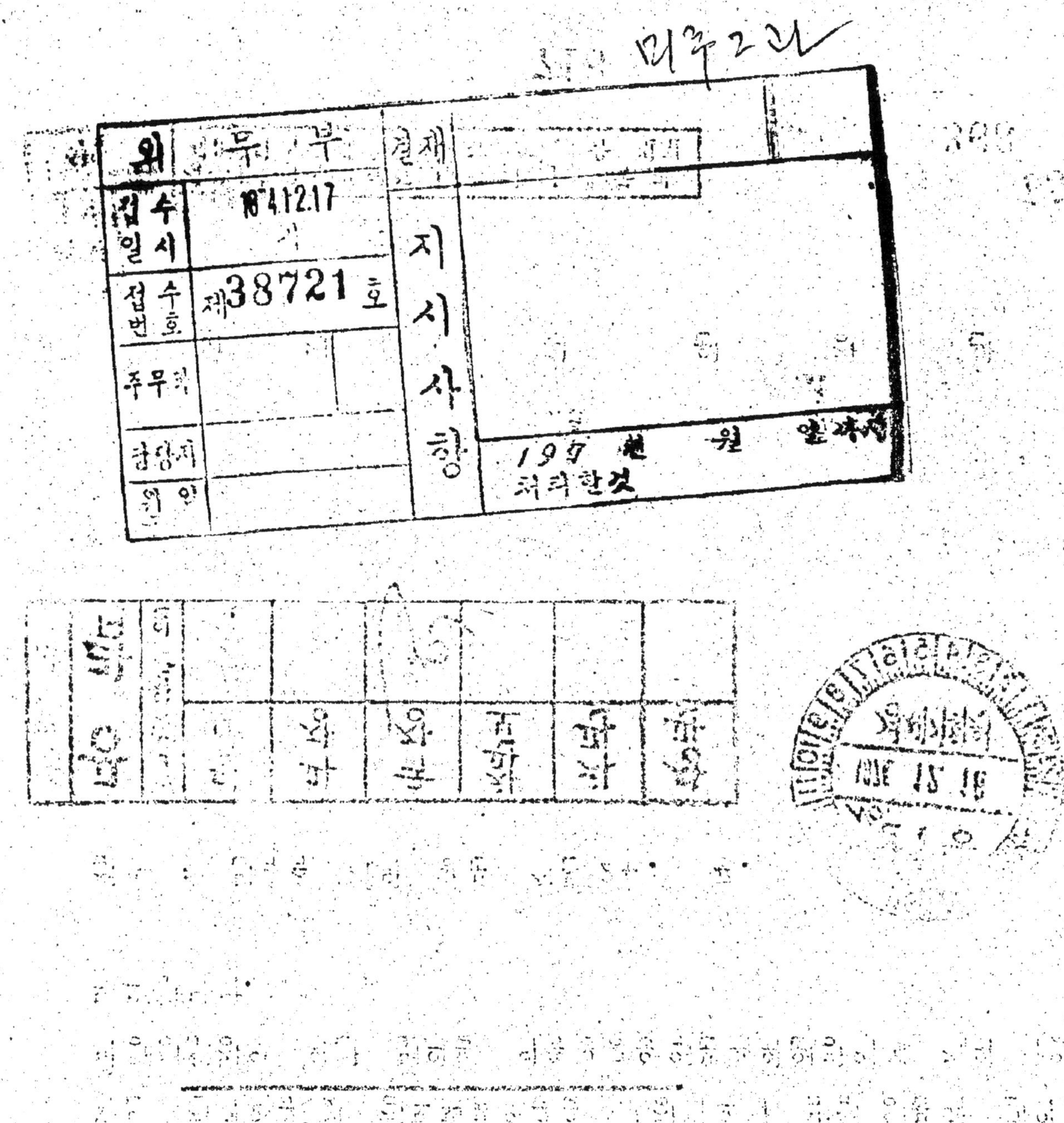
미주2과

외무부	결재
접수일시	1974.12.17
접수번호	제38721호
주무과	
담당자	
협조	

지시사항

197 년 월 일까지 처리할것

REPUBLIC OF KOREA-UNITED STATES
UTILITIES SUBCOMMITTEE

December 16, 1974

Subject : Change in Electric Power Rates Applicable to the US Armed Forces under Article VI of the Status of Forces Agreement.

To : Chairman, US Utilities Subcommittee.

1. Reference : Paragraph 2 and agreed Minute 1 of Article VI of the Status Forces Agreement.

2. The Government of the United States is informed through this written consultative process that the Republic of Korea proposes to change the following rates/tariffs at location indicated below;

Rate/Tariff	Location
Electric power rate schedule applicable to the US Armed Forces	the whole country

3. The following data is provided:

a. Effective date : December 13, 1974.
b. Rate Schedule showing rates that are charged all classes of users.
"attached"
c. Rate schedule of proposed change. Refer to item "b"
d. Calculation of old and new rate base. "attached"
e. Reason for revision of rates.
To secure operation costs according to increasing of oil price.

4. The Government of ROK advises the Government of the United States that priorities, conditions, and rates or tariffs being charged are no less favorable than those accorded any other user.

You may be assured that your views will be greatly appreciated.

Sincerely yours,

Kie Wook Lee
Kie Wook Lee
Director, Price Policy Bureau
Chairman, Republic of Korea
Utilities Subcommittee

366

COMPARISON

Contents of Revision

a. Rate category "General Service B" is separated into two kind of power service which are Government & Other Public Service and Commercial Service.
b. Demand charge in General Service B is reformed to single system, and energy charge in General Service A and B is reformed to block system.
c. Demand and energy charge rates are increased.

Old Rate Schedule	New Rate Schedule
1. GENERAL SERVICE A	1. GENERAL SERVICE A
Applicable: To residential service not restricted to any contracted demand, and to general service with the contracted demand under 4 KW.	Applicable: Same as the old.
Type of service: Single or three phase supply at any one of the Company's available voltages, 100V, 200V.	Type of service: Company's available voltages, 220V, 380V, or others are added, and others are same as the old.
Monthly bill: Basic charge: W213.00 per customer Energy charge: W20.19 per KWH for all energy consumed	Monthly bill Basic charge: W234.00 per customer. Energy charge: W22.12 per KWH for the first 50 KWH W27.39 per KWH for the next 100 KWH W35.05 per KWH for the excess.

769

2. GENERAL SERVICE B

Applicable:
To general service of 4 KW and over, except industrial and residential service excluding apartment houses.

Type of service:
Single or three phase supply at any one of available voltages, 150KV, 60KV, 20KV, 10KV, 6KV, 5.2KV, 3KV, 200V, 100V, or others.

Monthly bill: Demand charge

(a) Applicable to contracted demand of 4KW and over
W240.00 per KW for the first 50KW.
W190.00 per KW for the next 450 KW.
W142.00 per KW for the excess.

(b) Applicable to contracted demand of 500 KW and over, with supply voltage of more than 20KV.
W198.00 per KW for the first 500KW.
W132.00 per KW for the excess.

(c) Applicable to contracted demand of 1,000KW and over, with supply voltage of more than 150KV.
W132.00 per KW for the contracted demand.

Energy charge
W12.34 per KWH for all energy consumed.

2. GENERAL SERVICE B

Applicable:
Same as the old.

Type of service:
Available voltage 140KV is inserted in stead of the 150KV in the old.

Service classification:

A. Government & Other Public Service(A,B,C)
Applicable to the contracted demands for government and municipal offices, military facilities(including those for foreign army in Korea), embassy and similar diplomatic institutions, schools, broadcasting stations and press offices, hospitals, and residential apartment houses.

B. Commercial Service(A,B,D)
Applicable to the residual demands other than those mentioned in Govt. & Other Public Service.

C(1)Govt. & Other Public Service A, and Commercial Service A.
Applicable to contracted demand of 4 KW and over.

(2)Govt. & Other Public Service B, and Commercial Service B.
Applicable to contracted demand of 500KW and over, with supply voltage of more than 20KV.

(3)Govt. & Other Public Service C, and Commercial Service C.
Applicable to contracted demand of 1,000KW and over, with supply voltage of more than 140KV.

Monthly charge:

A. Govt. & Other Public Service(A,B,C)

Demand charge:

Govt. & Other Public Service A
W690.00 per KW for the contracted demand.

Govt. & Other Public Service B
W570.00 per KW for the contracted demand.

Govt. & Other Public Service C
W381.00 per KW for the contracted demand.

Energy charge:
W21.55 per KWH for the first 90 hours use of the contracted demand.
W22.98 per KWH for the next 90 hours use of the contracted demand.
W24.42 per KWH for the excess of 180 hours use of the contracted demand.

B. Commercial Service(A,B,C)

Demand charge:

Commercial Service(A,B,C)'s demand charge rate is same as Govt. & Other Public Service.

Energy charge:
W22.98 per KWH for the first 90 hours use of the contracted demand.
W24.42 per KWH for the next 90 hours use of the contracted demand.
W25.85 per KWH for the excess of 180 hours of the contracted demand.

368-1

REPUBLIC OF KOREA-UNITED STATES
UTILITIES SUBCOMMITTEE

December 16, 1974

Subject : Change in Freight Rates of Railroad Applicable to the US Armed Forces under Article VI of the Status of Forces Agreement.

To : Chairman, U.S. Utilities Subcommittee.

1. Reference : Paragraph 2 and Agreed Minute of Article VI of the Status of Forces Agreement.

2. The Government of the United States is informed through this written consultative process that the Republic of Korea proposes to change following rates/tariffs at location indicated below;

Rate/Tariff	Location
Freight rate schedule of railroad applicable to the US Armed Forces	the whole country

3. The following data is provided:

a. Effective date : December 15, 1974.
b. Rate schedule of proposed change. "Attached"
c. Rate schedule showing rates that are charged all classes of user.
Refer to item "b"
d. Calculation of old and new rate base. Refer to item"b"
e. Reason for revision of rates.
To secure transportation costs.

4. The Government of ROK advises the Government of the United States that the priorities, conditions, and rates being charged are no less favorable than those accorded any other user.

You may be assured that your views will be greatly appreciated.

Sincerely yours,

Kie Wook Lee

Kie Wook Lee
Director, Price Policy Bureau
Chairman, Republic of Korea
Utilities Subcommittee

369

Freight Change Rates of Railroad

(A) US Army

Description of rates	Unit	Present Rates	Change Rates KNR Proposed	Remark	Freight Rate	Roka
1.. Carload Freight						
a. Basic Rate Using Carrier's Car	Pre car/km	81	116	42% Increase	50km/t 1 : 210 2 : 181 3 : 159 4 : 139 5 : 125	116
b. Minimum Charge for carload	Per car	4,759	6,758		10,000	6,758
2. Special Train Service Minimum Charge	Per Train	173,250	246,015		468,413	246,015
3. Demurrage	6 hours/ Per car	1,386	1,969		2,680	1,969
4. Diversion or Reconsignment	Per car	2,772	3,937		3,937	3,937
5. Cancellation of Car Ordered	"	1,386	1,969		1,969	1,969
6. Switching Charge	"	721	1,024		Car/km 1,024	1024
7. Stop-off In-transit	"	1,294	1,838		-	1,838
8. Equipment Rental	Per car/ Perday	1,098	1,560		1,707	1,560

310

Description of rates	Unit	Present Rates	Change Rates KNR Proposed	Remark	Freight Rate	Roka
9. Dead head Movement of Rented or US Owned Car	Pre car/ Km	21	30	42% Increase	Ton/Km 139	30
10. Surcharge for Over-siqed Freight	"	60	86		Basic Rate 100%	86
11. Maintenance Service						
a. 24 Month Maintenance of US-Owned Freight	Per car	72,000	102,240		142,600	
b. Non-Scheduled Maintenance of US-Owned	"	49,000	69,580		184,600	
c. 24 Month Maintenance of US-Owned heavy	"	108,000	153,360		275,400	
d. Non-Scheduled Maintenance of US-Owned heavy duty Freight car	"	73,500	104,370		156,550	
e. Maintenance Operating Charges(other than Back Shop Maintenance)	Car/day	10.75	15.27		65.20	
12. Component Parts						
a. Wheel Set, Chilled Steel(an axle and wheels)		167,000	237,140		752,690	

0170

301

Description of Rates	Unit	Present Rates	Chang Rates KNR Proposed	Remark	Freight Rate	Roka
b. Wheel, Chilled Steel		61,047	86,687	42%	255,600	
c. Axle		43,890	62,324	Increase	269,800	
d. Coupler		46,284	65,724		139,160	
e. Draft Gear		35,910	50,993		184,600	
f. Triple Valve		27,930	39,661		248,500	
g. Bolster Spring (inner & outer)		37,107	52,692		56,800	
h. Side Frame		43,890	62,324		227,200	
i. Brake Beam		16,359	23,230		63,900	
j. Bolster		57,700	81,934		262,700	

372

외교문서 비밀해제: 주한미군지위협정(SOFA) 35

주한미군지위협정(SOFA) 공공용역 합동위원회 2

초판인쇄 2024년 03월 15일
초판발행 2024년 03월 15일

지은이 한국학술정보(주)
펴낸이 채종준
펴낸곳 한국학술정보(주)
주 소 경기도 파주시 회동길 230(문발동)
전 화 031-908-3181(대표)
팩 스 031-908-3189
홈페이지 http://ebook.kstudy.com
E-mail 출판사업부 publish@kstudy.com
등 록 제일산-115호(2000. 6. 19)

ISBN 979-11-7217-046-2 94340
979-11-7217-011-0 94340 (set)

책에 대한 더 나은 생각, 끊임없는 고민, 독자를 생각하는 마음으로 보다 좋은 책을 만들어갑니다.